AF840096

MONEY LAW, CAPITAL, AND THE CHANGING IDENTITY OF THE EUROPEAN UNION

This book addresses three questions: is money a way to create a European Union identity? If so, which type of identity is this? And in what ways is the EU identity changing? The book brings together experts from a variety of backgrounds and academic approaches to analyse the law of money and payments on the one side, and the law of capital and investments on the other.

The book is divided into two parts. Part I covers scriptural, electronic and digital money. It analyses the European framework for payment services users, explores limits and challenges of the Banking Union, and looks at the project for a digital euro. Part II investigates the policy and regulatory drivers of the EU's changing identity, from the early modern roots of the European law of money and capital to the regulatory strategy set in the Capital Markets Union and the role conferred on venture capital; from the FinTech-based developments of payment systems to the newly-established fiscal and monetary policies in the post-COVID phase.

The book will be of interest to researchers, academics and policy makers in the fields of law and regulation, as well as political economy and political sciences.

Money Law, Capital, and the Changing Identity of the European Union

Edited by
Gabriella Gimigliano
and
Valentino Cattelan

•HART•
OXFORD • LONDON • NEW YORK • NEW DELHI • SYDNEY

HART PUBLISHING

Bloomsbury Publishing Plc

Kemp House, Chawley Park, Cumnor Hill, Oxford, OX2 9PH, UK

1385 Broadway, New York, NY 10018, USA

29 Earlsfort Terrace, Dublin 2, Ireland

HART PUBLISHING, the Hart/Stag logo, BLOOMSBURY and the Diana logo are trademarks of Bloomsbury Publishing Plc

First published in Great Britain 2022

Copyright © The editors and contributors severally 2022

The editors and contributors have asserted their right under the Copyright, Designs and Patents Act 1988 to be identified as Authors of this work.

All rights reserved. No part of this publication may be reproduced or transmitted in any form or by any means, electronic or mechanical, including photocopying, recording, or any information storage or retrieval system, without prior permission in writing from the publishers.

While every care has been taken to ensure the accuracy of this work, no responsibility for loss or damage occasioned to any person acting or refraining from action as a result of any statement in it can be accepted by the authors, editors or publishers.

All UK Government legislation and other public sector information used in the work is Crown Copyright ©. All House of Lords and House of Commons information used in the work is Parliamentary Copyright ©. This information is reused under the terms of the Open Government Licence v3.0 (http://www.nationalarchives.gov.uk/doc/open-government-licence/version/3) except where otherwise stated.

All Eur-lex material used in the work is © European Union, http://eur-lex.europa.eu/, 1998–2022.

A catalogue record for this book is available from the British Library.

Library of Congress Cataloging-in-Publication data.

Names: Gimigliano, Gabriella, editor. | Cattelan, Valentino, editor.

Title: Money law, capital, and the changing identity of the European Union / edited by Gabriella Gimigliano and Valentino Cattelan.

Description: Oxford, UK ; New York, NY : Hart Publishing, an imprint of Bloomsbury Publishing, 2022. | Includes bibliographical references and index.

Identifiers: LCCN 2022018379 (print) | LCCN 2022018380 (ebook) | ISBN 9781509956791 (hardback) | ISBN 9781509956838 (paperback) | ISBN 9781509956814 (pdf) | ISBN 9781509956807 (Epub)

Subjects: LCSH: Money—Law and legislation—European Union countries. | Capital movements—Law and legislation—European Union countries. | Financial services industry—Law and legislation—European Union countries. | European Union.

Classification: LCC KJE7051 .M66 2022 (print) | LCC KJE7051 (ebook) | DDC 343.4/032—dc23/eng/20220629

LC record available at https://lccn.loc.gov/2022018379

LC ebook record available at https://lccn.loc.gov/2022018380

ISBN: HB: 978-1-50995-679-1
ePDF: 978-1-50995-681-4
ePub: 978-1-50995-680-7

Typeset by Compuscript Ltd, Shannon

To find out more about our authors and books visit www.hartpublishing.co.uk. Here you will find extracts, author information, details of forthcoming events and the option to sign up for our newsletters.

ACKNOWLEDGEMENTS

This study is a contribution to the project 'Jean Monnet Chair in EU Money Law' (EUMOL). Call for proposal 2018/EAC/A05/2017 – European Commission, Education, Audiovisual and Culture Executive Agency (EACEA). Project number 599983-EPP-1-2018-1-IT-EPPJMO-CHAIR.

CONTENTS

PART II
THE ENERGY OF CREDIT AND CAPITAL

LIST OF CONTRIBUTORS

Alexandra Andhov is an Associate Professor in corporate law and law and technology at the Center for Private Governance at Faculty of Law, University of Copenhagen. Dr. Andhov is a legal scholar with expertise in corporate law, capital market law, corporate social responsibility and technology both in academia as well as in practice. In 2019, Alexandra was a Fulbright Scholar at Cornell Law School. She has held visiting posts at various institutions, including the Oxford Law School, University of Turin, Lund University and CBS.

Luisa Brunori is Researcher at the French *Centre National pour la Recherche Scientifique* (CNRS). She is affiliated to the *Centre d'Histoire Judiciaire* of the University of Lille where she directs the Graduate Program in Humanities and Social Sciences. She is the Principal Investigator of the International Resarch Network PHEDRA (Pour une Histoire Européenne du DRoit des Affaires) which brings together 35 researchers from a dozen European, Turkish and North African laboratories. In 2016, her research on the history of European commercial law was awarded the prestigious CNRS Medal for Research.

Marta Božina Beroš is Associate Professor at the Faculty of Economics, Juraj Dobrila University of Pula (Croatia), where she teaches on EU finance and EMU law & governance. Božina Beroš graduated cum laude from the Faculty of Law, University of Zagreb and holds a PhD in Economics from the University of Ljubljana. Her primary research interests are in EMU integration dynamics and their effect on EU agencies' policymaking in a post-SSM framework. Her research interests also include the evolution of European payments in the context of an increasingly digitalised banking market.

Marin Beroš is Assistant Professor at the Faculty of Educational Sciences, Juraj Dobrila University of Pula and Head of the Regional Center in Pula of the Institute of Social Sciences 'Ivo Pilar'. He holds a PhD in Philosophy from the University of Zagreb (Croatia). His research interests intersect the fields of political philosophy, political and legal theory. He has published extensively on various issues of deliberative democracy, civil rights, and morality, as well as the relationship between education and cosmopolitanism more recently.

Marco Bodellini is an Assistant Professor in Banking and Financial Law at University of Bergamo. He has extensively published in the area of bank crisis management, central banking, sustainable finance and asset management law.

Valentino Cattelan is a Lecturer in Law at Birmingham City University (UK). He has widely published on Islamic law and finance, and his research interests span from comparative legal studies, EU law, contract law, financial markets, and the anthropology of money. He is currently completing an authored monograph on the topic 'Religion and Contract Law in Islam. From Medieval Trade to Global Finance' (Routledge).

Małgorzata Cyndecka is Associated Professor at the Faculty of Law at the University of Bergen (UiB), Norway. She is also affiliated with the Centre for the Science of Learning & Technology (SLATE) at the UiB. Privacy and data protection are the main fields she works on. Recently, she has joined the Norwegian Data Protection Authority's 'Sandbox for Responsible Artificial Intelligence' where she participates in a project concerning using AI in Norwegian schools.

Ursula M Dalinghaus is a Visiting Professor of Anthropology at Ripon College in Ripon, Wisconsin, USA. After receiving her PhD in sociocultural anthropology from the University of Minnesota, Twin Cities, she was a postdoctoral scholar at the Institute for Money, Technology, & Financial Inclusion (IMTFI) at the University of California, Irvine. In partnership with IMTFI and the International Currency Association (ICA), she has written two white papers on the role and importance of cash in society. She has more than five years of fieldwork experience in Germany, where she researched German experiences of the euro, currency unions, and central bank communications work with the public, and has published on the complex value translations of the 1990 currency union between East and West Germany.

Gabriella Gimigliano is a Lecturer in Business Law at the Business and Law Department of the University of Siena. She holds a PhD in Banking Law and Law of Financial Markets. From 2013 to 2016, she was the academic leader of the Jean Monnet Module on the Europeanisation of the Payment System, while more recently (2018–2022) she was Jean Monnet Professor in EU Money Law. At the University of Siena she teaches business and company law to bachelor and master degree students.

Alperen A Gözlügöl is an Assistant Professor in the Law & Finance Cluster of the Leibniz Institute for Financial Research SAFE, Frankfurt am Main, Germany. His research interests include comparative corporate law & governance, capital markets law and financial regulation. He has publications and forthcoming work in leading journals such as the *Journal of Corporate Law Studies* and the *European Business Organization Law Review*. His work is also featured on the *Oxford Business Law Blog* and the *CLS Blue Sky Blog*.

Gian Luca Greco is an Associate Professor of Economics Law at the University of Milan 'La Statale'. He holds a PhD in Banking and Securities Law and a Postgraduate Diploma from the SSBD (School of Specialization in Banking) from the University of Siena. He is a certified attorney at law and a certified chartered accountant. He is author of more than 90 scientific publications, including two monographs, journal articles and book chapters in the fields of financial regulation, tech law and banking contracts.

Johannes Lenhard, PhD, is Centre Coordinator, Research Associate and Associated Lecturer at the Max Planck Cambridge Center for Ethics, Economy and Social Change at the University of Cambridge and King's College Cambridge. His research is focused on understanding people experiencing homelessness and more recently the ethics of venture capital investors.

Lela Mélon is a Professor of Sustainability in Business Law at ESCI-UPF and the executive director of Planetary Wellbeing Institutional Framework at the UPF, and is active in the field of policy-making and scholarly work on the topic of environmental and social responsibility of business through individual projects (SCOM under the Marie Curie Fellowship) and broader institutional changes (for which she received the 2021 Emerging Sustainability Leader Award by World Sustainability Foundation). She is specialised in EU law, with a main focus on corporate conduct and sustainability, on which she published the book *Shareholder Primacy and Global Business* with Routledge in 2018. She is a lecturer at the Masters on Planetary Health (UPF, UOC, IS Global); at ESSEC Paris, at CEI Barcelona, ESCI-UPF and at the UPF.

Casimiro A Nigro is a Law & Finance Assistant Professor at the Center for Advanced Studies on the Foundations of Law and Finance, Goethe Universität, Frankfurt am Main, Germany. His research concerns comparative corporate law and governance, and securities regulation. His work currently focuses on the governance of private equity- and venture capital-backed firms from a corporate law perspective. His work has appeared, inter alia, in the *European Company and Financial Law Review* and *European Business Organization Law Review* and has been featured, inter alia, on the *Oxford Business Law Blog*.

Leo Rees is a Director at global advisory firm Milltown Partners and a Fellow for the UK think tank Onward. He advises actors across the technology ecosystem, from big tech to venture capitalists, and well capitalised startups, on their policy challenges. Alongside issues relating to venture capital, he has written extensively on innovation and data policy. Previously he worked for the British political party, the Liberal Democrats.

Marc Pilkington is currently Associate Professor of Business Administration and Dean of the Faculty of Economics and Administrative Sciences of Epoka University in Albania. He was formerly Associate Professor of Economics at the University of Burgundy, France. His interests include FinTech, blockchain technology and cryptocurrency, post-soviet economies, monetary policy and economic philosophy.

Maria Elena Salerno is Associate Professor in Law and Economics at Business and Law Department of the University of Siena. Since 2001 she has run courses on banking and financial law subjects in Bachelor and Master Degrees. Her academic publications focus on banking and financial supervision and regulation, pension funds, corporate governance, and financial investor protection. She is a member of the academic board of the PhD 'Diritto ed economia della società digitale', of the editorial board of 'IANUS' and 'Diritto della banca e del mercato finanziario'. She has been a member of the 'Economic Law Scholars' Association' (ADDE) since its inception.

Vittorio Santoro is Emeritus Professor of Business and Company Law at the Law Department of the University of Siena. Recently, he edited with Mario Chiti the monograph *The Palgrave Handbook of European Banking Union*.

Ruth Wandhöfer is an expert in the field of banking and one of the foremost authorities on transaction banking regulatory and FinTech innovation matters. After a distinguished career of over a decade with Citi, Ruth is now an independent Non-Executive Director on the boards of Permanent TSB, Gresham Technologies and Digital Identity Net as well as a Partner at Gauss Ventures. She is the Chair of the PSR Panel in the UK, Chief Innovation Officer at GC Partners, Co-Founder of Sinonyx and adviser to the UK BSI, the ETPPA, RTGS.global and the City of London Corporation. She holds several industry awards and is a published author and fellow of CASS Business School, where she obtained her PhD.

1

The *Life* of EU Money: Value, Credit and Capital as Societal Processes

VALENTINO CATTELAN

I. The Pure Energy of Money

In a fragment of his diary (*Tagebuch*), published posthumously in 1919/1920 (Kroner and Mehlis (eds)) and later in 1923 (Kantorowicz (ed)),[1] the great German sociologist Georg Simmel (1858–1918), author of *The Philosophy of Money* (1900),[2] writes that:

> [m]oney is society's only creation that is pure energy, completely disjointed from the material object it stands for, making it an absolute symbol. It is the most significant creation of our times to the extent that its existence has informed every theory and practice … Its being pure relation (and in this aspect representative, in fact, of its times), without incorporating any content of the relation, does not contradict it at all. Since in the reality, energy is nothing else than relation.[3]

If, as highlighted by the influential post-war German cultural theorist Hans Blumenberg,[4] it is certainly true that money stands as Simmel's proto-metaphor for *Life* in the latter's nascent *Lebensphilosophie*, the *Life* of money itself, as commented by Robert Savage, 'turns out to be pure circulation, sociation, and interactivity, an endless cycle of extensions and intensifications of value emerging through processes of social exchange'.[5]

[1] Respectively, G Simmel, 'Aus Georg Simmels Nachgelassenem Tagebuch' in R Kroner and G Mehlis (eds), *Logos, Internationale Zeitschrift für Philosophie der Kultur* (Vol VIII, Tübingen, Verlag von FCB Mohr (Paul Siebeck), 1919/1920) 121–51; G Simmel, *Fragmente und Aufsätze aus dem Nachlaß und Veröffentlichungen der Letzten Jahre* (ed G Kantorowicz) (Munich, Drei Masken Verlag, 1923) 1–46.

[2] G Simmel, *The Philosophy of Money* (trans T Bottomore and D Frisby) (London, Routledge, 1990).

[3] Passage quoted in A Deneault (ed), *Georg Simmel. L'Argent dans la Culture Modern et Autres Essais sur l'«Économie de la Vie»* (Paris, Hermann, 2006) 5; author's translation from French language.

[4] H Blumenberg, 'Money or Life: Metaphors of Georg Simmel's Philosophy' (2012) 29(7/8) *Theory, Culture & Society* 249–62 (trans from the German original of 1976 by R Savage).

[5] Blumemberg (n 4) 249.

Money, both as the 'matter' (the substance of *value*) and 'energy' (its inherent potential of being *credit*) of any exchange, enjoys the metaphysical quality of being an *absolute medium*, so 'to realize the possibility of all values as the value of all possibilities'.[6] At the same time, while projecting the singular (present or future) exchange in the whole of economic *Life* of a certain social group, it also mirrors this *Life* into the single *life* of each social relation[7] as the place of meaning for *value* at present, as well as for *credit* of future relations, where money, through a process of re-evaluation, becomes *capital*.

II. A Wave-Particle Duality

The chapters in this book cover a wide range of subjects. Looking at the European polity as a community in transition, this volume investigates the role of money both as 'matter' and 'energy' of this community, in terms of a core social institution whose understanding is vital to interpret the present (as well as the destiny) of the European polity itself.

'Matter' of any exchange, the *value* of EU money, affects the everyday *life* of EU (and non-EU) citizens dealing with payments and living in a changing economic environment increasingly dominated by technology (to the extent to which a new 'matter' of exchange has appeared in the form of the 'digital euro'). An economic environment whose *Life* – a reflection of a community in transition – is evolving through the ongoing ambitious project of a European Banking Union, whose fate is still uncertain in the aftermath of the COVID-19 pandemic (see Part I).

At the same time, as the 'energy' of commercial exchanges, with historical roots that can be traced back to early modern Europe, the present *Life* of EU money is also affected by urgent needs of sustainability, inclusion and protection of the environment acting themselves as drivers for change: accordingly, the changing nature of EU *credit* implies a re-definition of the directions taken by EU (venture) *capital*. Last but not least, in this dynamic context, issues of risk management and financial regulation – in relation to the role of national and European authorities – constitute an additional factor of analysis, as the 'institutional channels' that drive the 'energy' of money (see Part II).

Using a parallel allegory to introduce the contents of this book, if the project on EU Money Law constituted the 'shape' of the Jean Monnet Chair held by Gabriella Gimigliano (my co-editor and, I would say, real *domina* of this volume), the way in which this 'chair' has been moved by the contributors has largely depended on their own expertise, research interests and (as with any dinner guest) taste preferences.

[6] Simmel (n 2) 221.

[7] G Ingham, 'Money is a Social Relation' (1996) 54(4) *Review of Social Economy* (Special Issues on Critical Realism) 507–29; see also B Maurer, 'The Anthropology of Money' (2006) 35 *Annual Review of Anthropology* 15–36.

As a result, the Chair has multiplied its 'matter' as a medium fostering the 'energy' for this book, in a relational interaction between the different authors, where the *Life* of the volume has mirrored, to some extent, the scientific *life* of each of them.

At this point the reader may have already noted how much I rely, as a stylistic preference, on the semantic power of metaphors to approach complicated subjects: and indeed, there is no more complex topic of investigation for a social researcher (at least in my personal experience) than money – the protagonist of this book.

As highlighted above, with its position at the core of any economic exchange and business investment, not only does money represent the 'matter' of commercial transactions, but it is also the 'energy' that fosters the growth and development of a certain community. Moreover, '[f]ar from being a neutral medium of exchange, money [also] affects the daily practice of our economic dealings while being intrinsically connected to the whole of legal, social, and political interactions of the community to which we belong'.[8] Hence, as much as fiat money is backed by a normative order and a regulatory framework, the social use of money can vary in relation to multiple dynamics of public trust that may even lead to the creation of new instruments of payment, store of value, unit of account and tools of investment. Accordingly, under circumstances of inflation, mistrust or recession, the 'sovereign power (the beholder of the law) can hardly posit the use of "fiat money" by decree … [… which] is soon replaced by alternative "natural money" [i.e. money supported by public trust, independently from the action of a central regulator]'.[9] As will be clarified in the third section of this chapter, the impact of the COVID-19 pandemic on the European Union has given rise precisely to dynamics of re-definition of the role of the Euro as common currency; but, at the same time, technological advance offers alternative currencies to the public (the rise of cryptocurrencies, for example bitcoin, represents the most significant example) which are competing, in terms of 'shared trust', alongside fiat money in the same market.

Independently from its nature (legal or alternative currency), in all these cases the 'matter' of money is fuelled by an 'energy' that can multiply its *value* from the singular person to the provision of *credit* to others, in a process of societal relations which is potentially endless. It is in this way that money becomes *capital*, reproducing itself in a process of extension and intensification of value which, from the start of modernity, has shifted from the 'head' (in Latin, *caput*), the *name* of the person, to the *nominal* value of the impersonal loan. Not by chance, from the very start of Western capitalism, the notion of *credit* has been inserted within a de-personalised economy where 'credit-based honesty [casts] two incongruent textualities (personal reputation, impersonal paper) into discursive reciprocity'.[10]

[8] V Cattelan, 'Sacred Euro: Sovereign Debt(s) and EU's Bare Credit in the Corona Crisis' in W Gephart W (ed), *In the Realm of Corona Normativities* (Frankfurt, Klostermann, 2020) 195.

[9] ibid.

[10] S Sherman, 'Promises, Promises: Credit as Contested Metaphor in Early Capitalist Discourse' (1997) 94(3) *Modern Philology* 330.

> Derived from the Latin *credere* (to believe or to trust) and originally a reference to the quality of the person who could be trusted, the word [*credit*] now served to endow the untrustworthy thing – the loan – with the qualities of the person who could be trusted. Buttressed by the personal word of an individual and public acknowledgment of that bond, credit acquired substance, and only when trust failed would a borrower be obliged to pledge his plate or jewels …[11]

The reflection by Georg Simmel on the quality of money as the 'society's only creation that is pure energy, completely disjointed from the material object [but also from the human subject] it stands for, making it an absolute symbol' (see extract at the beginning of the chapter) reflects the intrinsic duality of money in the simultaneity of its static and dynamic components: in its substance, money has a *value*; in its potential, it is *credit*, and therefore, through the process of its re-evaluation, *capital*.

This inescapable interaction (*id est*, inherent complementarity) between the 'matter' and the 'energy' of money belongs to the essence of any monetary experience, independently from the form that money has assumed in the shape of currency in human history. In a recent article that I co-authored with Gabriella, I have underlined the nature of 'absolute symbol' that characterises *any* money by referring to a piece of installation artwork by Nicholas Mangan titled *Limits to Growth*, that forges 'interdependence between two (apparently distant, but actually much closer one another than expected) monetary currencies: *rai*, the ancient large stone coins from the Micronesian island of Yap, and *bitcoin*, the most popular crypto-currency currently in use in the global market'.[12] If the story of *rai* is popular among economists and has been mentioned, among others, by Keynes, Friedman, Tobin and Mankiw[13] – with Friedman drawing the correspondence of the symbolic value of *rai* stone to the gold stored in the central banks[14] – the *Life* of money in the European Union has already filled hundreds of research libraries. This book intends to add further reflection on the subject.

Before moving to some additional considerations on the changing *Life* of the EU, a final conceptual link may help in defining, I believe, the approach of this

[11] MC Howell, *Commerce Before Capitalism in Europe, 1300–1600* (Cambridge, Cambridge University Press, 2010) 28.

[12] V Cattelan and G Gimigliano, 'Digital Currency Schemes: More or Less Sustainable? *Limits to Growth* and Electronification of Money in Europe' (2020) 21 *Ianus – Diritto e Finanza* 12.

[13] ibid 15.

[14] 'The Yap islanders regarded stones quarried and shaped on a distant island and brought to their own as the concrete manifestation of wealth. For a century and more, the "civilized" world regarded as a concrete manifestation of its wealth metal dug from deep in the ground, refined at great labor, and transported great distances to be buried again in elaborate vaults deep in the ground. Is the one practice really more rational than the other? What both examples – and numerous additional ones that could be listed – illustrate is how important "myth," unquestioned belief, is in monetary matters. Our own money, the money we have grown up with, the system under which it is controlled, these appear "real" and "rational" to us. The money of other countries often seems to us like paper or worthless metal, even when the purchasing power of individual units is high': M Friedman, *The Island of Stone Money*. Working Papers in Economics, E-91-3 (Stanford University, The Hoover Institution, 1991) 4–5.

book to money: namely, what quantum mechanics describes in terms of 'wave-particle duality'. While *value* and *credit* cannot depict separately the nature of money, it is in their 'credit-value duality' that money's metaphysical quality of being an *absolute medium* for any possible socio-economic relation emerges in its entirety. The static (value) and dynamic (credit and, then, capital as process of re-evaluation) components merge in the intrinsic duality of what is the means of exchange, reserve of value and measure of price in a given society, as well as instrument of investment. As the two sides of the same coin (a metaphor which is certainly apt to the topic of discussion), money 'absorbs' and 'releases' value according to its use in societal processes. Being pure energy, nothing else than relation, it can be seen at the same time either as a specific 'particle' in the market, or as a 'wave' in the flow of credits and capital investments:[15] as Albert Einstein wrote in his comment to the wave-particle duality, 'separately neither of them fully explains the phenomena of light, but together they do!'.[16]

III. The *Life* of Money, Technology and the Changing Identity of the European Union

In the search to shed some light on the topic of money, this book concentrates on the European Union. More precisely, moving from the relational nature of money as a social institution (ie, how the *Life* evoked by Simmel affects the *life* of the single in a certain community), this book aims at presenting a critical study of the changing identity of the European Union *because of* the changing identity of its money, also in relation to the impact of new technologies and the scenario of radical transformation that the world is experiencing in the post-COVID-19 era. In fact, if there is undoubtedly a dimension of faith in the public trust that underlies the use of money (the trust that permits its *value* to become *credit* and *capital*),[17] the rise of new monetary tools, as well as of innovative dimensions of social interaction,

[15] The duality wave-particle that is intrinsic to money seems to be indirectly upheld by Levy in a recent article where he opposes the 'materialistic' conceptualisation of capital as a physical factor of production by defining capital as 'a particular kind of pecuniary process of valuation, associated with investment, in which capital may (or may not) become a factor of production': J Levy, 'Capital as Process and the History of Capitalism' (2017) 91 *Business History Review* 485. Indeed, I do not see any relevant contradiction in assuming both conceptualisations as valid tools to understand the nature of capital and money in a duality involving both the relational process and the matter of relation.

[16] A Einstein and L Infeld, *The Evolution of Physics. The Growth of Ideas From Early Concepts to Relativity and Quanta* (Cambridge, Cambridge University Press, 1938) 278.

[17] 'Money facilitates the rites and rituals we perform in everyday life. More than a mere medium of exchange or a measure of value, it is the primary means by which we manifest a faith unique to our *secular* age. But what happens when individual belief (*credo*, "I" believe) and the systems into which it is bound (*credit*, "it" believes) enter into crisis?': A Tynan, L Milesi and CJ Müller (eds), *Credo Credit Crisis. Speculations on Faith and Money* (London, Rowman & Littlefield International, 2017) synopsis (emphasis added).

if not of political nature (in terms of sustainability and environment protection), are certainly affecting the current *Life* of EU money.

As far as technological innovation is concerned, when looking at money in the form of a medium of exchange, some revealing considerations can be derived from media theory, and namely by referring to the famous sociologist Marshall McLuhan (1911–80). Paraphrasing a famous quote from his *Understanding Media: The Extensions of Man*,[18] we can agree that 'the personal and social consequences of … *money* – [as the] *economic* extension of ourselves – result from the new scale that is introduced into our affairs by … new technology', to the degree that exchanges are affected and amplified by any change in the design, pace, or pattern that financial technology introduces. So, as McLuhan sees the advent of electronic media in the twentieth century as the third major milestone in communication technology after the 'literacy revolution' (from oral and tribal culture into literate mentality, fifth century BC) and the 'Gutenberg revolution' (from calligraphy to printing, fifteenth century AD), correspondingly fiat money, which started to dominate global economy in the twentieth century, has revolutionised our lives by radically affecting economic exchanges. Specifically, as the third major technological advance in money technology, it has overcome commodity and representative money, whose respective impacts on mankind are comparable to literacy (from barter to trade) and printing (money as currency) in media theory. In this direction, by re-reading McLuhan's prophecy on the digital media's influence in constructing a 'global village' and the emergence of 'retribalisation' processes, we can also interpret the current age of 'global finance' as directly linked to the rise of fiat money technology, and the nature of new financial networks (from the sharing economy's crowdfunding to blockchain, cryptocurrencies, alternative and complementary currencies) as experiments of 'retribalised money', where economic *value* is imbued with the *values* of the communities that create money, and no longer backed by commodities or the authority of a state. In this regard, it is significant to note that, as Dodd has remarked in a recent article,[19] if the recent phenomenon of bitcoin is backed by a 'techno-utopia', where machine production and the mining process seem to replace the need for trust between persons, beyond this ideology it is in fact the existence of a peculiar 'bitcoin-community' that makes 'bitcoin-money'. 'Unwittingly, then, Bitcoin serves as a powerful demonstration of the relation character of money',[20] confirming Simmel's interpretation of the societal nature of money as a process: '[i]n his terms, money is a claim, if not on "society" then on *varying modes of shared existence and experience*'.[21]

[18] M McLuhan, *Understanding Media: The Extensions of Man* (New York, McGraw Hill, 1964).

[19] N Dodd, 'The Social Life of Bitcoin' (2018) 35(3) *Theory, Culture & Society* 35–56.

[20] ibid 35. 'In practice, … the currency has generated a thriving community around its political ideals, relies on a high degree of social organization in order to be produced, has a discernible social structure, and is characterized by asymmetries of wealth and power that are not dissimilar from the mainstream financial system': ibid.

[21] Dodd (n 19) 52; italics in the original text.

It is precisely with regard to these varying modes of shared existence and experience that the COVID-19 crisis, I believe, has also radically affected the nature of EU money, changing the character of the EU polity itself. Within a pandemic bringing mass death and economic catastrophe, the first semester of 2020 saw the conception of a Recovery Plan, the Next Generation EU (NGEU) fund (agreed to by the European Council of 21 July 2020) that for the first time in the history of the EU envisaged mechanisms of common European debt – paving the way for a new *Life* for Europe.[22] On this matter, Ferdinando Giuliano, *Bloomberg Opinion* Editor and former member of the editorial board of the *Financial Times*, has underlined how

> [t]he fund breaks a number of EU taboos. First, it raises significantly the amount the Commission can borrow on the financial markets. These are not 'euro bonds' in the classic sense of the word … However, it will be a very useful blueprint if the euro zone chooses to move closer to a much-needed fiscal union. The second big change is that two-thirds of the money would [be] given away as grants. This is the most controversial part of the plan … [b]ut the generous provision of grants is a step change from the European Stability Mechanism, the euro area's rescue fund, which only offers loans. The final taboo to be possibly broken is on EU-wide taxation.[23]

In the end, under these circumstances, where an age of monetary pluralism *in the EU* combines with the political metamorphosis *of the EU* (with the second process interlinked with the former), investigating the changing identity of the European community through its own money (*monies*?) becomes an imperative from which social researchers cannot escape.

IV. A Chair and a Banquet

Referring again to the metaphor of value-credit (becoming capital in the process of re-evaluation) as wave-particle duality – 'separately neither of them fully explains the phenomena of … [money], but together they do!'[24] – I believe that the ultimate meaning of this book can be probably depicted as a medium of understanding that the reader will employ to join the 'banquet' of investigations proposed by the contributors who have replied to this imperative.

If a chair is indeed of little benefit when kept in a storage closet, the *value* of the Jean Monnet Chair resides in the *credit* given by Gabriella to all the participants in the EU Money Law project. Acting separately, they would have never been able to

[22] With regard to the political implications of 'resurrection' related to this event, please refer to Cattelan (n 8).

[23] F Giuliano, 'The European Union is on the Brick of Historic Change' (*Bloomberg*, 31 May 2020) www.bloomberg.com/opinion/articles/2020-05-27/eu-pandemic-recovery-fund-puts-europe-on-brick-of-historic-change.

[24] Einstein and Infeld (n 16) 278.

capitalise their knowledge: their 'heads', isolated from each other, would have been like money put aside in a vault. On the contrary, this volume may start 'an endless cycle of extensions and intensifications' of intellectual discussion, of which the reader will hopefully take full advantage by enjoying the banquet of ideas that EU Money Law has prepared for the general public.

2

Monetary Identity of the EU and the Drivers of Regulatory Change

GABRIELLA GIMIGLIANO

I. Monetary Identity and the EU

This volume is one of the research activities promoted within the EUMOL project.

EUMOL stands for Jean Monnet Chair in EU Money Law, which I have held since 2018. In keeping with the general approach of Jean Monnet Actions, EUMOL activities address academicians as well as bachelor and master degree students, but also aim to reach professionals and the general public, through various teaching, research, and networking activities.[1]

This book, like many other project activities, takes an inter-disciplinary approach thanks to the cooperation of the key EUMOL Chair teaching staff members[2] and the invited lecturers who kindly joined the project's initiatives from time to time. They share a common research interest or professional expertise in the field of money and the European integration process, as well as a common approach to money as a social institution. Indeed, money

> (…) cannot be seen as a passive technical instrument of the market. It is an active institution in human societies that is socially and historically constructed. Far from being limited to a market function, money establishes comparative values in a range of circumstances – social, political and economic.[3]

[1] For an overview of EUMOL activities and output, please visit: www.eumol.com and also, on Twitter: @EumolM.

[2] Among the key teaching staff members, those who participated in this book as editors and/or contributors merit particular mention: Valentino Cattelan, Marc Pilkington, Vittorio Santoro, Ruth Wandhöfer, Luisa Brunori, and Marta Božina Beroš. Some other key teaching staff members have greatly contributed to the development of the ideas underlying this monograph, including Christos Gortsos, Gloria González Fuster, and Agnieszka Janczuk-Gorywoda.

[3] M Mellor, *Money. Myths, truths and alternatives* (Bristol, Policy Press, 2019) 136.

This means that money, rather than being a neutral device, is 'colored from the start', as Christine Desan argued, taking a constitutional approach:

> (…) money has an internal design: societies produce it by structuring claims of value in ways that make those claims commensurable, transferable, and available for certain private as well as public uses. That architecture, in all its intricacy, determines the way money works in the world. Moreover, that architecture varies. As societies change the way they engineer money, they change its character and the market it takes. (…) In fact, societies engineer money rather than discovering it. Their work is constant and collective, a matter that involves both public initiative and individual decision-making.[4]

In this process, money as a means of exchange is enabled by money as a unit of account. The latter works as an abstract measure that cannot be applied to the physical world, in terms of length or weight, which may raise a question about its substantive value. As Christine Desan writes in her piece,[5] 'what is the substantive value captured by a dollar, one that convinces people with different needs and means to understand it as a common measure?'.

Moving from the monetary experience in the Anglo-Saxon context at the heart of Desan's analysis to our domestic context, one might say that, in the EU, the governance strategy of money hinges on the day-to-day fulfilment of the policy priorities and the community values laid down in Article 3 of the Treaty on the European Union (TEU). Among other things, the article established that the Union works for

> the sustainable development of Europe based on balanced economic growth and price stability, a highly competitive social market economy, aiming at full employment and social progress, and a high level of protection and improvement of the quality of the environment,

promoting economic, social and territorial cohesion, solidarity among the Member States, and rich cultural and linguistic diversity. However, this challenging shared project is continuously subject to peer assessment. Therefore, the project – and the money – may be considered trustworthy to the extent that, for example, Europeans find it easy to send and receive payments domestically and across borders; businesses and consumers feel their data or their funds are protected any time they use payment services; money is not devalued or counterfeited, and so on.

However, it seems easier to empathise with a community project when it creates jobs, stimulates investments, and strengthens the economy, although the latest global financial crisis has demonstrated that supporting the banking system is not enough to stimulate sustainable economic and community growth. Hence, the European lawmakers have promoted the European Banking Union and launched

[4] C Desan, 'The Constitutional Approach to Money: Monetary Design and the Production of the Modern World' in N Bandelj, F Wherry and V Zelizer (eds), *Money talks: explaining how money really works* (Forthcoming, Harvard Public Law Working Paper No. 16-05), available at SSRN: https://ssrn.com/abstract=2724108.

[5] ibid.

the Capital Market Union (CMU). In 2015, President Juncker stated one of the key priorities: 'To strengthen investment for the long term, we need stronger capital markets. These would provide new sources of funding for business, help increase options for savers and make the economy more resilient'. This entails a focus on money as capital in terms of 'an economic process, governed by a form of pecuniary valuation, namely, capitalization; (...) associated with investment, in which capital may (or may not) become a factor of production'.[6]

The two-tier structure of money is acknowledged in the two Parts of this book. Part I concerns money as a means of exchange and unit of account, while Part II turns to money as capital; in other words, borrowing the approach followed by Valentino Cattelan in chapter one, Part I concerns money as a 'substance of value' or 'matter of exchanges', while Part II deals with money as 'energy' or 'inherent potential of credit'. Together, these elements form the monetary identity of the EU, an identity under pressure from three drivers of regulatory change: the COVID-19 pandemic, developments in FinTech developments (from Decentralised Ledger Technology or DLT to cryptoassets or CBDCs), and sustainable development goals. The framework and the drivers are the subjects of our contributors' analyses.

II. Money as a Matter of Exchanges

Thinking of money as a medium of exchange and a unit of account, money is simultaneously a settlement asset and a payment system; as such, there must be a secure way of transferring the asset. This leads us to the first feature of European monetary identity, ie, the two-tier structure of the regulatory context.

European policymakers carried out a long-lasting harmonisation process based on Articles 4 and 114 of the TFEU providing for a comprehensive and binding framework addressing money as funds. This definition comprises bank notes and coins, bank money and electronic money, as set forth in the EMI Directive.[7] In addition, the rules of EU law regarding information requirements as well as duties and obligations for the provision of payment services are also applicable to payment transactions in currencies other than the euro, which may be the currencies of Member States outside the Eurozone, and to some extent third countries' currencies.

However, there is still a duality between euro- and non-euro Member States in the construction of the internal market for payments. Indeed, within the broad legal framework regarding the payment system, there is a preponderance of secondary

[6] J Levy, 'Capital as a process and the history of capitalism' (2017) 91 *Business History Review* 483–510.

[7] Directive 2009/110/EC of the European Parliament and the Council, of 16 September 2009, on the taking up, pursuit and prudential supervision of the business of the electronic money institutions amending Directive 2005/60/EC and 2006/48/EC and repealing Directive 2000/46/EC [2009] OJ L267/10.

law provisions and business regulatory and technical standards tailor-made for transfers of funds in euro. These include the secondary law rules on execution time and value date laid down in the 2015 Payment Services Directive (PSD2),[8] the Regulations on cross-border credit transfers and direct debits in euro, and also the Single Euro Payment Area (SEPA) rulebooks,[9] all of which aim to bring about more stringent cooperation.

The second distinctive aspect of European monetary identity is the pro-competitive approach. European lawmakers have tried to curtail the oligopolistic position of credit institutions and major credit card issuers to help level the field in the internal market. In fact, since the 2007 Payment Services Directive (PSD1),[10] European lawmakers have sought to remove regulatory obstacles to market entry for non-banking payment service providers. Consistently, the legal framework for non-banking payment service providers has set own funds requirements and capital thresholds according to a risk-based approach, allowing payment institutions and electronic money institutions to overcome the principle of single corporate purpose; indeed, they may be established and authorised as either pure or hybrid business payment service providers. In addition, in the user-provider contract relationship, the European framework considered and considers information as a useful pro-competition tool. With a view to supporting antitrust action in the payment services market, the positive harmonisation process has sometimes tried to fill in some gaps. This is the case with regard to access conditions for the four-party payment system established in the PSD1 (and confirmed in the PSD2), the roof set for debit-card multilateral interchange fees (MIF),[11] and the principle of non-discrimination based on customers' nationality or place of residence in e-commerce transactions laid down in the 2018 geo-blocking Regulation.[12]

Closely linked to the pro-competition approach is the hybrid governance model, combining hierarchy, market, and network models.

Since hierarchy provides for a central authority leading a chain of subordinate units that are committed to performing specialised functions, this may not be fully applicable to EU law regarding money and payments. In fact, the positive harmonisation process is based on legislative jurisdiction being shared between the EU and the Member States, in compliance with Article 4 TEU, which

[8] Directive 2015/2366/EU of the European Parliament and the Council, of 25 November 2015, on payment services in the internal market, amending Directives 2002/65/EC, 2009/110/EC and 2013/36/EU and Regulation (EU) No 1093/2010, and repealing Directive 2007/64/EC [2015] OJ L337/35.

[9] See www.ecb.europa.eu/paym/integration/retail/sepa/html/index.en.html.

[10] Directive 2007/64/EC of European Parliament and the Council, of 13 November 2007, on payment services in the internal market amending Directives 97/7/EC, 2002/65/EC, 2005/60/EC and 2006/48/EC and repealing Directive 97/5/EC [2007] OJ L19/1.

[11] Regulation 2015/751/EU of the European Parliament and the Council, of 29 April 2015, on interchange fees for card-based payment transactions [2015] OJ L123/1.

[12] Regulation (EU) 2018/302 of the European Parliament and of the Council of 28 February 2018 on addressing unjustified geo-blocking and other forms of discrimination based on customers' nationality, place of residence or place of establishment within the internal market and amending Regulations (EC) No 2006/2004 and (EU) 2017/2394 and Directive 2009/22/EC [2018] OJ L60I/1.

established a dialectical relationship between the EU and the Member States and, to some extent, a degree of legal uncertainty. In addition, while European lawmakers largely give priority to the full harmonisation approach, the directives in force, especially the PSD2, leave some room for Member States and require complementary activity to be carried out by the European Banking Authority (EBA). In fact, Level 1 regulation includes European Parliament and Council directives and regulations, while the Level 2 normative framework accommodates the Binding Technical Standards developed by the EBA and endorsed by the Commission (and this endorsement makes them compulsory rules for national authorities), and also Guidelines and Recommendations, as well as Q&As, all gathered together in an interactive single rule To date, EBA measures have covered payment security, money laundering processes, payment data fraud, transparency, and comparison payment account fees, among others.

Since in the market model of governance, price is supposed to convey correct information, monetary identity is challenged by the dialectical relationship between European competition rules and the two-sided payment networks' agreements on price, such as multilateral interchange fees, the no-surcharge rule and the no-discrimination rule. This leads us to the last model, ie, network governance and the role it has played in the European regulatory context. Since the first soft rules were issued in the mid-1980s, the Commission has encouraged the interoperability of payment networks. However, the trade-off between intra- and inter- system competition has greatly challenged European antitrust actions, as the Visa, Mastercard, or *Cartes Bancaires*, cases suggest.

Finally, the last element of identity is the 'electronification' of funds. Since the Commission Recommendations and Communications of the mid-1980s, European lawmakers have encouraged Member States and financial institutions to shift all transfers of funds online. Since money as monetary consideration enters into all business transactions, the free movement of goods and services would work properly only if there were low (or no) technical, business, or regulatory obstacles to the free movement of current payments. In the Payment Services Directives, European lawmakers promoted fully integrated straight-through processing of payments and set paper-based drafts as well as banknotes and coins beyond the scope of the harmonisation process. This raised some degree of legal uncertainty on the discharge of monetary obligations, and whether bank money may be dealt with as legal tender. Recently, the European Court of Justice held that

> The third sentence of Article 128(1) TFEU … on the introduction of the euro must be interpreted as not precluding national legislation which excludes the possibility of discharging a statutorily imposed payment obligation in banknotes denominated in euro, provided (i) that that legislation does not have the object or effect of establishing legal rules governing the status of legal tender of such banknotes; (ii) that it does not lead, in law or in fact, to abolition of those banknotes, in particular by calling into question the possibility, as a general rule, of discharging a payment obligation in cash; (iii) that it has been adopted for reasons of public interest; (iv) that the limitation on payments in cash which the legislation entails is appropriate for attaining the public

interest objective pursued; and (v) that it does not go beyond what is necessary in order to achieve that objective, in that other lawful means of discharging the payment obligation are available.

This seems to sum up the background under discussion in this book, ie, the main features of the European monetary identity, which is now changing under the pressures of the health and financial crisis triggered by COVID-19, FinTech developments, and sustainability policy priorities.

At the beginning of Part I, chapter three aims to critically map the achievements of the European harmonisation process for payment service customers. To what extent has EU payment law created an inclusive community? How are risks and responsibilities in the transfers of funds allocated between service providers and users, or payers and payees?

From chapter four to chapter seven, the authors give an account of the feasible regulatory changes that may be induced by FinTech-based innovations.

Chapter four (Malgorzata Cyndecka) considers the open banking model from the standpoint of the 'silent parties', namely, those who do not know that their data are being processed. Indeed, the PSD2 provides for the application of GDPR regulations to payment services users' sensitive data, but at the same time accommodates open Application Programming Interfaces (APIs).[13] There, for the first time, the list of payment services comprises account information services and payment initiation services in the closed list of payment services, while the Directive compels their providers to adhere to some registration requirements, information requirements, and contracting duties and obligations.

In chapter five, Ruth Wandhöfer considers the international cross-border payments question and whether either the DLT or the option of a 'digital euro' may fill existing regulatory gaps. It is worth noting that the DLT entails removing the 'middleman', in full or to some extent, by promoting public, private, or hybrid blockchain-based systems. In contrast, any decision on whether and how to issue a European Central Bank Digital Currency involves institutional and identity side-issues. In fact, as Fabio Panetta, a member of the executive committee of the ECB, argued, the digital euro may not only ensure that public money remains widely accessible and usable for daily transactions, but also shield Europe's autonomy from non-European payment service providers.[14] It is a crucial policy-making choice: the ECB is still contemplating the *if, when, and how*, like many other central bankers throughout the world, with the exception of China, which has already made

[13] M Zachariadis and P Ozcan, 'The API Economy and Digital Transformation in Financial Services: The Case of Open Banking' (15 June 2017), SWIFT Institute Working Paper No. 2016-001, https://ssrn.com/abstract=2975199 or http://dx.doi.org/10.2139/ssrn.2975199.

[14] F Panetta, 'The ECB's case for central bank digital currencies' *Financial Times* (18 November 2021); F Panetta, 'Designing a digital euro for the retail payments landscape of tomorrow' (Brussels, 18 November 2021), www.ecb.europa.eu/press/key/date/2021/html/ecb.sp211118~b36013b7c5.en.html.

its choice. Issuing a CBDC brings many uncertainties, analysed in chapters six and seven by Ursula Dalinghaus, Vittorio Santoro and Gian Luca Greco, who look at the matter from different perspectives in keeping with their sociological or legal standpoints.

The last two chapters of Part I, authored by Maria Elena Salerno (chapter eight) and Marco Bodellini (chapter nine), take a normative and legal approach, and both concern commercial banking money, considering that

> such deposits are claims denominated in state money and payable on demand. The resulting convertibility into state money means that they all circulate at par, at an exchange rate of 1:1, despite having been issued by different banks with balance sheets that differ significantly in quality.[15]

There are several factors converging to keep the value of bank deposits uniform, from prudential supervision to deposit insurance, and from the lender of last resort to the banking insolvency management mechanism. Chapters eight and nine analyse some missing steps of the European Banking Union on the premise that the financial and economic crisis triggered by the COVID-19 pandemic has made regulatory and enforcement cooperation much more crucial for the European sustainable growth.

III. Money as Energy

Part II of this volume concerns money as capital, what was referred to in chapter one as the 'inherent potential of credit' or 'energy', consistent with Levy's construction of capital as a 'particular kind of economic process':

> Capital is property capitalized – a legal asset assigned a pecuniary value in expectation of its capacity to yield a likely future pecuniary income.[16]

From a normative standpoint, there is no definition of capital. In the second half of the 1980s, the European Court of Justice held that monetary transfers represent a broad category comprising both current payments and movements of capital; current payments are money consideration within the context of an underlying transaction, while movements of capital are financial operations essentially concerned with the investment of the funds in question rather than remuneration for a service.[17]

[15] C Zellweger, 'The right and duty of central banks to issue retail digital currency' in D Niepelt (ed), *Central Bank Digital Currency: Considerations, Projects, Outlook* (London, CEPR Press, 2021) 31–37.

[16] Levy (n 6) 494.

[17] A Landsmeer, 'Movement of capital and other freedoms' (2001) 28(1) *Legal Issues of Economic Integration* 57–69; JA Usher, *The Law of Money and Financial Services in the European Community* (Oxford, Oxford University Press 2000) 1–14, 15–38; JV Louis, 'Free movement of capital in the Community: the Casati judgement' (1982) 19 *Common Market Law Review* 443–52.

When the liberalisation of capital movements was fully achieved with the Fourth Capital Directive, Annex I merely provided a list of samples of capital movements,[18] ranging from the direct investment, ie:

> Investments of all kinds by natural persons or commercial, industrial or financial undertakings, and which serve to establish or to maintain lasting and direct links between the person providing the capital and the entrepreneur to whom or the undertaking to which the capital is made available in order to carry on an economic activity

to investment in real estate, operations in securities and other instruments normally dealt in on a money market, operations in units of collective investment undertakings, operations in securities normally dealt with on capital markets, and so on, as per the nomenclature in Annex I of the Fourth Capital Directive.

This means that the construction of an internal market for capital began later (in comparison with the other main freedoms) and still entails great effort in overcoming regulatory fragmentation with a view to reducing the cost of capital.[19] Indeed, in July 2021, the Commission stated that a 'well-integrated and efficient capital market should act as catalyst for effective mobilisation and allocation of capital towards sustainable investment'.[20] Therefore, the Capital Market Union (CMU) and the sustainable finance framework reinforce each other. At issue are ambitious objectives concerning the Union's identity: not only reducing overreliance on funding through banks, but also becoming the first climate-neutral continent by 2050 and reducing greenhouse gas emissions by at least 55 per cent by 2030 compared to 1990s levels. In addition, this is compatible with the need to provide individuals and small and medium enterprises with greater access to sustainable finance; making the financial sector more resilient and more consistent with the objectives of EU Green Deal; and enabling business operators across the economy to finance their transition plans. However, the economic recovery from the COVID-19 pandemic required European policymakers to make much greater financial resources available. In one of the last updates of the Capital Market Union Action Plan, in November 2021, the Commission stated that

> While the Recovery and Resilience Facility Plan will make a significant contribution to the recovery through structural reforms and publicly funded investment projects, strong and well-integrated capital markets will be essential to support future economic growth.[21]

[18] Council Directive 88/361/EEC of 24 June 1988 for the implementation of Art 67 of the Treaty [1988] OJ L 178/5 7.

[19] M Andenas, T Gütt and M Pannier, 'Free movement of capital and national company law' (2005) 16 *European Business Law Review* 757–86.

[20] See Commission, 'Communication from the Commission to the European Parliament, the Council, the European Economic and Social Committee and the Committee of the Regions, Strategy for Financing the Transition to a Sustainable Economy' COM (2021) 390 final.

[21] See Commission, 'Communication from the Commission to the European Parliament, the Council, the European Economic and Social Committee and the Committee of the Regions, Capital Market Union – Delivering one year after the Action Plan' COM (2021) 720 final.

In the end, despite uncertainties about the legal concept of capital, the free movement of capital plays a decisive role, especially for business law. Around the sixteenth and the seventeenth centuries, the economic and market evolution produced a radical change in the model of commercial partnership. Luisa Brunori, a commercial law historian, analyses the structural transformation of trade partnership and

> this evolution in the transition from partnerships characterized by the legal significance of the subjective element of the individuality of partners (*intuitus personae*) to a capital company in which the predominant legal importance is attributed to the size of the company's assets, that is, its monetary capital which has now become an independent centre for the imputation of legal effects (*intuitus pecuniae*).

This chapter outlines the starting point of Part II, what laid the foundations for the Capital Market Union providing us with the main regulatory framework to deal with now. This plan, launched in 2015, has recently pointed to three core policy objectives: (i) making financing accessible to EU companies, (ii) providing savers with Environmental Social Governance (ESG)-compliant products, and (iii) meeting the forthcoming challenges of the Digital Finance Strategy. With regard to (i), chapters eleven (Johannes Lenhard and Leo Rees) and twelve (Casimiro Nigro and Alperen Gözlügöl) focus, from different standpoints, on venture capital, which represents forms of alternative investment funds, intended to provide European entrepreneurship with sources of long-standing finance outside the banking channel; while concerning (ii), chapter thirteen (Alexandra Andhov and Lela Mélon) analyses Green CMU and regulatory challenges in terms of sustainability; and, chapter fourteen (Marc Pilkington) addresses the digital transition in terms of risk management with regard to the ambitious objective of digitalising the economy and applying the open finance model beyond the PSD2.

In conclusion, in chapter fifteen, Marta Božina Beroš and Marin Beroš investigate the role of European Central Bank and how the sovereign debt crisis first and the COVID-19 financial emergencies later, gradually expanded its powers. This chapter addresses the elephant in the room, ie, the redistribution issues running through the two-tier structure of money as a means of exchange and a unit of account on the one hand and a means of investment on the other.

Like members of an orchestra, the contributors touch different strings, but they play one melody, a critical reflection for the future of the EU; I hope the readers will feel fully involved.

PART I

The Changing Matter of Money

3

EU Law of Money and the Payment Service Consumers: Miles Done and the Challenges Ahead*

GABRIELLA GIMIGLIANO

I. Introduction

European harmonisation regarding payment and payment services was a lengthy process.[1] It began in the mid-1970s as a negative harmonisation,[2] and was transformed into a positive harmonisation around the mid-1980s by means of the Commission's communications and recommendations.[3] Only in the second half of the 1990s did the Council and the European Parliament pass the first binding rules, namely, the Directive on Cross-border Credit Transfers[4] and, a year later, the Settlement Finality Directive.[5]

It goes without saying that the 2007 Payment Service Directive[6] (hereafter, PSD1) was a turning point.[7] It was the first full harmonisation directive in this

* This chapter is written within the context of the Jean Monnet Chair in EU Money Law (2018–2021), held by Dr Gabriella Gimigliano.

[1] See overview in G Gimigliano, *Money, Payment Systems and the European Union. The regulatory challenges of governance* (Newcastle upon Tyne, Cambridge Scholars Publishing, 2016).

[2] See A Janczuk, 'Sources of EU payments law' in Gimigliano (n 1) 2–23.

[3] Commission Recommendation of 8 December 1987 on a European code of conduct relating to electronic payments [1987] OJEC L365/72. This was followed by the Commission Recommendation of 17 November 1988 concerning the contracting relationship between the card holder and the card issuer [1988] OJEC L317/55; Commission Discussion Paper of 26 September 1990 on 'Making payments in the internal market' [COM (90) 447 final]; Commission Recommendation 1997/489/EC of 30 July 1997, on transactions by electronic payment instruments, and in particular the relationship between the issuer and the holder [1997] OJEC L208/52.

[4] Directive 1997/5/EC of the European Parliament and the Council, of 27 January 1997, on cross-border credit transfers [1997] OJEC L43/25.

[5] Directive 1998/26/EC of the European Parliament and the Council, of 19 May 1998, on settlement finality in payment and securities settlement systems [1998] OJEC L166/45.

[6] Directive 2007/64/EC of European Parliament and the Council, of 13 November 2007, on payment services in the internal market amending Directives 97/7/EC, 2002/65/EC, 2005/60/EC and 2006/48/EC and repealing Directive 97/5/EC [2007] OJ L19/1.

[7] D Mavromati, *The Law of Payment Services in the EU* (The Netherlands, Kluwer International, 2007).

field and, although it was not intended to provide a fully comprehensive framework, it addresses the provision of payment services as a regulated activity[8] and covers three crucial areas: payment institutions, transparency of conditions and information requirements,[9] and rights and obligations concerning the provision of payment services.[10] The broad scope and, to some extent, the full harmonisation approach adopted made PSD1 the backbone of the European framework for payments. In turn, PSD2,[11] replacing the former, retains the same importance.

In the period between the two Payment Service Directives (PSDs), European policymakers passed directives and regulations that perform roles complementary to them. They address various specific aspects, including the revised framework for electronic money, multilateral interchange fees for debit card payments, the right to switch payment accounts throughout the Union and the right to access the payment system through a payment account with basic features.[12]

This chapter aims to analyse the European framework for payments from the consumers' standpoint, establishing their legal status. What type of 'community participation' has been formulated for payment service consumers? To the extent that the European policymaker is carrying forth a financial inclusion strategy,[13] what are its main legal instruments? Have EU policymakers ultimately taken a paternalistic and purely protective approach to the payment service consumer?

This chapter is made up of five sections following this introduction. Section II spotlights the user-consumer dichotomy in EU payment law; section III considers how consumers can access the payment system; section IV concerns consumers

[8] See: Title II, PSD2. With regard to the multi-layered framework for payment institutions made up of secondary rules and EBA technical regulatory standards, see CG Corvese, 'Sub Title II. Artt. 5 – 21, PSD2' in M Bozina Beros and G Gimigliano (eds), *The Payment Service Directive II: A Commentary* Elgar Commentaries series, (Cheltenham, Edward Elgar, 2021) 31–65.

[9] There is a common thread between the soft rules and the PSD2 provisions on transparency of conditions and information requirements. See: G Gimigliano, 'Sub Title IV. Chapter 2' in Bozina Beros and Gimigliano (n 8) 145–61.

[10] Title IV, PSD2.

[11] Directive 2015/2366/EU of the European Parliament and the Council, of 25 November 2015, on payment services in the internal market, amending Directives 2002/65/EC, 2009/110/EC and 2013/36/EU and Regulation (EU) No 1093/2010, and repealing Directive 2007/64/EC [2015] OJ L337/35.

[12] Directive 2009/110/EC of the European Parliament and the Council, of 16 September 2009, on the taking up, pursuit and prudential supervision of the business of the electronic money institutions amending Directive 2005/60/EC and 2006/48/EC and repealing Directive 2000/46/EC [2009] OJ L267/10 (hereafter, EMD2); Directive 2014/92/EU of the European Parliament and the Council, of 23 July 2014, on the comparability of fees related to payment accounts, payment account switching and access to payment accounts with basic features [2014] OJ L257/2014 (hereafter, PAD); Regulation 2015/751/EU of the European Parliament and the Council, of 29 April 2015, on interchange fees for card-based payment transactions [2015] OJ L123/1; Regulation (EU) 2018/302 of the European Parliament and of the Council of 28 February 2018 on addressing unjustified geo-blocking and other forms of discrimination based on customers' nationality, place of residence or place of establishment within the internal market and amending Regulations (EC) No 2006/2004 and (EU) 2017/2394 and Directive 2009/22/EC [2018] OJ L60I/1.

[13] CPMI – World Bank Group, *Payment aspects of financial inclusion* (April 2016) 1–82, www.bis.org/cpmi/publ/d144.pdf.

as transaction actors in contractual relationships with payment service providers (PSPs), addressing them as intelligent digital players, fully empowered with the ability to decide what is in their interests; section V turns to the potential shortcomings of an EU-based framework that protects the payment service consumer through the construction of the internal market; and finally, section VI draws some conclusions.

II. Consumers in EU Payment Law

Generally speaking, the European legal framework for payment services is addressed to 'users' rather than 'consumers'. In compliance with the principle of conferral, the Union identifies a Treaty provision as the legal basis for regulatory actions. Concerning European directives and regulations for payment services and systems, this is Article 114 of the Treaty of Functioning of the European Union (hereafter, TFEU). Therefore, consumer protection seems to be an indirect effect of the proper functioning of the internal market.[14]

The PSD2 outlines the difference between consumers, users and microenterprises. A consumer is 'any natural person who, in payment service contracts covered by this Directive, is acting for purposes other than his or her trade, business or profession', while the user can also be a trader, ie 'any natural or legal person who is acting for purposes relating to his trade, craft, business or profession and anyone acting in the name of or on behalf of a trader'. In between, there are micro-enterprises, namely, enterprises employing fewer than 10 people and whose annual turnover and/or annual balance sheet total does not exceed EUR 2 million. Like PSD1, PSD2 allows Member States to treat them in the same way as consumers. The legal framework was gradually built up matching soft rules with binding rules, as well as negative and positive harmonisation.

In the 1970s and 1980s, legal dispute focused on the four freedoms: matters of contention dealt with either small firms or consumers, but in any event always concerned the transfer of banknotes in a currency other than that of the State of origin, and the intent was to ascertain the extent to which freedom of payment was liberalised.

In those years, the free movement of payments was considered ancillary to the free movement of capital, and the latter had not yet been fully liberalised. In the

[14] The harmonisation process is made up of soft and binding rules, both aimed at building up or improving the internal market. It is argued that the 'four freedoms' are necessary for the unity of the internal market and, a fortiori, are necessary for the existence of the Union itself. In turn, harmonising rules and regulations, as well as competition and state aids rules, are necessary to create the conditions for the free movement of capital, goods, persons and services. See: S Cassese, 'La Costituzione Economica Europea' (2001) 6 *Rivista italiana di diritto pubblico comunitario* 907 ff.

Luisi and Carbone case,[15] the Court of Justice was asked to release a preliminary ruling on the interpretation of Article 106 of the Treaty of Rome. It held that

> any payments connected with the movement of goods or services are to be liberalised to the extent to which the movement of goods and services has been liberalised between the Member States.

In other words, the money consideration paid for exchanging goods or services (ie *current payments*) had been fully liberalised since the end of the transitional period. In addition, the Court stated that the

> physical transfer of bank notes may not therefore be classified as a movement of capital where the transfer in question corresponds to an obligation to pay arising from a transaction involving the movement of goods or services. Consequently, payments in connection with tourism or travel for the purposes of business, education or medical treatment cannot be classified as movements of capital, even where they are affected by means of physical transfer of bank notes.[16]

Later on, in the second half of the 1980s, harmonisation continued in the form of a framework of soft rules, and the consumers addressed included holders of debit or credit cards, e-money products or home banking accounts. In fact, the first Commission's communications and recommendations cover the contracting relationship between service providers and consumers, establishing information requirements prior and subsequent to the contract, as well as the basics of contracting duties and liabilities.[17]

In the mid-1990s, when the first binding rules were enacted, the attention of the European policymaker shifted from consumers to users, as in the case of the European Directive on cross-border credit transfers and the e-money directives of the 2000s.[18] PSD1 followed the same tack, but emphasised that consumers and enterprises are not in the same position in the contracting relationship with payment institutions. This is why whenever the users are consumers, PSD1 rules are compulsory for contracting parties, and Member States may provide for stricter rules in the directive transposition process.

In PSD2, provisions are addressed to payment service users rather than to payment service consumers, but with the same caveat provided in PSD1. It is

[15] Joined Cases 286/82 and 26/83 *Graziana Luisi and Giuseppe Carbone v Ministero del Tesoro* [1984] ECR 377. The joint '*Luisi and Carbone*' cases posed the following situation: two nationals of a Member State (Italy) moved to another Member State to enjoy tourist services or medical treatments and brought with them a quantity of physical banknotes in the foreign currency for use abroad, exceeding the maximum permitted by the home exchange law. Both Mrs Luisi and Mr Carbone were charged under national law, which imposed a penalty on them.

[16] *Luisi and Carbone* (ibid), paras 21–23.

[17] See n 3 above.

[18] Directive 2000/46/EC of the European Parliament and of the Council, of 18 September 2000, on the taking up, pursuit of and prudential supervision of the business of electronic money institutions and Directive 2000/46 and Directive 2000/28/EC of the European Parliament and of the Council, of 18 September 2000, amending Directive 2000/12/EC relating to the taking up and pursuit of the business of credit institutions [2000] OJ L275/37.

worth noting here that PSD2 sets out a broader definition of payment service consumers (in comparison with PSD1) consistent with its functional, territorial and currency scope. Indeed, Article 2 PSD2 establishes a shift from a double-leg to a single-leg principle. This means that for 'those parts of the payment transaction which are carried out in the Union', PSD2 also applies when the payment transactions are denominated in currencies other than Member States' currencies and one PSP (either the payee's or payer's PSP) is located in the Union.[19]

III. Accessing the Payment System

The next step is to take a closer look at legal means of accessing the payment system. One might initially think of traditional payment instruments, ie, banknotes and coins. However, neither banknotes nor coins seem to belong to the future development of the internal market for payment, where business transactions are largely carried out as remote operations. In fact, like paper-based negotiable instruments, banknotes and coins fall beyond the scope of harmonising rules.[20]

The previous section showed how, from the outset, the harmonisation process pushed forward the *electronification* of payment services, that is, the 'migration towards the provision of payment services on a fully electronic and highly automated basis'.[21] This has made the process of discharging monetary obligations a flow of digital information moving through the payment system as a whole or, more precisely, through interoperable payment systems, where the payment system is a

> funds transfer system with formal and standardised arrangements and common rules for the processing, clearing and/or settlement of payment transactions.[22]

Within such a legal framework, what are the options for regulating access to the payment system?

PSD2 provides for the following:

(i) Making a money remittance: the consumer brings with him banknotes and coins to hand over to a money remittance service provider to be sent and made available in cash to the beneficiary.[23]
(ii) Entering a framework contract that governs 'the future execution of individual and successive payment transactions and which may contain the obligation and conditions for setting up a payment account'.[24] This means

[19] See Art 2 PSD2. For further information, see G Gimigliano, 'Sub Title IV, Chapter 1, art. 61-63, PSD2' and 'Title III, Chapters 1, 2, 3 (Art. 38 – 58) PSD2' in Bozina Beros and Gimigliano (n 8) 132–44.
[20] See Art 3(a), (g) PSD2.
[21] ECB, 'Electronification of payment in Europe' (*ECB Monthly Bulletin*, May 2003) 61–72.
[22] Art 4(7), PSD2.
[23] See preamble (9) PD2.
[24] Art 4(21) PSD2.

that the PSP is bound to execute any payment order issued (by the payment service consumer) in compliance with the contract terms and conditions, but the consumer must bring with him and hand over the sum of money to the PSP.

(iii) Holding a payment account described in the Payment Service Directives (PSDs) as 'an account held in the name of one or more payment service users which is used for the execution of payment transactions'.[25] This is a type of framework contract upon which the holder may use the account balance for executing payment transactions.

(iv) Holding e-money, which means 'electronically, including magnetically, stored monetary value as represented by a claim on the issuer which is issued on receipt of funds for the purpose of making payment transactions as defined in point 5 of Article 4 of Directive 2007/64/EC, and which is accepted by a natural or legal person other than the electronic money issuer'.[26] In other words, as long as the electronic money institution concerned is also authorised to provide payment services, the e-money holder may use the monetary value stored as e-money to utilise all payment services listed in the PSD[27] Annex I.

A. The Payment Account as the Leading Means to Access the Payment System

Among the regulatory options listed above, there is little doubt that the payment account represents the paradigmatic means of access to payment systems at the Union level. The 2014 Payment Service Directive (or PAD)[28] provides for the principle of non-discrimination: Member States ensure that credit institutions do not discriminate against consumers legally resident in the Union on the grounds of their nationality, place of residence or personal legal status (European citizens as well as people seeking asylum) when they apply for or access a payment account within the Union.[29]

In 2014, the Payment Account Directive gave consumers the right to hold a payment account, at least in a basic form, in an attempt to compromise between the aim of financial inclusion and the risk of market distortion.[30]

This Directive establishes that the contracting parties may be credit institutions[31] – the only PSPs required to provide payment accounts with basic

[25] Art 4(12) PSD2.
[26] Art 2(2) EMD2.
[27] PSDs stands for Payment Service Directives.
[28] See n 12 above.
[29] Art 15 PAD.
[30] Art 16(1) PAD.
[31] The Member States may decide to apply Chapter IV of the 2014 Payment Account Directive to PSPs other than credit institutions (see Art 1(4) PAD).

features – and consumers, specifically both vulnerable and not-vulnerable consumers

> legally resident in the Union, including consumers with no fixed address and asylum seekers, and consumers who are not granted a residence permit but whose expulsion is impossible for legal or factual reasons.[32]

According to the PAD, credit institutions may refuse or unilaterally terminate the contract only in the following cases:

- When the consumer has deliberately used the payment account for illegal purposes: for example, on the grounds of a money laundering directive.
- The consumer is no longer resident in the Union.
- The consumer does not show a 'genuine interest' in the territory of the Member State concerned: beyond the consumer's residence, the 'genuine interest' should be interpreted in relation to the four freedoms of the European Treaties.
- The consumer holds a payment account – for example, a regular payment account – with a credit institution located in the same Member State, enabling the consumer to make use of the same payment services covered by the payment account with basic features. Similarly, credit institutions can refuse or unilaterally terminate the contract when there has been no transaction on the payment account for more than 24 consecutive months. In both cases, it is conceivable that the restraints imposed on the freedom of contract are allowed providing there is an actual need.
- The consumer has given the credit institution incorrect information in order to obtain a payment account with basic features 'where the correct information would have resulted in the absence of such right'. What cases does this specification cover? It does not concern residency or any other stable link with the territory of the Member State, nor the consumer's financial circumstances, ie employment status, level of income, credit history or personal bankruptcy, *ex* preamble 35, PSD2. It might refer to any further cases of permitted refusal and unilateral termination of the contract added on at the national level (Article 16(6) and Article 19(3) PAD).

European policymakers were also concerned with ensuring that the payment account with basic features not be treated as an 'inferior' form of access to the payment system. In bold letters, the preamble (38) disallows any form of visible discrimination (for example, differences in the appearance of cards, a different account number or card number), and encourages Member States to prioritise a territorial proximity relationship between the credit institution and the consumer. Moreover, the payment services covered allow the account holder to execute traditional payment transactions.[33]

[32] Art 16(2) PAD.
[33] Art 17 PAD.

However, the 2014 Payment Account Directive provides for some degree of *legal flexibility* in the process of implementation and application. Without proper regulatory coordination at Union level,[34] this may end up impairing consumers' access to the payment system and the proper functioning of the internal market for payment services.

Legal flexibility concerns service fees. Article 18 states that payment services are to be provided free of charge or applying 'reasonable fees' that take into account 'at least' (a) 'national income levels', and (b) 'average fees charged by credit institutions in the Member State concerned for services provided on payment accounts'.[35] In addition, Member States may require credit institutions to set up

> various pricing schemes depending on the level of banking inclusion of the consumer, allowing for, in particular, more advantageous conditions for unbanked vulnerable consumers.[36]

Jochen Hoffmann[37] has critically emphasised not only that this mechanism structure might trigger a price/quality race to the bottom to deter potential applicants, but that the principle of reasonableness does not effectively protect payment service consumers due to its uncertain enforceability, like – I might add – any 'general clause'. It goes without saying that both are likely results when there is not enough regulatory coordination at the Union level. This takes us to the next point.

Legal flexibility concerns the legislative leeway given to Member States in the implementation of the 2014 Payment Account Directive,[38] which prescribes that 'Member States shall ensure that the exercise of the right is not made too difficult or burdensome for the consumer'.[39] I fully agree with Hoffmann: with regard to articles 16(6) and 25 PAD

> The unfortunate wording of Art. 16 para. 6 PAD leaves the relationship between Art. 16 and Art. 25 PAD unsettled – it is not entirely clear if the free account mechanism may only be implemented in addition to the general right of access, or if it may also practically replace it.[40]

For example, UK law has made the joint reading of Articles 16(6) and 25 PAD the basis of a domestic system according to which the payment account with basic features must be free of charge, but is reserved for consumers who are ineligible for all other payment accounts offered by the credit institution concerned. This – as Hoffmann noted – may mean that 'the right to a free account therefore seems to be more a theoretical concept'.[41] It actually may spur credit institutions to

[34] For example, technical regulatory requirements or guidelines issued by the European Banking Authority.

[35] Art 18(3) PAD.

[36] Art 18(4) PAD.

[37] J Hoffmann, 'Implementation of the Payment Accounts Directive' (2019) 20 *ERA Forum* 241.

[38] See Articles: 16(3), (5), (6); 17(2), (6), (8); 18(4); 19(3), 25, PAD.

[39] Art 16(2) PAD.

[40] Hoffmann (n 37) 244.

[41] ibid.

offer regular accounts to any and all applicants in order to reduce the number of consumers taking advantage of a 'free lunch'.

B. Allocating the Costs of Scriptural Money

The entire harmonisation process has de facto prioritised scriptural money over cash in the discharging monetary obligations. But what costs does scriptural money have for payees and payers? There are, in fact, both direct and indirect costs for payees and payers.

The direct costs have to do with the execution of payment transactions; here, the European policymaker has made a clear-cut choice: when both the payer's and payee's PSPs are located in the Union, the payer and the payee pay the charges levied by their own PSP for the execution of the payment order.[42]

The indirect costs are closely connected to the indirect network externalities associated with payment services. This is the case of multilateral interchange fees (MIFs), centrally set by the platform acting as a matchmaker for the two sides of the market. The main point was that all payment services exhibit indirect network externalities, and MIFs were rolled over to the final customer. In fact, first and foremost, the MIF becomes the floor for the acquiring fee applied to the PSP-payee contracting relationship. Consequently, payees – with no chance of discriminating between payment instruments[43] – will rationally increase the item price, consistent with the acquiring fee (and, in turn, the MIF), impacting all payers, regardless of the payment instrument used. The scholarly debate on the antitrust effect of two-sided markets is still open, therefore in 2015 the European policymaker took the initiative in terms of regulation and passed an ad hoc regulation setting an upper limit for multilateral interchange fees for B2C debit and credit card payment transactions.[44] In the same year, PSD2 allowed payees to discriminate[45] among payment instruments.[46]

C. The Timeline for Discharging Monetary Obligations

A final point of discussion regards scriptural money questions about the timeline process of discharging monetary obligations. Taking into account payers

[42] This mechanism assumes that the provision of a payment service is a four-party operation with three layers: 1. The first begins with the payment order issuance (the consent may be given directly by the payer, but also via payee, or payment initiation service provider) and ends with debiting the payer's payment account; 2. The second begins with the transfer of funds from the payer's PSP and ends with the crediting of such funds to the payer's PSP; 3. In the third and last layer, the payee's PSP credits the sum of money to the payee's account.

[43] This concerns the 'honour all cards' rule.

[44] See Arts 3 and 4 Regulation 2015/751/EU.

[45] See Art 30(3) PSD2.

[46] See Arts 60 and 62(5) PSD2.

and the payees, can the regulatory pattern of scriptural money change the allocation of responsibility? The Court of Justice has applied a traditional approach to the discharging of monetary obligations. Indeed, in *Telecom GmbH v Deutsche Telekom AG*, the preliminary ruling dealt with the construction of Article 3, Directive 2000/35/EC on late payments. There, the Court held that it is

> explicit in the wording of that provision that a debtor's payment is regarded as late, for the purposes of entitlement to interest for late payment, where the creditor does not have the sum owed at his disposal on the due date. In the case of payment by bank transfer, only the crediting of the amount due to the creditor's account will enable him to have that sum at his disposal.[47]

However, it seems to me that this normative approach missed the big picture,[48] ie, the harmonisation process featuring a pro-competitive approach and made up of the institutional legal framework (soft and compulsory rules) as well as antitrust case law, converging to establish an architecture of money and payments in both the consumer-provider and payer-payee obligation relationships. Antonella Sciarrone Alibrandi argued that, since the 1997 Cross-border credit transfer Directive and, to an even greater degree, with the adoption of PSD1, the European framework has brought about an indirect harmonisation process with regard to monetary obligations, establishing that the moment of discharge of monetary obligation occurs when the sum of money is transferred from the payer's to the account of the payee's PSP rather than when it is credited to the payee's account. Looking ahead, it might be advisable for the harmonisation process for payments to cover the private law aspects of the payee-payer legal obligation as well.

IV. Addressing Payment Service Consumers as Digital Users

To sum up the initial results: legal analysis has addressed *electronification* as the mainstream in the construction of an internal market for payments where payment accounts are the leading means of accessing payment systems, indirectly prioritising scriptural money over cash as a means of discharging monetary obligations. Since the first phase of the harmonisation process, this regulatory approach has re-defined the contracting relationship for the provision of payment services and the payment service value chain. The entire normative approach seems to

[47] Case C-306/06 *Telecom GmbH v Deutsche Telekom AG* [2008] ECR I-1923.

[48] See A Sciarrone Alibrandi, 'L'adempimento dell'obbligazione pecuniaria tra diritto vivente e portata regolatoria indiretta della payment services directive 2007/64/CE' in M Mancini and M Perassi (eds), *Il nuovo quadro normativo comunitario dei servizi di pagamento. Prime riflessioni, Quaderni di ricerca giuridica della consulenza legale, n. 63* (Rome, Bank of Italy, 2008) 61–73.

address payment service consumers as smart users. There are four aspects to take into account:

- Concerning the way contracts for payment services are entered into, it is worth noting that, since the issuing of European directive on the distance marketing of consumer financial services,[49] consumers may make the payment account contracts by means of distance communication.[50] They have the same information requirements as brick-and-mortar payment services contracts, in addition to the right of withdrawal within 14 days from the contract date, unless the consumer concerned has expressly requested that the contract be carried out. Recently, the PSD2 confirmed the application of Directive 2002/65 where the two legal acts do not overlap;
- The role of 'durable medium' in the discharging of information duties set out in Title III PSD2. In the *Bawag* case, the Court of Justice held that the definition of durable medium comprises any device that

  > allows the payment service user to store information addressed personally to that payment user in a way accessible for future reference for a period of time adequate to the purposes of the information and allows the unchanged reproduction of the information stored. Furthermore, for a website to be regarded as being a 'durable medium' within the meaning of that provision, any possibility that the payment service provider or another professional to whom the management of that site has been entrusted could change the content unilaterally must be excluded;[51]

- In the end, PSD2 divides the payment service value chain into small parts with the aim of stimulating competition in monetary – and non-monetary – digital information processing. Indeed, PSD2 provides for two payment services, namely, the payment initiation service and the account information service, respectively described as a

  > service to initiate a payment order at the request of the payment service user with respect to a payment account held at another payment service provider,

  and an

  > online service to provide consolidated information on one or more payment accounts held by the payment service user with either another payment service provider or with more than one payment service provider.[52]

[49] Directive 2002/65/EC of the European Parliament and of the Council, of the 23 September 2002, concerning the distance marketing of consumer financial services and amending Council Directive 90/619/EEC and Directives 97/7/EC and 98/27/EC [2002] OJ L271/16.

[50] The 'means of distance communication' refers to 'any means which, without the simultaneous physical presence of the supplier and the consumer, may be used for the distance marketing of a service between those parties'.

[51] Case C-375/15 *BAWAG PSK Bank für Arbeit und Wirtschaft und Österreichische Postsparkasse AG contro Verein für Konsumenteninformation* [2017] 2 CMLR 35.

[52] See Art 4(16) and (17) PSD2.

Both are based on application programming interfaces (APIs) used for 'systems integration and data sharing within and across firms'.[53]

A. Empowered to Manage Data and Funds

Taking a closer look at the legal framework for payments, it seems that the European lawmaker refrains from taking a paternalistic approach towards payment service consumers. In fact, they are addressed as persons fully capable of managing their needs and consistently choosing the proper PSP and the most suitable framework contract. In the end, the main aspect of regulation is to ensure that they are provided with adequate information and tools for cutting short the research costs.[54]

This conclusion can be reached by analysing transparency rules as well as the rights and obligations relating to the provision of payment services laid down in PSD2 and in the PAD.

With regard to the right to be properly informed, PSD2 establishes that the PSP shall provide the customer with information on its organisation, the main features of the payment services concerned, charges and fees, means of communications and safeguarding measures, in addition to the PSP's right to terminate and revise the framework contract, and redress procedures. Such information must be provided by means of a durable medium before a contract is entered into. In addition, the terms and conditions of the payment service contract must correspond to the preliminary information given and, once the contract is made, any change to it must be proposed to and approved by the customers, save for the right to terminate the contract itself.

Thanks to the information provided, it is assumed that payment service consumers can ascertain the differences between PSPs. Indeed, removing the legal obstacle to entering the product market is certainly important to improving the efficiency of payment systems as well as the normative and economic contracting conditions for consumers. However, different PSPs apply different means of safeguarding consumers' funds. At the Union level, it is assumed that consumers, supplied with preliminary information, should be aware of the legal differences in the way their funds are safeguarded. In fact, payment account holders may enjoy the protection of the deposit guarantee scheme and central banks as lenders of last resort only when their funds are deposited in credit institutions. Conversely, with regard to funds placed in payment accounts held by payment institutions,

[53] M Zachariadis and P Ozcan, 'The API economy and digital transformation in financial services: the case of open banking' (2016) 1 *Swift Institute Working Paper* 1–26.

[54] The PAD compels the Member States to set up at least one comparison website free of charge. Such comparison websites must be independent: indeed, the information given on such websites must be 'trustworthy, impartial and transparent', striking the right balance between 'the need for information to be clear and concise and the need for it to be complete and comprehensive' (preamble (22), PAD).

safeguarding measures are largely based on private law tools: Article 10 PSD2 provides for: (i) depositing them in a separate account in a credit institution, but in that case they are not covered by deposit guarantee protection; (ii) investing them in secure low-risk assets as defined by the national competent authority; (iii) covering them with an insurance policy or a comparable instrument.

The more recent PSD2 gives payment service consumers the right to allow access to their monetary information to PSPs other than the account servicing PSPs (ASPSPs).[55] This is consistent with the right to data portability set forth in Article 20 GDPR.[56] In fact, the payment service consumer may enter into an agreement with an account information service provider (AISP) as well as with a payment initiation service provider (PISP),[57] even though no agreement is made between the account servicing PSP and the AISP or the PISP.

Contract information requirements are aimed at protecting consumers from hidden costs, but also at indirectly stimulating competition among PSPs. In fact, preliminary information should spur consumers to compare the proposed contract with competitors' terms and conditions. To this end, the PAD aims to minimise search costs: Article 7 PAD compels Member States to ensure that

> consumers have access, free of charge, to at least one website comparing fees charged by payment service providers

and the comparing website should cover at least the payment services included on the list of the most common services, which the Member States agreed upon, establishing a standardised terminology to utilise throughout Europe, in close cooperation with the EBA.[58]

Consistent with the right to be informed, the European legal framework gives payment services consumers the right to switch from one PSP to another across borders.[59] The right to switch, which may cover either the contracting relationship as a whole or single payment orders, is regulated as a transfer of information, wisely managed by the consumer/payment account holder who, having found a better offer, decides to transfer information concerning one or more incoming credit transfers, standing orders for credit transfers or direct debit mandates, from the transferring to the receiving PSP, based in the same Member State or in different Member States. There is no need for a contract relationship between the PSPs involved; it is sufficient that the consumer/payment account holder authorises the receiving PSP to request all associated information from the transferring PSP.

[55] See F Di Porto and M Maggiolino, 'Algorithmic information disclosure by regulators and competition authorities' (2019) *Global Jurist* 1–17.

[56] GDPR stands for Regulation 2016/679/EU of the European Parliament and of the Council of 27 April 2016 on the protection of natural persons with regard to the processing of personal data and on the free movement of such data, and repealing Directive 95/46/EC [2016] OJ L 119/1.

[57] Art 4(15) and (16) PSD2.

[58] Art 3 PAD.

[59] See Art 2(18) PAD.

B. Fully Accountable for the Proper Use of Payment Instruments and Personalised Security Credentials

Having empowered a payment service consumer to manage his funds and data, the payment service consumer is nonetheless accountable for correctly issuing payment orders: Article 88 PSD2 establishes that if a payment order is executed in compliance with the unique identifier, it is assumed that the PSP has properly executed the payment order, and if the unique identifier provided by the payment service user is incorrect, the PSP cannot be considered liable for non-execution or defective execution of the payment transaction. There is no duty of surveillance on the part of the PSP.

Furthermore, the payment service consumer must keep payment instruments and personalised security credentials safe, notifying the PSP of unauthorised payment transactions as well as incorrectly executed payment transactions.[60] In fact, PSD2 provides that payment service users must notify the PSP 'without undue delay on becoming aware of the loss, misappropriation or unauthorised use of the payment instrument' and no later than 13 months after the debit date.[61] This means that the payment service consumer is expected to regularly check the payment account statement. However, the more time has passed since a loss, misappropriation or theft, the more the consumer may be considered negligent in the contractual relationship with the payment instrument's PSP (or ASPSP).

The only legislative limitation of consumer liability is laid down in Article 74 PSD2, according to which the payer may not be liable for loss, theft or misappropriation of the payment instrument when this event was not 'detectable to the payer prior to a payment'. The definition of 'detectable' is fluid and subject to change because it depends on social and cultural background and therefore varies from one Member State to another. In addition, there are types of IT breaches or scams that, while initially new and unusual, eventually become common and widespread, therefore it is assumed that consumers applying due diligence can detect them.

V. Any Holes in the (Legislative) Net?

All in all, there seems to be no paternalistic approach taken towards payment service consumers.[62] One wonders whether the widespread use of mobile devices

[60] Confirmed by the following ECJ preliminary rulings: Case C-295/18 *Mediterranean Shipping Company – Agentes de Navegação v Banco Comercial Portguês SA, Caixa Geral de Depósitos SA* [2019] 2 All ER (Comm) 547; Case C-245/18 *Tecnoservice Int s.r.l. v Poste Italiane S.p.a.* [2019] 3 CMLR 12; Case C-480/18 *PrivatBank AS v Finanšu un kapitāla tirgus komisija* ECLI:EU:C:2020:274 [2020] not yet published.

[61] Arts 69 and 71.

[62] See G Colangelo and M Maggiolino, 'From fragile to smart consumer: shifting paradigm for the digital era' (2019) 32(5) *Computer Law & security Review* 173.

is enough to infer a good level of financial education among payment service consumers. However, this topic is beyond the scope of an analysis of the legislation. In addition, the rules and regulations for trusted third parties laid down in PSD2 raised some concerns regarding consumers' data: indeed, Article 66(g) and Article 67(f) PSD2 respectively forbid PISPs and AISPs to use, access and store any data for purposes other than performing the services explicitly requested by payment service users, in compliance with data protection rules. What exactly is the scope of the services to be provided?[63] That is a question to be discussed in the following chapter.

Here, however, we focus on the question of access to credit. The main point is the extent to which the new legal framework for payment service consumers can improve access to credit. In 2000, the Cruickshank report indicated overdraft facilities as a bottleneck in the payment services market, which at the time in the UK was still the banking market. The report showed that accounts with more expensive overdrafts were more popular than those offering cheaper ones. In other words, the price of overdrafts was not driving the choice of accounts, and '[a]s a result, a number of those consumers who make regular use of an overdraft facility are being charged higher prices than they could get by shopping around'.[64] The findings highlighted the presence of a *bundling effect* in payment account choices, and awareness of this anticompetitive effect spurred the European policymaker to allow payment institutions – newly established with PSD1 – to extend credit whenever it is closely linked to the operation of a payment transaction. Credit is granted from payment institutions' own funds and is to be repaid within a short period of time, not to exceed 12 months. This did not change with the introduction of PSD2.[65]

However, overdraft facilities and payday loans still lie at the root of European households' (over-)indebtedness problem. It has been observed that where vulnerable consumers are concerned, credit seems to replace income as a way of life; although the Union now provides higher levels of consumer protection, it must overcome 'narrow legal reasoning and incorporate ethical, economic and social norms'.[66] Recently, the 2020 Commission Report on the application of the 2008 Consumer Credit Directive underscored a still highly fragmented and State-based consumer credit market, where it is assumed that FinTech companies may greatly impact on the development of the internal market, but it is not clear how using a broader data set to carry out creditworthiness assessments of (potential) borrowers may help to break the debt chain.[67]

[63] PTJ Wolters and BPF Jacobs, 'The security of access to accounts under the PSD2' (2019) 35 *Computer Law & Security Review* 32 f.

[64] D Cruickshank, *Competition in UK Banking: A Report to the Chancellor of the Exchequer* (London, Stationery Office, 2000) 107 f.

[65] Art 16 PSD1 and now Art 18(4) PSD2.

[66] M De Munynck, 'Credit cards, overdraft facilities and European consumer protection' (2010) 6 *European Review of Private Law* 1181–241.

[67] Commission Staff Working Document, Evaluation of Directive 2008/48/EC on credit agreement for consumer, Brussels, 5.11.2020.

VI. Conclusions

The European policymaker has based the legal status of payment service consumers first and foremost on the right to access the payment system through a payment account, pushing scriptural money over banknotes and coins as means of payment, in compliance with the payment services electronification process, and, secondly, on the right to be adequately informed of the economic and normative terms and conditions of the payment service contract prior to and during contract execution, so that consumers can make well-informed business transactions and choose the most suitable offering on the internal market. But payment service consumers are increasingly becoming online users, thus the European policymaker has established the same level of information for brick-and-mortar framework contracts and distance contracts, and also considers online information devices such as websites to be fully analogous to traditional durable media like paper documents. Overall, there is no paternalistic regulatory approach towards payment service consumers; they are considered responsible and conscious users, fully empowered to manage their funds and their data.

Ultimately, an analysis of harmonising rules regarding payments, comprising institutional and self-regulatory acts as well as binding and soft rules, seems to demonstrate that many steps forward have been made in the construction of payment service consumers' status, despite some degree of fragmentation across national lines, especially with regard to ADR mechanisms for cross-border disputes. However, the main area for improvement falls outside the European framework for payments: it concerns the economic and regulatory conditions for overdraft facilities, which continue to undermine payment service consumers' ability to adequately fulfil their financial obligations.

4

The Interplay between the Framework for Payment Services and Data Protection: A Piece of European Community Identity

MAŁGORZATA CYNDECKA

I. Introduction

Data protection is a pillar of European citizens' empowerment and the EU's approach to the digital transition.[1] In February 2020, the European Commission ('the Commission') called for the creation of a 'single European data space' with 10 sectoral common European data spaces relevant for the twin green and digital transitions.[2] One of those sectors is the financial sector where open banking has created ground-breaking shifts in banks' business models.[3] For consumers, open banking may mean a boost to financial inclusion through access to innovative, cheaper, more targeted financial services.[4] The EU legislator's response to the emergence of new payment services was the adoption of the second Payment Services Directive (the PSD2) in 2015.[5] EU Member States were obliged to transpose the

[1] See Commission, 'Communication to the European Parliament and the Council, Data protection as a pillar of citizens' empowerment and the EU's approach to the digital transition – two years of application of the General Data Protection Regulation' COM (2020) 264 final.

[2] Commission, 'Communication to the European Parliament, the Council, the European Economic and Social Committee and the Committee of the Regions – A European strategy for data' COM (2020) 66 final.

[3] See eg M Zachariadis and P Ozcan, 'The API Economy and Digital Transformation in Financial Services: The Case of Open Banking' (2016) 1 *Swift Institute Working Paper* https://papers.ssrn.com/sol3/papers.cfm?abstract_id=2975199.

[4] See eg ChM Stiefmueller, 'Open Banking and PSD2: The Promise of Transforming Banking by "Empowering Customers"' in J Spohrer and C Leitner (eds), *Advances in the Human Side of Service Engineering. AHFE 2020. Advances in Intelligent Systems and Computing*, Vol 1208 (Cham, Springer, 2020).

[5] Directive 2015/2366/EU of the European Parliament and the Council, of 25 November 2015, on payment services in the internal market, amending Directives 2002/65/EC, 2009/110/EC and 2013/36/EU and Regulation (EU) No 1093/2010, and repealing Directive 2007/64/EC [2015] OJ L337/35.

PSD2 into their national legislations by 13 January 2018[6] – a few months before the General Data Protection Regulation (the GDPR or the Regulation),[7] came into force on 25 May 2018.[8]

Given the importance and value of personal data to financial services,[9] a harmonious interplay between the PSD2 and the GDPR is crucial. Such interplay is also a key feature of the EU identity and a way of improving one's sense of belonging to the EU. Yet, the GDPR and PSD2 seem to pursue contradicting objectives. The PSD2 regulates new market players that, for the purpose of providing payment services, have access to consumers' accounts and their personal data.[10] Payment providers are now obliged to share their customers' data with the providers of new payment services if the customer explicitly agreed to such disclosure.[11] Such data sharing increases competition and innovation, but potentially collides with the GDPR's objective of giving individuals more control over their personal data, including imposing restrictions on using and sharing such data.[12] Some stakeholders have thus raised the question whether full compliance with both legal acts is possible or whether compliance with one set of rules necessarily leads to breaching the other.[13] For European citizens, uncertainty concerning the interaction between the PSD2 and the GDPR may raise the question whether using the innovative, cheaper and more convenient payment services is offered at the expense of the protection of their personal data.[14] The success of the PSD2 will, after all, depend on consumers' willingness to share their personal data with the new payment services providers.[15]

[6] For information on the implementation of the PSD2, see www.ec.europa.eu/info/law/payment-services-psd-2-directive-eu-2015-2366/implementation_en. As regards EFTA EEA Member States, they were required to transpose the PSD2 into their national legislation once the Directive entered into effect under the EEA Agreement. The PSD2 was incorporated into the EEA Agreement on 14 June 2019 by decision of the EEA Joint Committee.

[7] Regulation (EU) 2016/679 of the European Parliament and of the Council, of 27 April 2016, on the protection of natural persons with regard to the processing of personal data and on the free movement of such data, and repealing Directive 95/46/EC (General Data Protection Regulation) [2016] OJ L119/1.

[8] As regards the EFTA EEA Member States Iceland, Liechtenstein and Norway, the GDPR entered into force on 20 July 2018 following the Joint Committee Decision incorporating it into the EEA Agreement on 6 July 2018.

[9] See eg EBA, EIOPA, ESMA, 'Joint Committee Discussions Paper on the Use of Big Data by Financial Institutions' (2016) JC/2016/86.

[10] See Arts 66(1) and 67(1) PSD2.

[11] See Arts 66(2) and 67(2)(a) PSD2.

[12] As pointed out by Schweitzer and Welker, the PSD2 is a sector-specific data access regime that goes beyond Art 20 GDPR, which lays down the right to data portability, see H Schweitzer and R Welker, 'A legal Framework for Access to Data – A Competition Policy Perspective' (2020) in German Federal Ministry of Justice and Consumer Protection Max Planck Institute for Innovation and Competition (eds), *Data Access, Consumer Interests and Public Welfare* (Baden, Nomos, 2020).

[13] See eg S McInnes and L Sampedro, 'EU: The interplay of PSD2 and GDPR – some select issues' (2019) *Data Guidance* www.twobirds.com/~/media/pdfs/eu-the-interplay-of-psd2-and-gdpr--some-select-issues.pdf.

[14] See Recital 89 PSD2.

[15] See M Bijlsma, C van der Cruijsen and N Jonker, 'Consumer willingness to share payments data: trust for sale?' (2020) 2020-015 *TILEC Discussion Paper Forthcoming* http://papers.ssrn.com/sol3/papers.cfm?abstract_id=3619988.

On these grounds, this contribution takes a closer look at the processing of 'silent party data' by the new payment services providers. 'Silent party data' are

> personal data concerning a data subject who is not the user of a specific payment service provider, but whose personal data are processed by that specific payment service provider for the performance of a contract between the provider and the payment service user.[16]

Examples of such data are data pertaining to the payee in the payer's credit transfer record. 'Silent parties' have no knowledge of their personal data being processed. Thus, they have no control over the scope or purpose(s) of such processing and no possibility to object to such processing. This is particularly problematic when the processing involves special categories of personal data within the meaning of Article 9(1) GDPR, ie data revealing racial or ethnic origin, political opinions, religious or philosophical beliefs, or trade union membership, genetic data, biometric data processed for the purpose of uniquely identifying a natural person, data concerning health, or data concerning a natural person's sex life or sexual orientation. Those types of data merit particular protection and their processing is strictly regulated.

In its Guidelines on the interplay of the PSD2 and the GDPR, the European Data Protection Board (EDPB), which safeguards a consistent application of the GDPR in the EU/EEA, adopted a strict approach to the processing of 'silent party data' and, in particular, when such data fall within Article 9(1) GDPR. While this resonates well with the objective of protecting such data, it may frustrate the process of offering the new payment services. Interestingly, the EDPB's Guidelines on the PSD2 and the GDPR seem to be more restrictive when it comes to special categories of personal data than its other Guidelines on the interpretation of GDPR. Moreover, it appears that there is no legal basis for the processing of such data.

The problem of the processing of 'silent party data' by new payment services providers is discussed as follows: Section II elaborates on the interplay of the PSD2 and the GDPR, introduces the new market players, and explains what legal basis they may rely on when processing personal data of payment services users. Section III elaborates on the processing of 'silent party data' with emphasis on the insufficient guidance from the EDPB, the difficulties of defining 'sensitive data', and inconsistencies in the EDPB's approach. The conclusions call for the EDPB's further guidance on 'silent party data'. Currently, it seems that the EDPB has overlooked how the new payment services work.

[16] See EDPB, 'Guidelines 06/2020 on the interplay of the Second Payment Services Directive and the GDPR' Version 2.0., 15 December 2020 ('Guidelines 06/2020'), point 45.

II. The Interplay of the PSD2 and the GDPR

A. Two Landmark Legal Acts, Two Different Approaches to Personal Data?

The GDPR repealed Directive 95/46/EC of 1995[17] where legal form led to a difference in levels of data protection in the EU/EEA. This Directive was furthermore outdated given the rapid technological development and globalisation of recent years. The strengthened data protection in the GDPR safeguards and increases transparency. It provides individuals with additional and stronger rights, and ensures that all those that handle personal data under its scope of application are more accountable and responsible. Personal data are defined as 'any information relating to an identified or identifiable natural person ('data subject'); an identifiable natural person is one who can be identified, directly or indirectly, in particular by reference to an identifier such as a name, an identification number, location data, an online identifier or to one or more factors specific to the physical, physiological, genetic, mental, economic, cultural or social identity of that natural person'.[18] A survey carried out by the European Union Agency for Fundamental Rights in 2020[19] clearly indicated that European citizens are 'increasingly aware of their rights of access, rectification, erasure, and portability of their personal data, the right to object to a processing, as well as enhanced transparency'.

Importantly, safeguarding a high level of protection of personal data is not the only objective of the GDPR. The Regulation also aims to contribute to economic and social progress and to the strengthening and convergence of the economies within the internal market.[20] Moreover, the GDPR makes it clear that while the protection of natural persons in relation to processing of personal data is a fundamental right,[21] it is not 'an absolute right; it must be considered in relation to its function in society and be balanced against other fundamental rights, in accordance with the principle of proportionality'.[22] Freedom to conduct a business is one of the freedoms to which the GDPR refers in this regard.[23]

[17] Directive 95/46/EC of the European Parliament and of the Council, of 24 October 1995, on the protection of individuals with regard to the processing of personal data and on the free movement of such data [1995] OJ L281/31.

[18] Art 4(1) GDPR.

[19] European Union Agency for Fundamental Rights, 'Fundamental Rights Survey 2019. Data protection and technology' (2020) www.fra.europa.eu/en/publication/2020/fundamental-rights-survey-data-protection.

[20] See Recital 2 and Art 1 GDPR.

[21] See Art 8(1) of the Charter of Fundamental Rights of the European Union [2012] OJ C 326/391; Art 16(1) of the Consolidated Version of the Treaty on the Functioning of the European Union [2016] OJ C 202/47.

[22] See Recital 4 GDPR.

[23] See Recital 4 GDPR. Freedom to conduct business is also guaranteed by Art 16 of the Charter of Fundamental Rights of the European Union [2012] OJ C 326/391.

While the GDPR is a milestone in both data protection and in EU law,[24] the PSD2 marked a momentous step towards open banking which holds the potential to reshape the financial sector by forcing more innovation and competitiveness.[25] The novel online payment services were not covered by the Payment Service Directive of 2007 ('the PSD').[26] Under the PSD, the banking incumbents could deny applications by new payment services providers to access their infrastructure and their customers' data.[27] The PSD2 not only closes the regulatory gaps, but also enhances security of new payment services by introducing an obligation for the providers of these services to apply strong customer authentication mechanisms.[28] Where the PSD addressed transfers inside the EU/EEA only and was limited to the currencies of the EU/EEA Member States, the PSD2 strengthens consumer rights when sending transfers and money remittances outside the EU/EEA or paying in non-EU/EEA currencies. Under the PSD2, rules on transparency also apply to 'one-leg transactions'. The PSD2 covers payment transactions to persons outside the EU/EEA with regard to the 'EU/EEA part' of the transaction.

The interaction between the two ground-breaking legislations has, however, raised a number of concerns. It was unfortunate that the Article 29 Working Party ('Article 29 WP') was not officially involved during the process of negotiating the PSD2.[29] The Article 29 WP was an independent EU Advisory Body on Data Protection and Privacy, composed of representatives from each of the EU Member States, the European Data Protection Supervisor (EDPS), and the representative of the Commission. The Working Party advised the Commission on any proposed amendment of Directive 95/46/EC, on any additional or specific measures to safeguard the rights and freedoms of natural persons with regard to the processing of personal data and on any other proposed EU measures affecting such rights and freedoms. Importantly, the Commission was made aware of the fact that the PSD2

[24] See Ch Kuner, LA Bygrave and Ch Docksey (eds), *The EU General Data Protection Regulation (GDPR). A Commentary* (Oxford, Oxford University Press, 2020) Editors Preface vii.

[25] At the same time, however, concerns have been expressed about alleged unintended consequences of data portability in financial markets. See eg O Borgogno and G Colangelo, 'The data sharing paradox: BigTechs in finance' (2020) 16 *European Competition Journal* 492–511. See, however, a critical assessment of the implementation of the PSD2 in Germany by AB Radnejad, O Osiyevskyy and O Scheibel, 'Learning from the failure of the EU Payment Services Directive (PSD2): When Imposed Innovation Does Not Change the Status Quo' (2021) 1 *Rutgers Business Review* 79. The authors consider the PSD2 'an exemplar of the gaining attention in literature phenomenon of "imposed innovation"'.

[26] Directive 2007/64/EC of the European Parliament and of the Council, of 13 November 2007, on payment services in the internal market amending Directives 97/7/EC, 2002/65/EC, 2005/60/EC and 2006/48/EC and repealing Directive 97/5/EC [2007] OJ L319/1.

[27] For more information on the differences between the PSD and the PSD2, see eg A Adeyemi, 'A new phase of payments in Europe: the impact of PSD2 on the payments industry' (2019) 2 *Computer and Telecommunications Law Review* 47.

[28] See Art 97(1) PSD2. See also J Peeters, 'Data Protection in Mobile Wallets' (2020) 1 *European Data Protection Law Review* 56–59.

[29] The same concerned Commission Delegated Regulation (EU) 2018/389 of 27 November 2017 supplementing Directive (EU) 2015/2366 of the European Parliament and of the Council with regard to regulatory technical standards for strong customer authentication and common and secure open standards of communication, C/2017/7782 [2018] OJ L 69/23 (RTS Regulation).

caused a number of data protection concerns. The PSD2 proposal was criticised by the EDPS, the EU's independent data protection authority, who also advises the Commission on proposals for legislation with impact on data protection and privacy. The EDPS' Opinion[30] recommended that references to applicable data protection law should be specified in concrete safeguards that would apply to any situation in which personal data processing is envisaged. The only response from the EU legislator was Recital 89 PSD2, acknowledging that the provision of payment services may entail processing of personal data. The said Recital also requires compliance with Directive 95/46/EC.

An important step towards clarifying the relationship between the PSD2 and the GDPR was made by a Member of the European Parliament, Sophie in't Veld. In a letter of 16 February 2018, she requested the Commission, the EDPS, and the Article 29 WP to provide clarifications on some of the most burning issues related to the obligation of compliance with both pieces of EU legislation. Those issues were addressed by the EDPB that replaced the Article 29 WP on 25 May 2018. In its response of 5 July 2018, the EDPB addressed: the processing of 'silent party data', the concept of 'explicit consent' within the meaning of Article 9(2)(a) GDPR and Article 94(2) of the PSD2, Regulatory Technical Standards on Strong Customer Authentication[31] that supplement the PSD2 and the position of banks.[32]

Another important question that arose almost immediately after the coexistence of the PSD2 and the GDPR became a fact, was whether the PSD2 could be considered a *lex specialis*.[33] Following explanations from the Commission and the EDPB, it is now established that the PSD2 must comply with the GDPR. In this respect, Article 94 PSD2 states that 'processing of personal data for the purposes of this Directive shall be carried out in accordance with Directive 95/46/EC, the national rules which transpose Directive 95/46/EC and with Regulation (EC) No 45/2001'.[34] As specified in Article 94 GDPR, 'References to the repealed

[30] EDPS, 'Opinion on a proposal for a Directive of the European Parliament and of the Council on payment services in the internal market amending Directives 2002/65/EC, 2006/48/EC and 2009/110/EC and repealing Directive 2007/64/EC, and for a Regulation of the European Parliament and of the Council on interchange fees for card-based payment transactions' 5 December 2013.

[31] RTS Regulation.

[32] EDPB, 'Letter to MEP Sophie in 't Veld', EDPD-84-2018 (5 July 2018) www.edpb.europa.eu/sites/default/files/files/news/psd2_letter_en.pdf.

[33] See eg AirPlus International, 'Comments on the EDPB's consultation on Guidelines 06/2020 on the interplay of GDPR and PSD2' (2020) www.edpb.europa.eu/sites/edpb/files/webform/public_consultation_reply/comments_on_the_interplay_of_the_second_payment_service_directive_and_the_eu-gdpr_-_airplus.pdf; D Helgadottir, 'The conflict concerning data sharing under PSD2 and obtaining consent to share such data under GDPR' (*Oxford Business Law Blog*, 31 July 2020) www.law.ox.ac.uk/business-law-blog/blog/2020/07/conflict-concerning-data-sharing-under-psd2-and-obtaining-consent.

[34] Regulation (EC) No 45/2001 of the European Parliament and of the Council, of 18 December 2000, on the protection of individuals with regard to the processing of personal data by the Community institutions and bodies and on the free movement of such data, repealed by the European Parliament and the Council Regulation (EU) 2018/1725 of 23 October 2018 on the protection of natural persons with regard to the processing of personal data by the Union institutions, bodies, offices and agencies and on the free movement of such data, and repealing Regulation (EC) No 45/2001 and Decision No 1247/2002/EC, PE/31/2018/REV/1 [2018] OJ L 295/39.

Directive shall be construed as references to this Regulation'. Moreover, as already mentioned, Recital 89 of the PSD2 declares that 'where personal data is processed for the purposes of this Directive, the precise purpose should be specified, the relevant legal basis referred to, the relevant security requirements laid down in Directive 95/46/EC complied with, and the principles of necessity, proportionality, purpose limitation and proportionate data retention period respected'.

As the EDPB's letter to MEP Sophie in't Veld merely touched upon the most controversial issues concerning the interplay of the PSD2 and the GDPR, a more comprehensive explanation was eagerly awaited. In July 2020, the EDPB issued Guidelines on the interplay of the PSD2 and the GDPR.[35] The Guidelines were subject to public consultation until 16 September 2020. On 15 December 2020, the EDPB adopted a revised version of the Guidelines after receiving input from individuals, organisations working with data protection and consumer rights, as well as representatives of both new payment services providers and the well-established market players.[36]

The EDPB's Guidelines are not legally binding, but they are issued by an independent EU body whose task it is to safeguard a consistent interpretation of the GDPR across the EU/EEA.[37] In light of the EDPB's competences, composition and role, its Guidelines are an authoritative source of guidance on the application of GDPR. The final version of the Guidelines on the PSD2 and the GDPR clarified the conditions for granting access to payment account information by the banks and for the processing of consumers' personal data by the new payment services providers, different notions of 'explicit consent' under the PSD2 and the GDPR, and the application of the main data protection principles set forth by the GDPR in Article 5. Yet, the processing of 'silent party data' and special categories of personal data remained very difficult if not impossible to handle by the new payment service providers. Adopting a very restrictive approach to the processing of such data, the EDPB seems to overlook how the new payment services are carried out. A comparison of the first version, subjected to an open hearing, and the final version of the Guidelines on the PSD2 and the GDPR reveals mere linguistic and punctuation changes with regard to the processing of 'silent part data' and special categories of personal data. Yet, in order to explain why the processing of 'silent party data' is problematic, it is necessary to first clarify what kind of new payment services the PSD2 regulates.

[35] EDPB, 'Guidelines 06/2020 on the interplay of the Second Payment Services Directive and the GDPR', Version 1.0, 17 July 2020.

[36] See www.edpb.europa.eu/our-work-tools/documents/public-consultations/2020/guidelines-062020-interplay-second-payment_en.

[37] The EDPB is composed of representatives of the EU national data protection authorities, and the EDPS. The data protection authorities of the EFTA EEA States Iceland, Liechtenstein and Norway are also members with regard to the GDPR-related matters, but without the right to vote and being elected as chair or deputy chairs. The Commission and – with regard to GDPR-related matters – the EFTA Surveillance Authority have the right to participate in the activities and meetings of the Board without voting rights.

B. New Payment Services and New Payment Service Providers under the PSD2

As chapter three provides details on new payment services, it suffices to mention that financial institutions maintaining payment accounts for payers are referred to as Account Servicing Payment Service Providers (ASPSPs). They are obliged to provide access to data, including personal data, to Payment Initiation Service Providers (PISPs) and Account Information Service Providers (AISPs), which are collectively referred to as Third Party Providers (TPPs).[38]

A 'PISP' initiates a payment order at the request of the payment service user (PSU) with respect to a payment account held at another payment service provider. When a PSU initiates a payment order online, it is no longer obliged to interact directly with its ASPSP. A commissioned PISP will request the relevant ASPSP to provide access to the PSU's account and will initiate the transaction on behalf of the user. An 'AISP' provides consolidated information on one or more payment accounts held by the PSU with either another payment service provider or with more than one payment service providers.[39]

In order to provide the relevant payment services, PISPs and AISPs must process personal data. In this respect, Article 66 PSD2 provides rules on access to payment accounts by PISPs while Article 67 PSD2 provides rules on access to and use of payment account information by AISPs. As regards PISPs, they shall 'not request from the payment service user any data other than those necessary to provide the payment initiation service',[40] and shall 'not use, access or store any data for purposes other than for the provision of the payment initiation service as explicitly requested by the payer'.[41] As regards AISPs, they shall 'not use, access or store any data for purposes other than for performing the account information service explicitly requested by the payment service user, in accordance with data protection rules'.[42]

Under the GDPR, PISPs and AISPs may process the relevant personal data either as controllers or as processors.[43] Article 4(7) GDPR defines a controller as 'the natural or legal person, public authority, agency or other body which, alone or jointly with others, determines the purposes and means of the processing of personal data; where the purposes and means of such processing are determined by Union or Member State law, the controller or the specific criteria for its nomination may be provided for by Union or Member State law'. Article 4(8) GDPR

[38] See Art 4 PSD2; Guidelines 06/2020 6.
[39] Annex 1 PSD2 contains the eight payment services that are covered by the PSD2.
[40] Art 66(3)(f) PSD2.
[41] Art 66(3)(g) PSD2.
[42] Art 67(2)(f) PSD2.
[43] See point 12 of the Guidelines 06/2020. See also EDPB, 'Guidelines 07/2020 on the concepts of controller and processor in the GDPR', Version 1.0., 2 September 2020.

establishes that a processor 'means a natural or legal person, public authority, agency or other body which processes personal data on behalf of the controller'. The concept of controller and its interaction with the concept of processor determine who is responsible for compliance with the data protection rules, and how data subjects can exercise their rights in practice. In this respect, the GDPR explicitly introduces the accountability principle in Article 5(2) according to which the controller shall be responsible for, and be able to demonstrate compliance with, the principles relating to processing of personal data provided in Article 5(1).[44] Yet, the GDPR also introduces more specific rules on the use of processor(s) and some of the provisions are directed at not only controllers, but also processors.

A controller must identify an appropriate legal basis for the processing of personal data amongst those stated in Article 6(1) GDPR and ensure compliance with all requirements posed by the relevant legal basis.[45] When choosing an appropriate legal basis, the controller must take into account, amongst other things, the characteristics of the data subject; the relationship between the data subject and the controller; the nature of personal data that are to be processed; the purpose of their processing; and the circumstances in which the relevant personal data are to be processed. The next section elaborates on the legal basis for processing of personal data of PSUs by TPPs.

C. Legal Basis for the Processing of Personal Data of a PSU by TPPs

The principle of lawfulness requires the controller to identify at least one legal basis under Article 6(1) GDPR.[46] Article 6(1) provides for an exhaustive and restricting list of six legal bases. In this regard, one may distinguish between the data subject's consent (Article 6(1)(a))[47] and five situations where the processing of personal data is necessary for achieving a given purpose. Relying on the latter is thus contingent on the fulfillment of the condition of necessity. The following purposes are included in the condition of necessity: performance of a contract to which the data subject is party, or taking steps at the request of the data subject prior to entering into a contract (Article 6(1)(b)); compliance with a legal obligation to

[44] Those are the principles of: lawfulness, fairness and transparency (Art 5(1)(a)), purpose limitation (Art 5(1)(b)), data minimisation (Art 5(1)(c)), accuracy (Art 5(1)(d)), storage limitation (Art 5(1)(e)), integrity and confidentiality (Art 5(1)(f)).

[45] See Art 6(1) GDPR.

[46] According to Art 5(1)(a) GDPR personal data shall be processed lawfully. This requires not only that every processing of personal data has a legal basis in accordance with Art 6(1), but also that other principles for the processing of personal data are fulfilled, see W Kotschy, 'Article 6. Lawfulness of processing' in Kuner, Bygrave and Docksey (n 24) 325.

[47] For more information on consent and its evolvement, see EDPB, 'Guidelines 05/2020 on consent under Regulation 2016/679', Version 1.1., 4 May 2020 ('Guidelines 05/2020').

which the controller is subject (Article 6(1)(c)); protecting the vital interests of the data subject or of another natural person (Article 6(1)(d)); performance of a task carried out in the public interest or in the exercise of official authority vested in the controller (Article 6(1)(e)); or for the purposes of the legitimate interests pursued by the controller or by a third party, except where such interests are overridden by the interests or fundamental rights and freedoms of the data subject which require protection of personal data (Article 6(1)(f)).

As regards the processing of personal data of a PSU by a TPP, the appropriate legal basis is Article 6(1)(b) GDPR. Processing is necessary for the performance of a contract to which the PSU is party or in order to take steps at the request of the PSU prior to entering into a contract. The payment services that are a requirement for the existence of a contract that allows for relying on Article 6(1)(b) GDPR are defined in Annex 1 of the PSD2.

In 2019, the EDPB issued Guidelines on the processing of personal data under Article 6(1)(b) GDPR in the context of the provision of online services to data subjects.[48] Therein, the EDPB clarified how the condition of necessity should be interpreted in terms of the performance of a contract or when taking pre-contractual steps at the request of the data subject. The controller must identify the purpose for the processing, which must be clearly specified and communicated to the data subject in line with the controller's purpose limitation[49] and transparency obligations.[50] The appraisal of the necessity condition involves 'a combined, fact-based assessment of the processing "for the objective pursued and of whether it is less intrusive compared to other options for achieving the same goal".[51] If there are realistic, less intrusive alternatives, the processing is by definition not "necessary"'.[52] Article 6(1)(b) GDPR will thus not provide a valid legal basis for the processing of personal data that are useful to the controller but not objectively necessary for the performance of the contractual service or for taking relevant pre-contractual steps at the request of the data subject.

Article 6(1)(b) GDPR is, however, not the only legal basis that may be appropriate when TPPs are processing personal data of a PSU. As provided in Article 94(1)

[48] EDPB, 'Guidelines 02/2019 on the processing of personal data under Article 6(1)(b) GDPR in the context of the provision of online services to data subjects' Version 2.0., 8 October 2019 ('Guidelines 02/2019').

[49] According to the principle of purpose limitation, personal data must be collected for specified, explicit and legitimate purposes and not further processed in a manner that is incompatible with those purposes. See also Art 29 WP, 'Opinion 03/2013 on purpose limitation', 2 April 2013.

[50] Guidelines 02/2019, point 24.

[51] See EDPS Toolkit: 'Assessing the Necessity of Measures that limit the fundamental right to the protection of personal data' 5 (EDPS Toolkit).

[52] See point 25 of Guidelines 02/2019. In this respect, the Guidelines refer to: Joined Cases C-92/09 and C-93/09 *Volker under Markus Schecke GbR and Hartmut Eifert v Land Hessen* [2010] ECR I-11063; Case C-13/16 *Valsts policijas Rīgas reģiona pārvaldes Kārtības policijas pārvalde contro Rīgas pašvaldības SIA 'Rīgas satiksme'* (*Rīgas satiksme*) [2017] 3 CMLR 39; EDPS Toolkit 7.

PSD2, Member States shall permit processing of personal data by payment systems and payment service providers when necessary for safeguarding the prevention, investigation, and detection of payment fraud. The processing of personal data considered strictly necessary for the purposes of preventing fraud may be lawful under Article 6(1)(f) GDPR. In this respect, such purposes may constitute a legitimate interest on the part of the payment service provider in question if they are not overridden by the interests or fundamental rights and freedoms of the data subject.[53] As explained in the following section, relying on Article 6(1)(f) GDPR always requires a careful case-by-case assessment by the controller in accordance with the accountability principle.[54]

As mentioned in section III, Articles 66(3)(g) and 67(2)(f) PSD2 limit further processing of PSU's personal data by PISPs and AISPs. These limitations must be taken into account when considering Article 6(4) GDPR, which lays down conditions for further processing. The wording of Articles 66(3)(g) and 67(2)(f) PSD2 exclude the possibility of considering new purposes of the processing of personal data being compatible with the purposes for which the PSU's data were collected. Therefore, the processing of personal data by a PISP for purposes other than the provision of the payment initiation service as explicitly requested by the payer or by an AISP for purposes other than performing the account information service explicitly requested by the PSU, is legal only if the processing is laid down by the EU/EEA law or national law to which a PISP or AISP is subject[55] or if such processing is based on the PSU's consent.

The appropriate legal basis on which ASPSPs rely when providing access to their customers' accounts, is Article 6(1)(c) GDPR, which refers to a legal obligation imposed on the controller ie, an ASPSP. As specified in Articles 66(1) and 67(1) PSD2, Member States shall ensure that a payer has the right to make use of a payment initiation service provider to obtain payment services and the right to make use of services enabling access to account information, respectively. The obligation of the Member States corresponds to the obligation of ASPSPs to provide access to personal data of their clients. This obligation does not depend on the existence of a contractual relationship between a PISP or an AISP with the given ASPSP.

[53] See Recital 47 GDPR.

[54] Guidelines 06/2020, point 20.

[55] eg all PISPs and AISPs are obliged entities under Art 3(2)(a) Directive (EU) 2015/849 of the European Parliament and of the Council of 20 May 2015 on the prevention of the use of the financial system for the purposes of money laundering or terrorist financing of the anti-money laundering Directive. These obliged entities are therefore compelled to apply the customer due diligence measures as specified in the Directive. The personal data processed in connection with a PSD2 service are, therefore, further processed based on at least one legal obligation resting on the service provider. See point 24 of the Guidelines 06/2020.

III. The Problem of Processing of 'Silent Party Data' and Special Categories of Personal Data by TPPS

A. The Legal Basis for Processing of 'Ordinary' 'Silent Party Data'

The provision of payment services by PISPs and AISPs may result in the processing of 'silent party data': personal data of a data subject who is not the user of the given payment service. Those may be data on the payee in the payer's credit transfer record such as personal data of employees in cases where a company pays out the monthly salary with a wire transfer. More examples may be found in the EDPB Guidelines on the interplay between the PSD2 and the GDPR. In cases where a PSU, data subject A, makes use of the services of an AISP, and data subject B has made a series of payment transactions to the payment account of data subject A, data subject B is regarded as the 'silent party' and the personal data (such as the account number of data subject B and the amount of money involved in these transactions) relating to data subject B, are regarded as 'silent party data'.[56]

Notwithstanding, the processing of this type of data is usually either necessary or unavoidable. Therefore, TPPs must have a legal basis for such processing. According to the EDPB, the appropriate legal basis here is Article 6(1)(f) GDPR. This provision allows for the processing of personal data of a data subject when this processing is necessary for purposes of the legitimate interests pursued by a controller or by a third party. Still, such processing may only occur when the legitimate interest of the controller is not 'overridden by the interests or fundamental rights and freedoms of the data subject which require protection of personal data'. The legitimate interest of a PISP or an AISPs is to perform the contract with the PSU. As regards a TPP balancing its own or a PSU's legitimate interest against the interests or fundamental rights and freedoms of a 'silent party', the Guidelines provide that 'the necessity to process a "silent party data" is limited and determined by the reasonable expectations of these data subjects'. It is, however, not explained how one should understand or assess the reasonable expectations of a 'silent party' considering that he or she is unaware of his or her personal data being processed and that they have no relation to the relevant TPP. Given the specific situation in which 'silent party data' are processed, the Guidelines are quite sparse and would benefit from an elaboration on factors that should be taken into account when carrying out the balancing test under Article 6(1)(f) GDPR. The Article 29 WP did provide a detailed Opinion on the notion of legitimate interests of the data controller under Article 7 of Directive 95/46/EC.[57] This Opinion was, however, not

[56] Guidelines 06/2020, point 45.

[57] Article 29 WP, 'Opinion 06/2014 on the notion of legitimate interests of the data controller under Article 7 of Directive 95/46/EC' (WP217).

acknowledged by the EDPB. Furthermore, the wording of Article 6(1)(f) GDPR differs from Article 7(1)(f) of Directive 95/46/EC. More explanations on the issue of reasonable expectations should clarify why, unlike in the case of processing personal data of PSU, the EDPB seems to have excluded the possibility that the processing of 'silent party data' may be necessary or indispensable for the purposes of preventing fraud. It is unclear why this purpose was omitted and why it would fall outside of the reasonable expectations of a 'silent party'.[58]

Moreover, while the EDPB clarifies that a PISP or an AISP must establish the necessary safeguards for processing in order to protect the rights of a 'silent party' and, if feasible, that encryption or other techniques should be applied to achieve an appropriate level of security, it is doubtful that encryption should be recommended. This is simply because it may render the provisions of TPPs' payment services inoperable.

As regards any further processing of 'silent party data', the EDPB rightly concludes that it is allowed only on the basis of EU/EEA law or national law to which the controller is subject. The consent is not legally feasible, for obvious reasons, while the compatibility test under Article 6(4) GDPR would not be passed given the specific situation of a 'silent party'. In this respect, the argument that further processing 'silent party data' is essential for developing open banking does not sound convincing in light of the balancing test in Article 6(1)(f) GDPR, even if the EDPB does not elaborate on it.

B. The Challenging Definition of Special Categories of Personal Data

As provided in Recital 51 GDPR, 'Personal data which are, by their nature, particularly sensitive in relation to fundamental rights and freedoms merit specific protection as the context of their processing could create significant risks to the fundamental rights and freedoms.' Therefore, the processing of special categories of personal data as they are referred to in Article 9(1) GDPR is strictly regulated.[59] Article 9(1) GDPR prohibits 'Processing of personal data revealing racial or ethnic origin, political opinions, religious or philosophical beliefs, or trade union membership, and the processing of genetic data, biometric data for the purpose of uniquely identifying a natural person, data concerning health or data concerning a natural person's sex life or sexual orientation'. This prohibition is, however, not absolute; it may be lifted if one of the derogations provided for in Article 9(2)

[58] Guidelines 06/2020, points 49–50.

[59] On the evolving contours of sensitive data in data protection law, see P Quinn and G Malgieri, 'The Difficulty of Defining Sensitive Data. The concept of sensitive data in the EU data protection framework' (2020) *German Law Journal* (Forthcoming) http://papers.ssrn.com/sol3/papers.cfm?abstract_id=3713134.

GDPR applies alongside a legal basis under Article 6(1) GDPR. The question of what derogation TPPs may rely on is dealt with in section III(D).

The processing of the Article 9(1) data entails a greater threat to fundamental freedoms and rights of data subjects than does the processing of 'ordinary' personal data. This must be considered by a controller when assessing appropriate measures according to Articles 24, 25, 28, and 32 GDPR. These provisions require that the controller implements appropriate technical and organisational measures to ensure compliance with the GDPR and a level of security appropriate to the risk; that every processing of personal data involves data protection by design and by default; and that the controller chooses a processor that will meet the requirements of the GDPR. Moreover, a controller who processes Article 9(1) data may be required to carry out a data protection impact assessment as provided in Article 35(3)(b) and to designate a data protection officer as stated in Article 37(1)(c). Finally, pursuant to Article 83(5)(a) GDPR, infringements of Article 9 GDPR may lead to an administrative fine of up to 20,000,000 EUR, or in the case of an undertaking, up to 4 per cent of the total worldwide annual turnover of the preceding financial year, whichever is higher.

Given the obligations resulting from the processing of special categories of personal data, determining whether one is processing such data is crucial. As the list contained in Article 9(1) is exhaustive, one may not add any new types of special categories of personal data.[60] Yet, the scope of Article 9(1) GDPR is wider than it may appear at first sight. Article 29 WP stated that: 'The term "data revealing racial or ethnic origin, political opinions, religious or philosophical beliefs, trade union membership" is to be understood that not only data which by its nature contains sensitive information is covered by this provision, but also data from which sensitive information with regard to an individual can be concluded.'[61] In other words, information that indirectly indicates special categories of personal data will also fall within the scope of Article 9(1). This leaves room for interpretation, which may widen the scope of Article 9(1).

In this respect, the EDPB provides some useful clarifications in its Guidelines on the targeting of social media users.[62] The EDPB distinguishes between: (1) explicit special categories of data, and (2) inferred and combined special categories of data.[63] The former refers to cases where personal data will clearly fall within Article 9(1) GDPR such as when a data subject directly declares himself or herself a member of a given political party. Yet, not all seemingly 'explicit' cases of sensitive data fall within Article 9(1) GDPR. For example, a photograph or an image may reveal a data subject's racial or ethnic origin or religious beliefs. Still, Recital 51 GDPR stipulates that 'The processing of photographs should not

[60] As it was the case under the Directive 95/46/EC.

[61] Article 29 WP, 'Advice paper on special categories of data (sensitive data), 20 April 2011.

[62] EDPB, 'Guidelines 08/2020 on the targeting of social media users', Version 2.0., 13 April 2021 (Guidelines 08/2020).

[63] ibid, points 119–26.

systematically be considered to be processing of special categories of personal data as they are covered by the definition of biometric data only when processed through a specific technical means allowing the unique identification or authentication of a natural person.'

As regards 'inferred and combined' special categories of data, the EDPB explains that 'Assumptions or inferences regarding special category data, for instance that a person is likely to vote for a certain party after visiting a page preaching liberal opinions, would also constitute a special category of personal data. Likewise, (...) profiling can create special category of data by inference from data which is not special category of data in its own right, but becomes so when combined with other data. For example, it may be possible to infer someone's state of health from the records of their food shopping combined with data on the quality and energy content of foods.'[64] Yet, while the 'processing of a mere statement, or a single piece of location data or similar, which reveals that a user has (either once or on a few occasions) visited a place typically visited by people with certain religious beliefs will generally not in and of itself be considered as processing of special categories of data', it may be the case 'if these data are combined with other data or because of the context in which the data are processed or the purposes for which they are being used'.[65]

Although the idea of 'inferred and combined' special categories of data creates questions of interpretation of the scope of Article 9(1),[66] the EDPB seems to establish a certain threshold for qualifying personal data as special categories data. It appears that the EDPB operates with two criteria that delimit the scope of Article 9(1): (1) the purpose of the processing as indicated by the controller making assumptions, and (2) the context in which processing takes place as indicated by the amount of data that are available to the controller. This resonates with the observation made by Quinn and Malgieri who point out the difficulties with delimiting the scope of sensitive data and the evolvement of Article 9(1) GDPR.[67] A similar *de minimis* approach in determining whether given personal data qualify as Article 9(1) data may be found in the EDPB's Guidelines on the processing of personal data through video devices.[68] Therein, the EDPB specifies that 'video surveillance is not always considered to be processing of special categories of personal data'.[69] As an example, the EDPB refers to video footage showing a data subject wearing glasses or using a wheel chair. Yet, if the objective of processing the video footage is to deduce special categories of data, Article 9(1) applies. For

[64] Art 29 WP, 'Guidelines on Automated individual decision-making and Profiling for the purposes of Regulation 2016/679' (WP251rev.01) 15, referred to by the EDPB in Guidelines 08/2020, point 121.

[65] Guidelines 08/2020, point 122.

[66] See L Georgieva and Ch Kuner, 'Article 9. Processing of special categories of personal data' in Kuner, Bygrave and Docksey (n 24) 374.

[67] Quinn and Malghieri (n 59).

[68] EDPB, 'Guidelines 03/2019 on processing of personal data through video devices', Version 2.0, 29 January 2020.

[69] ibid, point 62.

example, political opinions could be deduced from images showing identifiable data subjects taking part in an event or engaging in a strike. Another example concerns a hospital that installs a video camera in order to monitor a patient's health condition. Once again, the purpose of deducing sensitive data is crucial. As Quinn and Malgieri note, however, both criteria raise questions. As regards the context, one may argue that the computational power and amount of accessible data may render all data sensitive. As regards the purpose, the question is how to prove the purpose of the controller. Moreover, the purpose of processing may change. Notwithstanding, in both sets of Guidelines, the EDPB adopted a seemingly realistic, although not entirely precise and clear approach in determining whether a given set of personal data constitutes special categories of personal data that makes it possible to avoid or at least attempt to avoid an overly broad definition. The question is whether the same approach was taken in the Guidelines on the interplay of the PSD2 and the GDPR.

C. A Stricter Definition of Special Categories of Personal Data in the Guidelines on the Interplay of the PSD2 and the GDPR?

In its Guidelines on the interplay of the PSD2 and the GDPR, the EDPB states that financial transactions can reveal sensitive information about a data subject, including special categories of personal data. The EDPB provides examples such as donations made to political parties or organisations, churches, or parishes that, depending on the transaction details, may reveal political opinions and religious beliefs. Likewise, trade union membership may be revealed by the deduction of an annual membership fee from a person's bank account, while personal data concerning health may be gathered from analysing medical bills paid by a data subject to a medical professional (for instance a psychiatrist). Information on certain purchases may reveal information concerning a person's sex life or sexual orientation.[70] According to the EDPB, even single transactions can contain special categories of personal data. Moreover, the EDPB notes that AISPs might rely on profiling that 'can create special category of data by inference from data which is not a special category of data in its own right, but becomes so when combined with other data'.[71] The EDPB concludes that, 'through the sum of financial transactions, different kinds of behavioural patterns can be revealed, which may include special categories of personal data. Therefore, the chances are considerable that a service provider processing information on financial transactions of data subjects also processes special categories of personal data'. The EDPB recommends that a

[70] Guidelines 06/2020, point 52.
[71] WP251rev.01 15.

TPP at least maps out and categorises precisely what kind of personal data will be processed by carrying out a data protection impact assessment as stipulated in Article 35(3)(b) GDPR.[72]

In this regard, one should note that a TPP processes only those personal data that are provided by a PSU. They may result from: (1) the PSU's choice of words in the free-text-fields provided in the payment reference, or (2) by means of the quality of the recipient of the payment. In both cases one might argue that the EDPB's understanding of processing of special categories of personal data may be too broad or oversimplified. As regards the information provided by the PSU in the free-text-fields, it may in some cases reveal sensitive data. This would, however, require a case-by-case analysis. In the course of public consultation on the first version of the Guidelines, a number of stakeholders provided examples that demonstrate that seemingly 'explicit' special categories of data are not necessarily special categories of personal data. The Austrian Savings Banks Association referred to a situation in which a PSU transferred money to a 'Cancer Treatment Center'. This alone does not necessarily reveal any sensitive data about that data subject who could have simply donated the money or paid a bill for someone else.[73] Any assumption about the PSU's health condition would require a confirmation by combining data from other sources unless one accepts a potential inaccuracy. Similar concerns may be raised with respect to characteristics of the recipient of the payment. The mere fact that the recipient is a hospital is not in itself indicative of the data subject's health condition. Along the same lines, one may question whether payments to political parties or religious organisations automatically reveal the data subject's political views of beliefs.

In its Guidelines on the targeting of social media users and Guidelines on processing of personal data through video devices, the EDPB avoids a sweeping approach in determining whether the processing of personal data involves special category data. Conversely, in the Guidelines on the PSD2 and the GDPR, the EDPB simply notes that 'the chances are considerable that a service provider processing information on financial transactions of data subjects also processes special categories of personal data'.[74] This is interesting because it is unclear why, in the case of financial transactions, the EDPB apparently rejects the above-mentioned *de minimis* approach by not considering the context and purpose of processing. At the same time, the EDPB states in the Guidelines that 'Personal data concerning health may be gathered from analysing medical bills paid by a data subject to a medical professional (for instance a psychiatrist)'.[75] The word 'analysis' seems to indicate purpose. Should we assume that a TPP (always) aims to deduce sensitive data? Obviously, if the manner in which the PSU formulated the text leaves

[72] Guidelines 06/2020, point 53.

[73] Sparkaasse Verband Österreich, 'Response to the EDPB consultation 06/2020 on the Guidelines on the interplay between PSD and GDPR' 2.

[74] Guidelines 06/2020, point 52.

[75] ibid.

no doubt that the data are sensitive, denying the processing of such data may lead to an insufficient level of protection. Still, the question is how to verify this. Moreover, as already pointed out, TPPs may process personal data only for the purpose of carrying out the relevant payment. As regards the context in which data are processed, the EDPB claims that 'through the sum of financial transactions, different kinds of behavioural patterns can be revealed, which may include special categories of personal data'. While this may be the case for some PSUs, should one assume that this is always the case, even when a given PSU engages with a given PISP for the first time? Such a strict approach in the Guidelines on the PSD2 and the GDPR in effect means that TPPs must simply assume that they process sensitive data. The immediate consequence of this is that they need to identify an appropriate derogation under Article 9(2) GDPR.

If TPPs cannot rely on Article 9(2) GDPR, the question is whether they may avoid processing special categories of personal data as suggested by the EDPB.[76] This seems to be impossible. First, any such data are received by a TPP following actions taken by the PSU. TPPs do not ask for such data. Secondly, an ASPSP has no obligation or right to filter sensitive data when giving TPPs access to its customer's account. Under the PSD2 and under Article 36(1)(a) of the Regulatory Technical Standards for strong customer authentication and common and secure open standards of communication (RTS Regulation), ASPSPs must grant AISPs access to the same data they make available to the PSU.[77] Therefore, by applying any restriction or filtering as proposed by the EDPB, the banks would directly violate their obligations under PSD2 and the RTS Regulation. Thirdly, the identification of sensitive data may be either very difficult or inaccurate. Fourthly, in many cases, such data must necessarily be processed if they for example identify the recipient of the payment. In this respect, the EDPB recommends that 'payment service providers may explore the technical possibilities to exclude special categories of personal data and allow a selected access which would prevent the processing of special categories of personal data related to silent parties by TPPs'. The question is, however, whether the industry has such technical possibilities at their disposal, and if such measures will not disrupt the quality of payment services provided by the TPPs. Moreover, they may delay the execution of the payment services and make them more expensive.

D. The Basis for the Processing of Special Categories of Personal Data

If the given 'silent party data' qualify as special categories data and their processing is either necessary or unavoidable, a TPP must rely on one of the derogations

[76] ibid, point 58.
[77] See Art 36(1)(a) of the RTS Regulation.

included in the exhaustive list provided under Article 9(2) GDPR. In addition to explicit consent given by a data subject (Article 9(2)(a)), the said provision allows for the processing of personal data of special categories when it is necessary for the achievement of a given purpose or purposes. Those are: the purposes of carrying out the obligations and exercising specific rights of the controller or of the data subject in the field of employment and social security and social protection law (Article 9(2)(b)); the protection of the vital interests of the data subject or of another natural person where the data subject is physically or legally incapable of giving consent (Article 9(2)(c)); the establishment, exercise or defence of legal claims or whenever courts are acting in their judicial capacity (Article 9(2)(f)); reasons of substantial public interest (Article 9(2)(g); the purposes of preventive or occupational medicine, for the assessment of the working capacity of the employee; medical diagnosis; the provision of health or social care or treatment or the management of health or social care systems and services (Article 9(2)(h)); reasons of public interest in the area of public health (Article 9(2)(i)); and for archiving purposes in the public interest, scientific or historical research purposes, or statistical purposes (Article 9(2)(j) GDPR). Moreover, the processing of special categories of personal data is allowed in two situations: when processing is carried out in the course of its legitimate activities with appropriate safeguards by a foundation, association or any other not-for-profit body with a political, philosophical, religious, or trade union aim and on the condition that the processing relates solely to the members or to former members of the body or to persons who have regular contact with it in connection with its purposes and that the personal data are not disclosed outside that body without the consent of the data subjects, (Article 9(2)(d)), and when processing relates to personal data which are manifestly made public by the data subject (Article 9(2)(e)).

According to the EDPB, the processing of Article 9(1) data could be based on an explicit consent (Article 9(2)(a)) or reasons of substantial public interest (Article 9(2)(g)). Contrary to what the EDPB assumes, an 'explicit consent' is not possible. As regards a PSU, if the provision of a payment service were dependent on obtaining consent in order to process special categories of data, such consent would not be freely given, and thus invalid.[78] Article 7(4) GDPR indicates that the situation of 'bundling' consent with acceptance of terms and conditions is highly undesirable. As for a 'silent party', an explicit consent would not be feasible for obvious reasons.

As regards the reasons of substantial public interest, the EDPB merely reiterates that all the conditions of Article 9(2)(g) GDPR must be met. The processing of the special categories of personal data has to be addressed in a specific derogation to Article 9(1) GDPR in EU/EEA or national law. This provision will also have to address the proportionality in relation to the pursued aim of the processing and contain suitable and specific measures to safeguard the fundamental rights and

[78] Guidelines 05/2020, points 13–39.

the interests of the data subject. Obviously, the processing of the special categories of data must be necessary on the grounds of substantial public interest, including interests of systemic importance.[79] The question whether this derogation applies to 'silent party data' is not answered. While the EDPB cannot assess relevant national legislations, it could have specifically assessed whether the PSD2 provides for such a derogation. The processing of such data is necessary based in the argument that functioning payments systems are a 'substantial public interest, including interests of systemic importance'. As stated in Recital 5 PSD2, 'The continued development of an integrated internal market for safe electronic payments is crucial in order to support the growth of the Union economy and to ensure that consumers, merchants and companies enjoy choice and transparency of payment services to benefit fully from the internal market.' Moreover, 'Payment services are essential for the functioning of vital economic and social activities'.[80]

IV. Conclusions

As noted by Open Banking Implementation Entity, '[t]he GDPR and the PSD2 are key legislative frameworks that must co-exist holistically ensuring that personal data is protected, while at the same time enabling the provision of payment services and driving competition and customer benefits'.[81] Yet, the current EDPB Guidelines on the interplay of the PSD2 and the GDPR indicate that not aspects of processing of personal data under the PSD2 seem to have been considered by the EU legislator. This creates legal uncertainty for both payment services providers and European citizens. In Q4 2021, the Commission initiated the review of PSD2, so it may be adjusted where necessary, in order to support the implementation of the retail payments strategy policies.[82] As part of that review, the Commission called for advice from, amongst others, the European Banking Authority (EBA), that should deliver its report by 30 June 2022 at the latest.[83] It is uncertain whether data protection issues may be included in the review, but clarifying the processing of sensitive data would be welcome. The bill for lack of cooperation between EU bodies when negotiating the PSD2 should not be paid by the TPPs or their customers. A smooth interplay of the PSD2 and the GDPR is also crucial to European citizens, the sense of community belonging and community construction.

[79] Guidelines 06/2020, point 56.

[80] See Recital 7 PSD2.

[81] See www.edpb.europa.eu/sites/default/files/webform/public_consultation_reply/obie_submission_to_edpb_on_guidelines_06.2020_on_the_interplay_of_psd2_and_gdpr.pdf.

[82] Commission, 'Digital Finance package: Commission sets out new, ambitious approach to encourage responsible innovation to benefit consumers and businesses' Press release, 24 September 2020.

[83] See https://ec.europa.eu/info/sites/default/files/business_economy_euro/banking_and_finance/documents/211018-payment-services-calls-advice-eba_en.pdf.

5

Boosting Economic Growth in Europe with the Help of Technology: Innovation and the Role of FinTechs in Payments

RUTH WANDHÖFER

I. Introduction

As we navigate through the COVID-19 economic aftermath, Europe needs to have a clear strategy on how to boost economic growth in order to help lead to recovery.

One of the growing key pillars of the European economy over the last number of years is represented by the financial technology (FinTech) sector. Within that context financial services and more specifically the payment space has become of particular interest, driven to a significant degree by the evolving EU regulatory regime on payments, which encouraged an opening up of the market to enable more competition and choice for users.

A lot of progress has been achieved at the level of the EU in terms of payment system harmonisation and the delivery of associated efficiencies and customer benefits. An example of this is the huge success of the Single Euro Payments Area (SEPA), which is now driving the market into real time payment adoption with SEPA Instant Credit Transfers.

However, FinTech payments are still struggling across both regulatory and infrastructure related areas in Europe, often due to the slow pace of change by banks and the existence of significant barriers to competition, despite the second Payment Services Directive (PSD2)[1] being in place.

[1] Directive 2015/2366/EU of the European Parliament and the Council, of 25 November 2015, on payment services in the internal market, amending Directives 2002/65/EC, 2009/110/EC and 2013/36/EU and Regulation (EU) No 1093/2010, and repealing Directive 2007/64/EC [2015] OJ L337/35.

From an EU perspective, another area where more progress is required is regarding international cross-border payments, which is also underlined from a more global perspective by the work of the Financial Stability Board (FSB) and the Bank for International Settlements (BIS). The combination of innovative technologies and new business models is ripe for addressing the challenges of cross-border payments, which are represented by cost, speed, reach and overall efficiency.

From a wholesale cross-border payments perspective, technologies such as Distributed Ledger (DLT) and cloud computing, with a view to speeding up velocity of liquidity in the context of interbank payments going across central bank accounts, are currently being worked on in the market.

The continuing focus by central banks on the potential creation of Central Bank Digital Currencies (CBDC) is another piece of the puzzle. Over time with delivery of such an instrument across key jurisdictions one could imagine that we could see cross-border interoperability and connectivity as another way to improve cross-border payments. It remains to be seen whether a digital euro would have the effect of increasing competitiveness in the European payments market or if such an instrument might compete with the existing landscape of bank and non-bank payment service providers (PSPs), which could defeat the purpose of PSD2.

As new technologies mature, FinTech will inevitably become a more critical ingredient in the sustainability of the European economy. We have seen the growth of several FinTech hubs in Europe, but a lot still needs to be done in order to ensure more consistent and accelerated growth of this sector. We have repeatedly observed that successful FinTechs (once they reach a certain size) tend to look to US financing and in several cases listing, rather than exploring the opportunity to remain in Europe. The Kalifa Review[2] in the UK has addressed a number of ways to encourage FinTechs to remain in the UK, ideas that are also largely relevant for Europe. Equally, the potential for more FinTech sandboxes will need to be emphasised going forward as a means of supporting FinTech growth in Europe.

This chapter will review payments developments in Europe over the last decade as well as cast a light on the current initiatives in play, which are all focused on further increasing the efficiency of intra-European payments with a view to supporting trade and individual consumer payment transactions.

We will then discuss how well the arrival of FinTechs, as well as the evolving regulatory regime for payments, is supporting the growth of innovative solutions and innovative players that our market so badly needs. A number of measures that can help FinTechs to grow and scale will be discussed.

Lastly we will examine the field of cross-border payments, specifically looking at how the EU transacts with other markets and where there is room for improvement in these payment structures. Again, we will see that FinTechs are starting to play a more important role, both as drivers of innovation by banks, which still

[2] R Kalifa, 'Kalifa Review of UK Fintech' (2021) https://assets.publishing.service.gov.uk/government/uploads/system/uploads/attachment_data/file/978396/KalifaReviewofUKFintech01.pdf.

constitute the rails on which wholesale payments flow cross border, but also where innovative ideas on reengineering cross-border payment rails are evolving further.

II. A Recap of Europe's Payment Journey and the Role of FinTechs

The efficient working of intra-EU payments is essential for Europe's post-COVID-19 recovery plans.

The last two decades have seen the payments industry in Europe together with the European Central Bank (ECB) and EU regulators pursuing a joint agenda of payment system harmonisation and service innovation, underpinned by common conduct of business legislation. The building blocks of SEPA, the Payment Services Directive (PSD),[3] as well as the alignment and modernisation of Automated Clearing Houses (ACH) and central bank settlement capabilities have underpinned the introduction of new euro currency-based payment instruments to the market, namely SEPA Credit Transfers, SEPA Direct Debits and SEPA Card payments.

As a further step, SEPA Instant Credit Transfers (SEPA Inst) have been launched in November 2017, delivering a cross-border instant payment solution for the euro. The ECB is supporting this scheme with a specially developed central bank settlement offering in the form of the TARGET Instant Payment Service, or in short TIPS. SEPA Inst is also an enabler of new payment solutions such as 'request to pay' (RTP), which drives the removal of frictions in the e-commerce space.

One area that has become the beating heart of economies around the world in the last decade or so is FinTech, or financial technology. The FSB defines FinTech as 'technologically enabled financial innovation that could result in new business models, applications, processes or products with an associated material effect on financial markets and institutions and the provision of financial services'.[4]

In Europe FinTechs have really come to the fore as a consequence of the opening up of the payments market since PSD in 2007. Broadly speaking FinTechs tend to provide faster data processing and information sharing technology in a way that reduces the costs of payment and of aims to disrupt the incumbents, in terms of credit, payments, investment and overall servicing.

In Europe we have seen the emergence of money transfer service operators that quickly became European 'Unicorns' and significantly helped provide fairer

[3] Directive 2007/64/EC of European Parliament and the Council, of 13 November 2007, on payment services in the internal market amending Directives 97/7/EC, 2002/65/EC, 2005/60/EC and 2006/48/EC and repealing Directive 97/5/EC [2007] OJ L19/1.

[4] Financial Stability Board, 'FinTech' (*FSB*, 28 June 2021) www.fsb.org/work-of-the-fsb/financial-innovation-and-structural-change/fintech/.

and more transparent pricing as well as speedier and more seamless services to consumers and businesses. We can also observe that legislative change has been a key catalyst for innovative payments FinTechs to develop. The Payment Services Directive 2 (PSD2) in particular has led to a proliferation of FinTechs, some of which have also became 'Unicorns'.

Newly introduced third-party providers (TPPs) are permitted by PSD2 to access the payment account information of customers (subject to consent) that hold their accounts at Account Servicing Payment Service Providers (ASPSP), ie a credit institution or an e-money institution (ASPSPs can also act as TPPs). Services such as payment initiation (PIS) and account information (AIS) are enabled and can insert themselves into the broader digital payments economy, where Application Programming Interfaces (APIs) can be leveraged as a tool to allow account-related data transfers between ASPSPs and third parties. This opening up of payment account data unlocks the opportunity to develop new services going far beyond the payment itself; eg data driven services will allow for automation of mortgage applications, improved credit scoring of individuals, instant consumer loans, SME lending, foreign exchange (FX) transactions and much more.

As part of the PSD2 Level 2 requirements on Secure Customer Authentication and Communication (SCA), ASPSPs will have to provide a secure communication interface, which can be an API, that TPPs can connect to in order to allow them access to the account information to enable them to offer these new types of services.

However, TPPs are still being challenged by the shortcomings of the current implementation of PSD2 by many banks as well as some of the PSD2 and EBA Regulatory Technical Requirements. The European banking industry still has not consistently implemented the required technological modifications – in particular APIs are often not up to expected standards – and at the same time maintains unnecessary barriers to TPP service provisions, forcing customers to be redirected to their web portal or app, creating unexpected system downtimes, or requesting multiple SCAs during one transaction journey etc. Creating a harmonised European API has also been somewhat elusive and the European Payments Council (EPC), under the supervision of the European Retail Payment Board, chaired by the ECB and the EU Commission, has begun work in earnest in order to create a SEPA API scheme, which aims to deliver both regulatory and value-added standardised API journeys that will help all players to make the most of PSD2 and its new services.

Beyond this, the European Retail Payments Strategy[5] laid out the principles for the future development of retail payments in Europe. The development of a pan-European retail payment solution at the point of interaction that is governed at the European level is at the centre of this strategy, in addition to a continued focus on

[5] European Central Bank, 'The Eurosystem's retail payments strategy' (2021) www.ecb.europa.eu/pub/pdf/other/ecb.eurosystemretailpaymentsstrategy~5a74eb9ac1.en.pdf.

improved cross-border payments beyond the EU as well as the overall innovation and the digitalisation of the European payment ecosystem.

Another recently announced strategy comes in the shape of the European Payments Initiative (EPI) – a plan to create a European owned and operated card scheme, digital wallet and P2P real-time payments system with full pan-European interoperability. However, looking at the EPI project, initially envisaged by some of the leading EU banks and markets, it should not be forgotten that the remaining 5,000 banks and hundreds of third-party providers have just spent three years and a huge amount of money in developing the PSD2 infrastructure across the whole of Europe and have done so at the request of the authorities. PSD2 mandated all Member States to ensure that payers can pay directly from their account, either using their own bank or any other licensed PISP. This means that today, all EU citizens having an online accessible payment account at any bank (or any other ASPSP) and across all EU markets can use this infrastructure for any retail payment.

To make this work in practice, especially at an in-store point of sales, requires further improvements which are currently in the making. With SEPA Inst becoming the new normal across Europe and SCA becoming frictionless as the remaining EBA-recognised API obstacles have been removed by the end of 2020, the EU is getting very close to becoming independent of any currently dominating cards or wallets. The so-called European Retail Payments Framework (ERPF), which is the market initiative of the bank-independent European TPPs, represented by the European Third Party Provider Association (ETPPA), is proposing how to complete the final stages of PSD2 implementations and then use this already existing infrastructure in combination with SEPA Inst to allow all, not just some, EU citizens to pay directly from their bank account, anywhere in Europe and without the need for any additional tool, app, card or wallet.

Both EPI and ERPF, by leveraging SEPA Inst as the underlying payment mechanism, will be able to divert flows from international card schemes to the pan-European account-based SEPA process, which will strengthen the European market by ensuring that the EU is in control of its payment systems: the lifeblood of any economy.

III. Thoughts on the Potential for a Digital Euro

The arrival – at a global level – of private cryptocurrencies such as Bitcoin, Ether, Dash Coins and thousands of others has opened up a new chapter for the world of money and payments. These cryptocurrencies are a special form of private digital money that operates on a distributed ledger, where encryption technologies are used to manage the generation of units as well as their verification and transfer. The underlying systems are outside governments' and the banking system's control. The move from centralised to decentralised systems that achieve seamless payment transactions across the globe is hailed as a financial revolution. At the same time cryptocurrencies have the potential to challenge the role of commercial and central banks when it comes to the provision of retail payment services.

All of the retail payment instruments listed in the previous section and the laws that apply to them relate to commercial bank money/credit. As the market evolves further towards digitisation and as physical cash will continue its decline – a process that has significantly accelerated as a consequence of the COVID-19 pandemic – a new question has come to the fore, which is whether the Eurosystem should consider issuing a digital version of what is today the only direct link it has to its citizens, cash.

We have been observing for a few years now that central banks around the world are researching and experimenting with the topic of Distributed Ledger Technology (DLT) and cryptography, where the theme of Central Bank Digital Currency (CBDC) is coming to the fore. Whilst Sweden is preparing a plan to potentially launch the 'e-Krona', the local government of Dubai has emerged as the first to launch a DLT based cryptocurrency, 'emcash', which has been declared legal tender and can be used for payments at both government related and non-governmental entities.[6] Japan has designated Bitcoins and other cryptocurrencies as payment instruments and Christine Lagarde, formerly Head of the International Monetary Fund (IMF), has made a public statement underlining the need for governments to take cryptocurrencies more seriously as there is a risk that weaker countries may be inclined to opt for cryptocurrencies in order to reduce their dependency on the US dollar (USD).[7] Furthermore, she also underlined the importance of central banks to reconsider their role as money issuers in the digital age, emphasising many of the key principles and design considerations discussed in this chapter.[8] Since she took the helm of the ECB, the focus on CBDC has clearly emerged as a strategic priority for the EU.

The ECB began work on Proofs of Concepts (PoCs) internally and with other central banks as early as 2016 as a way to both learn about the emerging technology and to identify areas where its application could result in efficiencies, better control, better data etc.

In recent years, however, the ECB has increasingly focused its attention on the potential for a retail CBDC, a digital euro, something that I thematised in my PhD where I presented a proposal for Euro cryptocash to the ECB annual conference in 2017.[9] In 2020 the ECB then issued a consultation on a digital euro, which

[6] J Buck, 'Dubai will issue first ever state cryptocurrency' (*Cointelegraph*, 1 October 2017) https://cointelegraph.com/news/dubai-will-issue-first-ever-state-cryptocurrency.

[7] C Lagarde, 'Central Banking and Fintech – a brave new world? (30 September 2017)' in IMF, *The Power of Partnership – Selected Speeches by Christine Lagarde, 2011–2019* (Washington, International Monetary Fund Publication Services, 2019) 67 ff.

[8] C Lagarde, 'Winds of Change: The Case for New Digital Currency (14 November 2018)' in IMF (n 7) 37 ff.

[9] R Wandhöfer, 'The future of digital retail payments in Europe: A role for central bank issued crypto cash?' (2017) www.ecb.europa.eu/pub/conferences/shared/pdf/20171130_ECB_BdI_conference/payments_conference_2017_academic_paper_wandhoefer.pdf.

attracted a lot of responses from industry as well as citizens. Taking this process forward the ECB in October 2021 set up the ECB Digital Euro Market Advisory Group, composed of 30 market experts as well as representatives from the EU Commission and from National Central Banks of the Eurosystem, with the task of advising on design and distribution of a potential digital Europe in a way that would add value to the Euro Area as whole.

Some argue that a digital euro success could contribute to the overall competitiveness and attractiveness of the European market, and this in turn could contribute to the main direction of the European Retail Payments Strategy. However, a digital euro would naturally compete with both commercial banks and non-bank PSPs and it is currently not clear whether that competition would be facilitated based on a level-playing-field.

At a general level there are several reasons as to why a central bank should investigate the topic of CBDC. Key motivations cover the areas of monetary policy, eg the ability of imposing negative interest rates and improving the monetary policy transmission mechanism; currency competition (in this instance with private cryptocurrencies); efficiency of central banks' currency function; reduction of costly physical cash; payment system efficiency; security and back-up system provision; and provision of legal tender once physical cash is phased out, to name a few.

There are different models for CBDCs, where the CBDC is either token-based and thus lends itself to anonymous or pseudonymous transactions where data control is more in the hands of the user, whilst the account-based model would effectively see CBDCs issued into accounts that everyone holds directly with the central bank. Unsurprisingly some central banks are favouring the account-based model with a view to issuing accounts to all types of users, ranging from consumers to businesses and government entities themselves. In such a model data transactions would be fully visible to the central bank, which in turn would be responsible for ensuring AML/CTF regulatory compliance and the like.

A digital euro could provide a digital step up to existing digital payment solutions in the commercial space by being built on the latest state of the art technology, deliver instant settlement – hence removing any financial stability risk or credit risk – and be able to offer distinct features through programmability; a way to smarten up the Euro.

70.3 billion real-time payment transactions were processed globally in 2020, a surge of 41 per cent over the previous year.[10] The world is moving towards instant liquidity management, on-the-spot settlement of payments and an overall real-time economy. Thus, instant payments should be used as a basis for payment services, irrespective of the underlying back-end technology. The provision of a

[10] ACI Worldwide, 'Prime Time For Real-Time' (2021) https://go.aciworldwide.com/rs/030-ROK-804/images/2021-Prime-Time-Report.pdf.

digital euro would also be able to reduce and even remove the dependency on international card schemes, which impinge on the Eurozone's payments sovereignty. However, so too could the ERPF discussed above.

As the digital future is wide open, more and more features and elements could be considered in light of a potential digital euro. For example, for many years the market has been demanding a Digital Identity solution. If Europe could develop a standardised pan-European version of a Digital Identity, this could be linked to each user's digital euro wallet and transactions would be easily identifiable. Through linking and automating data in such a way it will also be possible to fully automate taxation and thus achieve a significant reduction in tax evasion, in particular in light of the continued decline in cash usage observed across several European markets. At the same time the topic of privacy has to be carefully addressed. Many European citizens use physical cash in order to maintain their privacy. The full digitisation of payments under a digital euro that would ultimately replace physical cash would potentially remove the privacy preserving nature of cash. Sufficient controls and balances of power will need to be ensured to avoid a fully centralised money and data infrastructure, which by its very nature would be open to abuse, hacks and mistakes. Another key dimension to keep in mind is the broad set of PSPs in Europe, which all play different roles in the payments value chain and have been encouraged to enter the market via regulatory stimulus under PSD and PSD2.

IV. Supporting the European FinTech Ecosystem

FinTech has many strands to it, ranging from its objective to broaden access to finance and promotion of financial inclusion to deepening the EU's capital markets, increasing operational efficiency and automation as well as supporting regulatory reporting and compliance. Some FinTechs are also providing digital identity services, a topic highlighted above that is a crucial ingredient for the full digitisation of financial services, payments and money.

Over the last decade more than 1,500 FinTechs have established themselves in the EU, with most business headquarters and activity being located in the UK. Post-Brexit there has been some adjustment to this, however the UK is taking significant measures to remain attractive to European FinTechs, including special measures to ease access to capital and promoting an attractive environment for talent in this area.

Depending on the FinTech business model and whether any regulations are applicable (or not) FinTech either focuses on growing domestically or expanding at a pan-European level. What can be observed overall is that FinTech is still not scaling at the European level and several companies, having reached a certain size, have sought access to US capital markets, in particular listing on Nasdaq or NYSE, rather than listing on a European venue. In fact, according to a KPMG study discussed as part of the Kalifa Review in the UK,[11] these two US exchanges have absorbed more than 55 per cent of FinTech IPOs between 2015 and 2020, thus illustrating the significance of the US capital market.

The European Commission's Digital Finance Strategy for Europe, launched in 2020, is primarily focused on determining areas where regulatory measures will need to apply to FinTechs, including the more recent developments in the crypto asset market but also emphasising the need for operational resilience of players. A key area to hopefully benefit the FinTech ecosystem is the data sharing space, where the Commission is advocating for the emergence of Open Finance and safe data sharing between businesses.

However, in order to more actively support FinTechs in their growth as an ever more important pillar of the European economy, there are other key areas that the EU could focus on. It is encouraging to see the updated EU Commission FinTech Action Plan of 2020,[12] which spells out a number of measures ranging from financial support to the ability to test solutions in regulatory sandboxes and encourage cross-industry collaboration.

Regulatory sandboxes have been proven as an area that has been very effective for many FinTechs. Initially launched by the UK Financial Conduct Authority in 2016, FinTech Regulatory sandboxes have taken a tour around the world. They are controlled 'safe spaces' where services and products as well as business models and ways to deliver them can be executed in a test mode, without requiring those solutions and processes to be compliant with relevant regulatory requirements. In this way, it can be established whether services and processes work from a technical perspective, whilst also identifying potential improvements to architecture and governance. This makes it easier to navigate regulatory requirements at a later stage as well as enabling business models to align with them before live services are offered in the market.

Another important advantage of regulatory sandboxes is the fact that they allow regulators themselves to find out about new technologies and processes and how they can be deployed to create new and improved services for consumers and businesses.

In the meantime, various national regulatory sandbox initiatives have emerged, but at EU level the European Commission, as part of its Digital Finance Package published end 2020,[13] has proposed a Regulation on a Pilot Regime for Market Infrastructures based on Distributed Ledger Technology (labelled as 'PilotR'). This will mark the beginning of an EU-wide approach to fostering the delivery of Pan-European FinTech innovation.

[11] Kalifa (n 2) 61.

[12] European Commission, 'Communication to the European Parliament, the Council, the European Central Bank, the European Economic and Social Committee and the Committee of the Regions – Fintech Action Plan: For A More Competitive And Innovative European Financial Sector' COM (2018) 109 Final.

[13] European Commission, 'Digital Finance Package' (*ec.europa.eu*, 24 September 2020) https://ec.europa.eu/info/publications/200924-digital-finance-proposals_en.

A considerable challenge with the FinTech space in Europe is that divergence in regulatory and supervisory practice will result in potentially significant risk of arbitrage and fragmentation. At the same time this fragmentation could further promote innovation at domestic rather than European or global level, which risks curtailing FinTech's potential for European innovation and growth. The EBA as part of its FinTech Knowledge Hub continues to identify best practices in the design and operation of sandboxes and is expected to publish recommendations for the core design of a sandbox.

V. International Cross-border Payments: A P(l)ay for FinTechs?

An area of payments that is of critical importance in today's globalised world are wholesale cross-border payments. These underpin international trade and constitute a systemically important area of business, with financial institution (FI) and corporate transactions representing 80 per cent of the cross-border transaction value, 20 per cent of the overall transaction volumes and 40 per cent of global revenue.[14] As the world is growing closer and digitisation is effectively removing physical borders, this space is ripe for innovation.

Empirical evidence shows that there are major shortcomings in cross-border payments at a global level. In July 2020, a task force coordinated by the Bank of International Settlement's Committee on Payments and Market Infrastructures (CPMI) published a report[15] tabling recommended 'building blocks' for improved cross-border payments. The report came as part of a task force on the subject instigated by the G20, and led by the Financial Stability Board, which had observed in a preceding report that cross-border payments face four major challenges today: they are slow, expensive, opaque and inaccessible. These deficiencies cause negative implications to global growth, trade, development and financial inclusion.

From a European perspective, ensuring the smooth functioning of cross-border payments is as important as an efficient intra-European payments space. International trade and significant exposures of banks to each other in terms of cross-border credit lines necessitates a look at what can be done to make these flows more transparent, speedy and less vulnerable to financial stability concerns.

Improvements have been made to international payments via, for example, the SWIFT network, with the arrival of global payment initiative (gpi). This innovation ensured that correspondent banking payments across the vast network of

[14] McKinsey, 'Global Payments 2016: Strong Fundamentals despite Uncertain Times' (2016) McKinsey & Company Report, Financial Services Practice.

[15] Bank for International Settlements, 'Enhancing cross-border payments – building blocks of a global roadmap' (Stage 2 Report, 2020) www.bis.org/cpmi/publ/d193.pdf.

SWIFT members can now be tracked in real time, making it easier to act upon situations where payments suddenly get stuck.

However, the FinTech space in not asleep when it comes to the topic of cross-border payments. One FinTech is currently in the process of developing a cross-border wholesale payments platform that effectively connects participating banks' reserves accounts (held specifically for the purpose of this system) at their respective central banks with each other, enabling them to transact cross-border wholesale payments in form of High Quality Liquid Assets (HQLAs). This would for the first time not only remove the cost of banks holding risk weighted assets (RWAs) in relation to their correspondent banking nostro/vostro balances, including the overall cost and operational risk of maintaining those types of accounts, but also provide central banks with visibility into a portion of their banks' reserves accounts, where until now no such visibility exists. We shall see where this ambitious project will lead us, but it is already clear that financial stability can only benefit from such a solution. Despite the fact that this approach relies on central banks both recognising the quality of liquidity – ie HQLA – as well as the legality of ownership change of central bank reserves, as banks transact with each other, it is clear that such a solution would provide central banks with an important tool, both in terms of monitoring the transaction flows as well as being able (in the case of a bank resolution) to immediately have access to all necessary information in terms of which balances a bank really owns in its reserves account.

Other FinTechs in the cross-border payment space have focused on the deployment of crypto coins and Stable Coins, a form of cryptocurrency pegged to a national fiat currency or basket of currencies, via which banks can exchange payments. This approach is more complex as it involves participating banks exchanging fiat currency into the designated crypto coin or Stable Coin first, then transacting between each other in this medium and ultimately reconverting back to fiat currency. This operationally more convoluted with currency volatility risk depending on the nature of the Stable Coin's backing (single currency, currency basket, types of fiat underlying etc).

VI. Conclusion

Despite the roll out of SEPA and PSD2, the European Single Market still has potential to improve in efficiency when it comes to payments. Mass adoption of SEPA Inst, accelerating the speed of payments, is one key pillar to achieving this. However, what we still continue to lack is an end-to-end enablement of Open Banking, such that all different PSPs can effectively engage in competition with each other, driving the evolution of better services to all users.

Practical ways to address this are in motion with the SEPA API Access Scheme development, under the umbrella of the EPC. The focus on developing competitive value-added customer journeys and services on the basis of the open API architecture is a key community project of cross-collaboration between different parts of the payments industry at EU level.

The European Payments Initiative (EPI) is another community initiative, aimed at enabling broad adoption of SEPA Inst, such that more and more efficient account-based payments can be executed across the Union.

Both projects can enable the EU to control its payment systems, where the latter are the rails for the life blood of the economy to flow efficiently across the Single Market. As such, the issue of payments is a strategic priority for the EU in an age where the dominance and dependency on international card schemes has reached its peak.

Beyond this, the continued focus on exploring new technologies and business models should remain a priority. In particular, the exploration around a potential digital euro is expected to continue to garner more focus. Building on the evolving distributed ledger technology, smart contracts and richer data flows, new technologies can make the European and global financial system more inclusive, transparent and efficient in support of trade and growth.

In particular, the cross-border opportunity of leveraging new technologies in payments is an area of increased attention, where FinTech is playing a key role. For Europe to become a global leader in this space, it is this potential that needs to be explored with more vigour. In addition to initiatives based on Stable Coins as well as the opportunity for a future digital euro to be interoperable and therefore easily connectable to other emerging national CBDCs, the idea of enabling banks to exchange central bank reserve liquidity via a global synthetic ledger that facilitates legal ownership change of liquidity between participants in a real time environment would truly have a substantial positive impact on banks' balance sheets, by making these types of transactions much more efficient and cheaper as well as greatly increasing financial stability.

6

A Substitute without Substitute: Cash Money, Digital Euros, and the Shifting Futures of Currency Communities

URSULA M DALINGHAUS*

I. Introduction

A truism, reiterated by central banks and critical theorists alike, is that fiat currency lives from trust – from the 'faith' that we as members of currency communities are compelled to place in it – as we use it to make payments now and store value for the future. Until recently, physical cash issued by independent central banks has occupied the centre of this currency imaginary. Physical cash is the only tangible link between everyday consumers and central banks. With the rise of digital payments, cryptocurrencies, FinTech-based applications, and distributed ledger technologies, central banks including the European Central Bank (ECB), are exploring the design and policy implications of digital fiat, otherwise referred to as Central Bank Digital Currency (CBDC).

This chapter examines the future of the euro single currency in relation to the changing politics of payment forms and infrastructures.[1] Nowhere is more at stake for the future relationship of central banks to discrete currency communities and individual consumers alike than in the euro zone. Because all Member States share

* I am indebted to Gabriella Gimigliano (EUMOL Jean Monet Chair at University of Siena) for guidance and comments on earlier drafts, and for the invitation to participate in the 2019 EUMOL Winter School in Siena, Italy. This chapter has greatly benefitted from ongoing conversations with currency and cash industry experts – you know who you are. All errors and arguments are my own.

[1] The arguments presented here draw upon evidence presented in two white papers for the International Currency Association (ICA)/Cash Matters Movement in collaboration with the Institute for Money, Technology, & Financial Inclusion (IMTFI) at UC Irvine: U Dalinghaus, 'Keeping Cash: Assessing the Arguments about Cash and Crime' (2017) *White Paper Cash Matters*, www.escholarship.org/uc/item/8tj0678b; U Dalinghaus, 'Virtually Irreplaceable: Cash as Public Infrastructure' (2019) *White Paper Cash Matters*, https://cashmattersrebuild.s3.amazonaws.com/documents/IMTFI_Whitepaper_US_Download.pdf.

the same banknotes and coins, physical cash has played a key role in concretising a European identity, unifying payment infrastructures, and enabling greater mobility of persons across national borders. Membership in the euro binds disparate communities to transnational monetary governance and financial markets independent of national fiscal and social policy making. How might a move to digital fiat impact the long-term prospects and sustainability of this ongoing euro project? Scholarship on the euro has taken for granted the substitution of physical euro cash with digital payments.[2] However, design proposals for a future digital euro are bringing into sharper focus how the materiality of currency actually plays a central role in differentiating the relationship between central banks, commercial banks, and consumers in the global monetary system.[3] This chapter will explore current research and discussions around a future 'digital euro' and describe how CBDCs have the potential to disrupt these interrelationships with uncertain outcomes.

Currently the ECB and the national central banks in the Eurosystem maintain a commitment to physical cash as a complementary payment form.[4] The Bundesbank particularly communicates to a lay audience how the bank maintains and secures the cash cycle on behalf of the public's payment and savings needs.[5] But will cash remain viable in the future if cash use declines and people turn increasingly to digital payment options? I argue that this turn to digital over cash is not solely an expression of payment choice, but reflects growing challenges to the acceptance of cash payments, which at scale threatens the sustainability of a cash infrastructure dependent on widespread circulation and use of cash. Greater consideration is needed of the role and importance of physical currency for financial inclusion as well as monetary and market stability in the EU. As numerous financial crises and monetary failures exemplify, trust in currency is immensely fragile. Monetary failures not only intensify conditions of precarity and deepen inequality, but also harm the reputational profiles of central banks as people lose trust in their ability to safeguard value.[6] I consider the design implications of digital euros in the context of current evidence about how trust and instability play out differently across specific payment forms, drawing evidence from interdisciplinary and anthropological research on money and payments, specifically the ECB's

[2] In contrast to Sweden, which does not use the euro, the implications of a shift to a fully digital fiat system in the euro monetary arrangement where Member States share the same physical cash is under-theorised. My conceptualisation of 'substitution' has greatly benefitted from feedback at a 2019 conference panel on ethnographies of substitution organised by Nandita Badami and Katie Ulrich.

[3] European Central Bank, 'Report on a Digital Euro' (2020).

[4] See the Eurosystem Cash strategy available at www.ecb.europa.eu/euro/cash_strategy/html/index.en.html.

[5] Deutsche Bundesbank, 'Bargeld' (*Deutsche Bundesbank*) www.bundesbank.de/de/aufgaben/bargeld.

[6] See M Tankha and U Dalinghaus, 'Mapping the Intermediate: lived technologies of money and value' (2020) 13(4) *Journal of Cultural Economy* 345–52, www.tandfonline.com/doi/full/10.1080/17530350.2020.1779112.

initial 2020 report on a digital euro.[7] The ECB report outlines the core principles that a digital euro would need to meet, speculates on possible scenarios warranting its issue, and elaborates on economic, technical, and legal requirements and effects. To what extent can digital euros exist alongside physical cash? What are the policy mandates necessary for securing the long-term stability of, and access to central bank money as a basic right and public good? Given the acceleration into digital, largely private, payment networks due to the COVID-19 pandemic, what stance should the ECB take in maintaining a cash infrastructure alongside digital forms? Answers to these questions entail different stakes for diverse actors who maintain the cash infrastructure, for currency communities, and ultimately, central banks.

II. The Shift from Competing Currencies to Competing Payment Forms

Current efforts to secure the future stability of public (central bank) money as distinct but complementary to commercial bank or 'private' money turn around the political and ethical stakes of *who should issue* money, and *what forms* public money should take. In the current global financial system, especially in developed markets, central banks are viewed as public institutions acting as a third term between States and commercial banks to safeguard the national unit of account through the issuance and management of physical national currency. When modern States define the unit of account in the form of a physical unified national currency, physical cash constitutes a promise made by the State to all its money holders to secure current as well as future value.[8] In turn, money holders bind their future fates and economic fortunes to the stability and welfare of the corresponding national economies.[9]

Although cash is issued by States, it has the capacity to be autonomous from States in how people use it, store it, manipulate it, and give it meaning. As economist Pierre Lemieux has noted, 'It is an intriguing fact that the availability of government currency provides protection against government intrusion itself'.[10] Here, 'government currency' applies only to physical cash, where physical cash has the status of legal tender. Currently, legal and regulatory measures ensure at-par settlement of cash payments (ie, one euro equals one euro) and fees cannot be charged above face value. Electronic payments entail fees and tolls, which mean

[7] European Central Bank (n 3).

[8] B Maurer, 'The Gift of Money: Dematerialization, Demonetization, and Money's Pedigree' (2018) 2(52) *La Découverte Revue du Mauss* 173.

[9] G Peebles, 'Inverting the Panopticon: Money and the Nationalization of the Future' (2008) (20)2 *Public Culture* 234.

[10] 2016, cited in Dalinghaus, 'Virtually Irreplaceable' (n 1) 10.

that a euro or a dollar is not really a euro or a dollar when people must pay to pay. Analyses of cash in relation to the potential characteristics of CBDCs affirm the threshold properties of physical cash: that physical cash has qualities and features that are difficult to replicate in a digital form and that cash acts as a barrier to the use of the zero lower bound as a monetary policy tool.[11]

Importantly, cash, unlike digital options, can be held outside the formal financial system. When people hold cash as national, or in the case of the euro, transnational currency, they can assert claims upon States through participation in the market economy and through forms of national or supranational citizenship. The distributed affordances of physical cash make it a convenient mode of payment for poor and wealthy alike provided that people trust in its stability to store and transfer value. This can be true of global currencies like the US Dollar or the euro as well as soft currencies that people depend on for domestic use.[12] Precisely these qualities of physical currency, enabled by good governance practices of central banks, and the logistical and infrastructural support of currency and cash-in-transit professionals, support physical cash as a 'public good'.[13] Cash is the only form of public money not controlled by a private entity. Cash is non-excludable because it exists to enable value transfer at par, rather than to make a profit off its transfer (either as fees or data). Cash is non-rivalrous because everyone can use the cash system at the same time, in contrast to other digital payment forms, which require bank accounts or are based on creditworthiness.[14]

With the rise of digital payments and FinTech, and a decline in cash payments (though not necessarily of cash in circulation), there is growing concern at a wider societal level in the US, UK, EU, and elsewhere, about the potential for the complete privatisation of payments if central banks do not step in and offer a digital version of central bank money. To this end, significant research and experimental testing of central bank digital currency options is underway.

Central Bank Digital Currency (CBDC) refers to digital forms of money issued by a central bank, though the phrase digital currency is used as an umbrella term for the various digital money and payment options that central banks around the world are researching and analysing.[15] At a general level, the types of digital money a central bank might offer have been discussed in binary terms, as either token-based money that could be held on an external device, in a digital wallet, or on a smart card, which could represent cash-like features in digital form, or as an accounts-based model, which could take on a variety of forms, including individual accounts held with a central bank. Most proposals foresee supervised

[11] Dalinghaus 'Virtually Irreplaceable' (n 1) 29.

[12] J Guyer, 'Soft currencies, cash economies, new monies: Past and Present' (2012) 109(7) *PNAS* 2214–21.

[13] Dalinghaus 'Virtually Irreplaceable' (n 1) 20–21.

[14] ibid. Thanks to Bill Maurer, Andrea Nitsche, Sean Mallin, and Jenny Fan for contributions to formulating this argument.

[15] Dalinghaus 'Virtually Irreplaceable' (n 1) 27.

intermediaries such as commercial banks taking on the onboarding and customer services aspects of managing these accounts that would hold value as a liability of the central bank rather than a liability of commercial banks.

An accounts-based form of digital 'retail' central bank money held directly by the central bank, or by commercial banks on behalf of the central bank, poses the greatest challenge to the current division of labour between central and commercial banks. Researchers and expert commentators worry that deposits might leave commercial for central banks, posing a threat to commercial banks' business model as well as overwhelming the central banks' balance sheet. In current discussions, it seems more likely that whatever form a retail CBDC might take, the management, maintenance, and day-to-day regulatory compliance would be handed over to commercial banks or payment providers as intermediaries in a two-tier system, as is currently the case for physical cash.

What this arrangement might mean for public and private sectors in a context where a digital fiat potentially replaces physical cash is unclear. Insofar as central banks determine the unit of account in a given currency community, the change from a physical to a largely (or exclusively) virtual form of representation and means of payment has wide implications for ongoing historical shifts in the nature of national and territorial currencies.

III. Cash, Currency Communities, and Identity

Historical perspectives on the development of territorial currencies and cash design offer new lessons for the present digital age. Because of the diverse ways in which cash denominations have been designed, used, exchanged, held, and distributed across societies over time, people have turned to cash as a deliberative tool in shaping economic, political, and social life.[16]

As Gustav Peebles has presciently argued, in the State-sponsored project – beginning in the mid-1800s at the advent of the Industrial Revolution – of persuading citizens to translate privately hoarded international signs of wealth to fiduciary paper money indexing collectively-held wealth in the form of national reserves, 'people became bound, in unison, to the nation-state's future'.[17] Where once people could translate the metallic content of silver and gold into values on the international market, with the shift from commodity-based money to a

[16] B Maurer, 'Distributed Accounts: Money as token and record' in NJ Enfield and P Kockelman (eds), *Distributed Agency: The Sharing of Intention, Cause, and Accountability* (New York, Oxford University Press, 2017) 109–16; C Desan, *Making Money: Coin, Currency, and the Coming of Capitalism* (New York, Oxford University Press, 2015); K Hart, 'Heads of Tails? Two Sides of the Coin' (1986) 12(1) *Man* 637–56; E Helleiner, *The Making of National Money: Territorial Currencies in Historical Perspective* (Ithaca, Cornell University Press, 2003).

[17] Peebles (n 9) 234.

fiduciary paper money system, people's economic wellbeing became tied to the future of the nation-state. Peebles argues that this created an 'inverted panopticon, wherein the citizens must be constantly gazing back into the nation's centre, for their own economic self-interest has now become attached to the management of the national currency'.[18] In this way the future value of money is inherently tied to the stability of the State and reliability of banking institutions. 'Horizons of spatial mobility and future planning' are tied to the boundary-making activities of the State as 'public authority'.[19] Whether digital accounting or material cash, money is always 'denominated' in terms of a particular currency – in other words, particularised in a unit of account tied to territories, nation-states, colonial, imperial, and/or transnational orders.[20]

In the contemporary euro area, the right to issue banknotes resides with the European Central Bank, whereas the right to issue coin resides with each Member State ('subject to approval by the European Central Bank of the volume of the issue'). Thus, while Member States retain the ability to design nation-specific euro coins (with special or commemorative coins only permitted as payment in their country of issue), the denomination of euro bills famously feature examples of generically 'European' architecture that do not actually exist in an effort to create unity out of diversity. Indeed the most controversial and complex dimension of euro membership has to do with the splitting off of monetary policy from national-level fiscal and social policy, and the location of monetary governance at a different 'supranational' level above the national political electoral process. Thus, in this arrangement, monetary union exists while other forms of political and fiscal union do not. The euro single currency is therefore an unprecedented monetary experiment, one that currently ties European citizens together through shared but opaque monetary governance that sits uneasily alongside nationally and locally specific – and more democratic – forms of governance.

Throughout the early years of the euro's inception and implementation, 'the euro in your pocket' was widely proclaimed by European institutions, politicians, advocates, and scholars as the single most important material object that brings the EU into being for Europe's citizens. When physical euros were rolled out to the public in 2002, the convenience of shared cash that seamlessly crosses national borders of euro Member States was a key 'selling' point to the broader European public. The affordances offered by a shared physical currency in the form of euro banknotes and coins could act as a constant and tangible reminder to Europeans of their place in a new transnational currency community.

[18] Peebles (n 9) 234.

[19] Peebles (n 9) 260.

[20] Thank you to Taylor Nelms for theorising 'denomination' in these terms. TC Nelms, 'Dollarization, Denomination, and Difference: Rounding Up in Quito, Equador' (2017) *Working Paper*, www.dropbox.com/s/ep0wc447121clrm/Nelms-Dollarization%2C%20Denomination%2C%20and%20Difference.docx?dl=0.

National central banks charged with governing the euro underscored this relationship in a different way. In my research with the Deutsche Bundesbank in the early years of the euro, I observed how tangible cash was important in educating the public about the role and authority of central banks as guarantors of the reliability and value of the new euro currency.[21] In keeping with their mandate of independence and neutrality, the Bundesbank emphasised those aspects of physical cash most closely tied to their mandate of ensuring a stable currency as well as the security features embedded in physical cash. The materiality of euro cash was central to communicating about the underlying claims on the central bank as guarantor of the public trust. In this way, euro cash acted as calling cards of the euro system of central banks and helped to materialise the unique monetary arrangement of the euro community.

In my larger work, I argue that this monetary governance works in part through the medium of physical cash (a claim further underscored by current ECB President Christine Lagarde's December 2021 announcement that the ECB will redesign euro banknotes by 2024 'to make them more relatable to Europeans of all ages and backgrounds').[22] This aspect led me to investigate how the euro project necessitated and made possible the need for a shared conversation between monetary authorities and the general public about monetary policy – typically an arcane and abstract concern of select experts – as a shared domain of knowledge and practice. As a distributed material infrastructure that circulates across formerly national boundaries, euro cash is a constant index of the shared membership across national boundaries, and the collective – even shared fate – that binds Europe's publics to the project. Introducing the 50-euro banknote in 2017, ECB president Mario Draghi emphasised the importance of physical euros distributed across the European payments landscape and polity: 'Holding a euro banknote and knowing that it can be used in 19 countries is a reminder of the deep integration Europe has attained'.[23]

Because physical euros can be held outside the jurisdiction of the euro zone, people living in politically and economically unstable circumstances have also seen euro notes as a safe haven to store value as a hedge against domestic uncertainty and a claim on the future convertibility of value. In the event that a digital

[21] I conducted research on German experiences of the euro and currency unions during the timeframe of 2005–2010. U Dalinghaus, 'Accounting for Money: Keeping the Ledger of Monetary Memory in Germany,' (Minneapolis, 2014) Ph.D. Dissertation. See also U Dalinghaus, 'Between memorialization and monetary re-valuation: the 1990 currency union as a site of post-unification memory work,' in M Lindemann and JC Poley (eds), *Money in the German-Speaking Lands* (New York, Berghahn Books, 2017) 283–302.

[22] U Dalinghaus, 'When Cash is the Tie that Binds: Denominating Affective Monetary Attachments in Germany and the Euro Zone' (n.d.) Unpublished Manuscript; European Central Bank Press Release, 'ECB to redesign euro banknotes by 2024' (ECB, 6 December 2021) www.ecb.europa.eu/press/pr/date/2021/html/ecb.pr211206~a9e0ba2198.en.html.

[23] M Draghi, 'Address to mark the Issuance of the new Issuance of the new €50 banknote' (*ECB*, 4 April 2017) www.ecb.europa.eu/press/key/date/2017/html/sp170404.en.html.

euro sits side by side with, or replaces euro cash, to what extent, if at all, will small-value holders outside Europe be eligible to access and store digital euros?

A fundamental political question, then, that respective central banks will need to address in designing a digital central bank currency concerns who would be eligible to have an account with a given national central bank or hold a sovereign digital token. The ECB report on a digital euro suggests that eligibility would be based on euro area residency, with accommodations made for tourists or temporary residents, and cross-border access and use governed by multilateral agreements.[24] However, current expert discussions on the potential accessibility of CBDCs to individuals outside domestic jurisdictions raise doubts about the feasibility of multilateral agreements between central banks or the interoperability of different CBDCs with one another.[25]

Euro cash is therefore an important site for examining the materially binding power of money and the affective attachments it constitutes to the market, to political projects, to identity politics. What are the implications of substituting physical euros with digital payments that no longer signal any obvious connection to an issuing central bank? And to what extent could digital fiat replace physical cash?

IV. Euro Cash and Digital Euros – Complementary or Competing Forms?

The precise features of a digital euro remain highly speculative. As the 2020 ECB report on the digital euro explains, the core principles and goals for a digital euro must come first, with the specific design features to follow at a later time (form follows function).[26] The digital euro should

> replicate some key features of cash that are useful in the digital economy, such as the ability to make offline payments. However, it should also provide online payment capabilities that could support the fulfilment of the mandate or the Eurosystem in other areas.[27]

In line with a stated core principle that a digital euro should not replace physical cash, the design of the digital euro must therefore ensure at a fundamental level that physical and digital euros are mutually interchangeable to avoid situations of currency substitution and ensure on-par exchangeability. However, one of the possible scenarios outlined in the report describes a situation where cash is no

[24] European Central Bank (n 3) 14; 18–22; 28–29.

[25] D Beckworth, 'Interview on Macromusings, "Megan Greene on the Future of CBDC and How Central Banks should respond to Climate Change"' (*Mercatus*, 20 September 2021) https://macromusings.libsyn.com/megan-greene-on-the-future-of-cbdc-and-how-central-banks-should-respond-to-climate-change.

[26] European Central Bank (n 3).

[27] ibid 4.

longer used or accepted, and the reason for issuing a digital euro is to replace cash as an outcome of consumer 'choice' to no longer use cash.[28] There is a definite tension between the stated core principal to preserve cash as a public payment form and the adherence to a payment-neutrality ethos wherein a decline in the role of cash is ascribed primarily to changing consumer choices rather than a weakened institutional mandate to secure the cash infrastructure.[29]

Left outside this discussion is the impact of non-acceptance of cash on the part of businesses and retail establishments, such that consumer 'choice' reflects external limitations on the ability to pay in cash rather than a fully voluntary decision by consumers to use digital over cash. Moreover, many people who have the ability to choose among different payment methods are generally unaware of the implications of not using cash. As the volume and value of cash transactions decline at scale, the more costly it becomes to maintain the cash infrastructure. Consumers may only become aware of what they have lost when cash is no longer widely accepted, as is the case in Sweden, where Riksbank survey data from 2020 shows 'only nine percent of the population' paying regularly in cash.[30] Gustav Peebles describes the exclusionary impact of cashless-ness on elderly, homeless, and disabled members of Swedish society, not to mention non-residents without Swedish bank accounts who cannot access the widely used payment application Swish.[31] However, the ability to pay in cash is not only important for unbanked and underbanked residents and non-residents, but also for those who can comfortably select between a variety of payment tools. If these latter types of consumers understood the importance of continuing to use cash as a complement to digital, this could impact payment choice as well as demand for widespread cash acceptance.

Therefore central banks and State authorities need to communicate more explicitly on the systemic dimensions of a potential loss of the cash infrastructure to the public, and what this would mean to people's payment choices in the future. The Riksbank is raising awareness on these issues, explaining that the capacity of the cash infrastructure to aid in times of emergency or crisis depends on reliable cash usage in 'normal situations'.[32] In order to secure the cash infrastructure, the Riksbank has proposed new legislation to strengthen the status of cash as legal tender in Sweden, to mandate that commercial banks support cash services, and to secure consumers' 'right to pay' in cash.[33]

The ECB also anticipates how the introduction of a digital equivalent to euro cash would require an update to the legal tender status of different forms of the

[28] ibid 9–11.

[29] ibid 11, note 14.

[30] Sveriges Riksbank, '2021 Payments Report' (2021) www.riksbank.se/globalassets/media/rapporter/betalningsrapport/2021/engelska/payments-report-2021.pdf, 5.

[31] G Peebles, 'Banking on Digital Money: Swedish Cashlessness and the Fraying Currency Tether' (2021) 36(1) *Cultural Anthropology* 13, https://journal.culanth.org/index.php/ca/article/view/4743.

[32] Sveriges Riksbank (n 30) 32.

[33] ibid 32–34.

euro to discharge monetary obligations.[34] A January 2021 ruling of the Court of Justice of the European Union (CJEU) affirmed 'in principle' that physical euro cash is the only form of legal tender in all euro Member States.[35] This means that there is a strong, but not absolute mandate for the acceptance of euro-denominated banknotes as payment. A second principle allows for Member States to introduce restrictions on payments in cash 'for reasons of public interest,' but such measures would require proportionality in relation to the reasons for limitations and the availability of other legal forms of payment.[36] The European Cash Management Companies Association (ESTA) interprets the ruling as favourable to the strict acceptance of cash.[37] If a digital euro with legal tender status were to be introduced, how strict acceptance of physical forms of the euro would continue to be mandated alongside digital euros to ensure general acceptance of cash payments is unclear.

Privacy should be a central feature; in public consultations, concerns over privacy rank highest.[38] Digital payments, unlike cash, require a third party or set of intermediaries to enable final settlement, which leaves behind traces that allow for things like the identity of the payee, the date, time, and place to be recorded and tracked (for good or for ill).[39] Due to the regulatory, legal, as well as technical parameters that would be required for a digital form of cash to work, there would be no possibility of full anonymity. Due to Know your Customer (KYC) Anti-Money Laundering (AML) and Counter-terrorist financing (CFT) regulatory requirements, some form of identity authentication would likely be required at some point in the onboarding process, even where offline use is possible. So while layers of privacy could be designed in, the authentication necessary to guarantee security, stability, and compliance would limit anonymity.[40]

Depending on the design of a CBDC, users might meet with greater constraints on use compared to physical cash. In the current system, cash acts as a guarantee that citizens can exercise their right to determine how they store wealth and how they make decisions about spending and consumption. Digital forms of the euro will likely require that certain limits and restrictions on the value of digital euro holdings, where or how it can be transferred or spent (such as domestic vs

[34] European Central Bank (n 3) 33, see also 57.

[35] CJEU, Judgment of the Court (Grand Chamber), 26 January 2021, Joined Cases C-422/19 and C-423/19 *Johannes Dietrich and Norbert Häring v Hessischer Rundfunk* [2021] 2 CMLR 23; See also Cash Matters, 'European Court of Justice Delivers Judgment on Cash Acceptance Case' (*Cash Matters*, 4 Feb 2021) www.cashmatters.org/blog/european-court-justice-delivers-judgment-cash-acceptance-case.

[36] ibid.

[37] ESTA, 'Position of ESTA on the Ruling of the European Court of Justice' (2021) www.esta-cash.eu/wp-content/uploads/2021/02/4a7639ab55c0451ea51b2346bcffec80d831a903-601bcd00dff17-2021-01-26-Note-on-EUCJ-ruling-c-422-4-423-19-final.pdf.

[38] European Central Bank (n 3) 11; 27.

[39] A Guseva and A Rona-Tas, 'Money talks, Plastic Money tattles: The new sociability of money' in N Bandelj, FF Wherry and VA Rotman Zelizer (eds), *Money Talks: Explaining How Money Really Works* (Princeton, Princeton University Press, 2017) 215–29.

[40] European Central Bank (n 3) 29, note 51.

cross-border contexts) are programmed into the initial design, potentially limiting flexibility for everyday users in a manner that cash does not. The use cases for digital euros (compared to cash) may be more narrowly defined and less inclusive in terms of access (such as the conditionality that will apply to non-euro residents). Satisfaction with, and trust in the digital euro user interface may depend more substantively on supervised intermediaries to ensure a seamless and reliable user-experience than is the case with physical cash, with more potential for blame to fall directly on the central bank in times of failure.

How will the European Central Bank ensure that commercial banks and other intermediaries do not undermine the viability of digital euros in favour of upselling private and more profitable alternatives, as is currently the case with cash? Currency and cash in transit professionals argue that commercial banks, which are core distributors of physical cash, do not have an interest in maintaining cash and prefer to offer their own, more profitable alternatives to customers, where fees can contribute to profitability for commercial banks.[41] In other words, the commercial banks and private sector are, in practice, not committed to the core central bank principle of market neutrality when it comes to cash. To what extent would the ECB be able to guarantee the same for the digital euro, and would commercial banks have an interest in providing add-on services that increase profits rather than ensure convertibility and on-par settlement between different forms of the euro?

Trust in the euro, whether physical or digital, is key to the reputational success of the ECB and the national central banks in the euro system. The ECB report on the digital euro anticipates some of the potential challenges to central banks' reputational identities in designing, implementing, and communicating about the role and goals of digital representations of central bank money.[42] While a number of functions and forms of a digital retail euro can coexist with cash, it remains to be seen how 'end-users' will adopt, use, and accept a digital euro. More importantly, how will digital and cash forms of the euro continue to coexist and be sustained in an increasingly digital-centric payments environment? This is an urgent question as the viability of the physical cash infrastructure depends upon availability, circulation, use, and acceptance of cash.

V. Substitutability, Design, and the Ethos of Choice in Framing Digital Payments

Everyday citizens in developed, relatively stable economic markets are largely unaware of the difference between physical cash (a claim on central banks) and

[41] ESTA, 'Report to the ERPB Working Group on Access to and Acceptance of Cash' (2021) www.esta-cash.eu/wp-content/uploads/2021/06/e698207585e540b1db037791dc563303b050596a-60c7c064566d3-2021-06-10-ESTA-report-to-the-ERPB-final.pdf.

[42] European Central Bank (n 3) 20.

digital money (a claim on private entities recorded in electronic ledgers of commercial banks and other financial institutions).[43] Physical cash is the only central bank money that ordinary citizens can hold (with digital central bank money restricted to operations between central banks and the commercial banking sector).

The substitutability of different payment forms within a domestic currency community underlies the notion of payment choice, which is a dominant framing in research on payments. Proponents of digital payments emphasise the substitutability of payment methods as a consumer choice, but frame digital as more convenient than cash.[44] In this view, the ability to substitute one method of payment for another allows consumers flexibility and choice. Tracking data on payment methods used in point of sale transactions shows the share of relative frequency, volume, and value attributed to payment methods, such as cards, contactless payments, and cash.[45] A growing preference for digital over cash is often taken as evidence for their relative convenience in comparison to cash.

However, when tracked across different countries or localities, or at the level of different payment venues such as convenience and grocery stores, the picture can look quite different. In the US cash still dominates low-value payments.[46] People are more likely to pay cash when the charge is for smaller amounts. Some have shown the precise thresholds at which the shift from cash to card occurs. Nonetheless, data on payment transactions and the growing shift is often taken uncritically as a measure of convenience. Convenience here becomes synonymous with speed and efficiency. Payment diaries are shedding some light on consumer motivations.[47]

A 'banknote paradox' is increasingly discussed in central bank research on currency in circulation.[48] New data shows that while cash used for transactions is declining, cash in circulation is rising, primarily because euro banknotes are being kept as a store of value at home, outside the banking system. This can be seen based on observations in the data that cash issued does not quickly return to the banks. In the context of the pandemic, and at a time when many private card networks

[43] Peebles (n 31); G Peebles, 'Privatizing Cash: Currency and Public Goods in Sweden' (2021) *Accounting, Economics, and Law: A Convivium*.

[44] B Scott, 'Gentrification of Payments: Spreading the Digital Financial Net' (*TNI Longreads*, 15 January 2019) https://longreads.tni.org/stateofpower/digital-payment-gentrification.

[45] H Esselink and L Hernández, 'The Use of Cash by Households in the Euro Area' (2017) 201 *ECB Occasional Paper Series* www.ecb.europa.eu/pub/pdf/scpops/ecb.op201.en.pdf.

[46] O Shy, 'How the ATM affects the way we Pay' (2019) 2 *Working Paper Federal Reserve Bank of Atlanta* www.econstor.eu/bitstream/10419/200540/1/1067490302.pdf.

[47] Esselink and Hernández (n 45); C Greene and J Stavins, 'The 2019 Diary of Consumer Payment Choice' (2019) 20(4) *Research Data Reports Federal Reserve Bank of Atlanta* http://docs.publicnow.com/viewDoc.asp?filename=68444%5CEXT%5CF1FA54E2B247172C94D9D92D9BFA6F4AF03E18E8_23367707595B387A8AAC6886F00ADD814D4317B2.PDF.

[48] A Zamora-Pérez, 'The Paradox of Banknotes: Understanding the Demand for Cash Beyond Transactional Use' (2021) 2 *ECB Economic Bulletin* www.ecb.europa.eu/pub/economic-bulletin/articles/2021/html/ecb.ebart202102_03~58cc4e1b97.en.html; see also Sveriges Riksbank (n 30) 7.

and other entities were claiming that cash transactions should be reduced to stop the spread of COVID-19, many consumers were confronted with limitations on their ability to pay in cash. Despite research demonstrating that cash surfaces were no more (indeed less) likely to transmit the virus than other payment surfaces with which customers might interact at the point of sale, a widespread response across business and retail was to nonetheless scale down the acceptance of cash payments. In some cases, this was tied to the reduction of employees who work on-site to accept payments. In spite of these increased limitations, public demand for cash stayed constant and grew in many currency communities across the globe, as even during the pandemic, when there were more limited opportunities to spend cash due to lockdowns and greater reliance on online payments, people nonetheless turned to cash as an emergency store of value to keep on hand at home. A hedge against emergencies where ATM access might be reduced, cash on hand guaranteed that money could be accessed in time of need.[49]

The relative substitutability of different payment forms depends upon an underlying stable *unit of account* backed by States together with central banks and monetary authorities.[50] Arguably, this backing underlies trust in State-issued physical currency. From a legal standpoint, physical cash is currently the only form of legal tender, settles at par, and is the primary instrument accepted in the settlement of debts. The ability of private citizens to convert electronic funds into physical cash at par helps to maintain this important distinction. While everyday consumers may not question the convertibility between the private money deposits in their bank accounts and central bank issued cash, the guarantee that they can translate their money holdings into physical State-issued cash at par in the domestic economy underpins trust in the relative long-term stability of the financial system as a whole. In times of crisis, central banks and regulatory bodies have measures in place to reassure consumers that their money is safe, even if individual banks might fail.

In designing a central bank digital 'public money', monetary authorities must confront the ways in which consumers might experience a CBDC as one of many interchangeable payment options, to the potential detriment of, or decline in trust of central banks in cases where access to digital public money is interrupted, unwieldy, complicated, or inaccessible for a variety of reasons. How central banks might create the tangible tie to digital forms of central bank money in a way that complements the experiential ties to physical banknotes and coins remains uncertain. While consumers may not interact with physical national currency daily,

[49] These findings are based on presentations of central bank and other payment professionals at a virtual Global Currency Forum event, 'The Evolution of Payments during the Pandemic and the Resilience of Cash,' held by the International Currency Association on 28 January 2021. See also F Panetta, 'Cash still King in Times of Covid-19' keynote speech (*European Central Bank*, 15 June 2021) www.ecb.europa.eu/press/key/date/2021/html/ecb.sp210615~05b32c4e55.en.html.

[50] Dalinghaus, 'Virtually Irreplaceable' (n 1) 28.

there exists nonetheless a tacit, embodied connection to national cash as a material reference point (as the ECB's proposed redesign of euro banknotes attests). Physical cash can be used in unofficial ways; a folded origami banknote can invoke the specificity of a gift and the fungibility of abstract value. What aesthetic affordances will a digital euro have, and on what terms might people invest tacit meaning in digital central bank holdings? These are the kinds of attachments that the ECB or national central banks may wish to activate in order to communicate about the back-end architectures that guarantee digital forms of the currency in a complementary form to physical euro banknotes and coins.

VI. The Payment Neutrality Paradox

The ECB's current cash policy holds that physical and digital euros should remain complementary and does not foresee the digital euro as replacing cash. At the same time, however, the ECB holds to its policy of payment neutrality and while promising the *availability* of cash, does not step up directly to mandate the *acceptance* of cash at the point of sale. Cash is a product of central banks but is outsourced to a variety of actors that ensure its logistical and infrastructural distribution. From the point of view of the currency and cash management and cash-in-transit industries, whose business models depend on supporting the work of central banks in the design and supply of banknotes and coins, and in contributing to the resiliency of the wider cash infrastructure, this creates a paradox.[51] Central banks are key to the relationship of creating physical cash as a public good, but once cash is issued, central banks defend payment neutrality even as this stance undermines cash. Growing limitations on cash acceptance, heightened by the COVID-19 pandemic, increase the costs and undermine the viability of the cash infrastructure. While commercial banks are key distributors of cash, they profit more from customers who use their own products instead of cash, and are key contributors to the decline in cash acceptance.

What seems imperative for the future viability of cash, then, is that it continues to be not only widely *available* but also widely used *and accepted* as a form of payment. As cash transactions decline combined with increased limitations on acceptance at the point of sale, the costs of the cash infrastructure will become unsustainable. Currently, seigniorage for the issuance of physical banknotes is a source of public revenue for central banks that supports the mandate to issue and supply cash. Whether central banks would continue to ensure availability of physical cash is uncertain if decreasing use of cash for transactional purposes entails a financial loss that must be offset by other funding sources.

[51] This argument is informed by discussions with industry and research participants at the ESTA Business conference in Seville Spain, 24–26 October 2021.

VII. Maintaining the Euro Cash Infrastructure as a Public Good

The underlying cost of these payment systems (and who bears the costs) poses potential challenges for the future of cash, especially if the use of the cash infrastructure declines in favour of digital central bank money forms. In practice, the cost of payments can be highly variable, difficult to quantify, and largely invisible to ordinary consumers. This is as true of electronic payments as for the underlying costs of providing a cash infrastructure. Policy and industry actors wanting to underscore the singular status of physical currency (cash) as a public good raise questions about the infinite substitutability of money via its payment forms. If completely dismantled, the physical cash infrastructure will not be available in any meaningful way in times of emergency, political or environmental disruption, or other crises. The complementarity of physical and digital euros must therefore be at the centre of ensuring universal access, affordability, privacy, and widespread acceptance to physical cash.

Insofar as the extension of digital forms of the euro to the public open up a conversation about present and future use-cases of physical cash alongside digital versions of the euro, the potential for greater inclusion is possible, but not guaranteed. Part of the novelty of central bank issued physical cash is precisely in its affordances to be representationally tied to the issuer yet completely detached in physical terms. Unlike cash, which can be used independently and anonymously from its issuer, digital euros will not be able to offer the same independence, anonymity, and multiplicity of use. The results of a newly published Bundesbank survey show that few members of the German public are even aware of the discussions about a digital euro.[52] How these changing forms of public money will be perceived by the general public as contributing to, or undermining of trust in central banks as authorities that work on behalf of the public good remains an open question.

[52] Deutsche Bundesbank, 'Wie stehen private Haushalte in Deutschland zum Digitalen Euro? Erste Ergebnisse aus Umfragen und Interviews,' (2021) 10 *Deutsche Bundesbank Monatsbericht* 65–85, www.bundesbank.de/resource/blob/878908/8222f73e033984d0e346dbe1b51bc4a8/mL/2021-10-digitaler-euro-private-haushalte-data.pdf.

7

Thinking of the Digital Euro as Legal Tender

GIAN LUCA GRECO AND VITTORIO SANTORO*

I. Introduction

The jurist rarely understands the importance of money problems, generally preferring to leave solving these problems to the economists. This attitude may be justified by the fact that the rules governing money have spontaneous daily application, to the point that they appear to be inherent in the very nature of social life.[1] On the other hand, Hicks significantly states that for economists

> Money is not a mechanism; it is a human institution, one of the most remarkable of human institutions. Even the simplest forms of money, even metallic coinage, even the use of metals as money that preceded coinage, none can function without some minimum of trust.[2]

Considering the regulation of money as an expression of legal systems to be historically determined, jurists turn their attention to the great upheavals that mark said history; in contemporary history, for example, the transition from convertibility to inconvertibility of banknotes, and now, preparations for the creation of central bank digital money. The launch of a digital euro may challenge the stability and financial cohesion of the Eurozone, raising concerns about monetary policy management, the proper functioning of the banking system and consumer rights protection. Then again, the 'forthcoming' digital euro may encourage jurists to revise their approach to money and legal tender on the premise that money is first and foremost a social process rather a legal construction.

* The work is the result of joint conception, elaboration and revision. However, sections IV and V can be attributed to Gian Luca Greco and sections I, II, III, VI, VII, VIII and IX to Vittorio Santoro.

[1] *cf* J Dalhuisen, *Dalhuisen on Transnational Comparative, Commercial, Financial and Trade Law, Volume 3*, 6th edn (Oxford, Hart Publishing, 2016) 333 ff.

[2] *cf* J Hicks, *Critical Essays on Monetary Theory*, 2nd edn (Oxford, Clarendon Press, 1979) 59. See also K Polanyi, *The Livelihood of Man* (New York, Academic Press, 1977) (we read the Italian translation, Einaudi 1977) 143 ff.

II. Money as Legal Tender

The legal literature regarding the construction of money as legal tender mirrors changes in social contexts and legal systems.

The first phase was accompanied by the development of two opposing theses. The first relates currency exclusively to State sovereignty:[3] In Carbonnier's opinion 'la monnaie est un meccanisme d'Etat';[4] and Ascarelli wrote: 'Nel mondo moderno … l'ordinamento valutario corrisponde a quello statale';[5] Mann believed that: 'Only those chattels are money to which such character has been attributed by the law i.e. by or with the authority of the State',[6] therefore Mann refused to consider the ECU as money, since the currency could not be matched with any 'national currency system'. In other words the ECU lacked correspondence with a 'state' which could justify its existence as a 'distinct unit of account'.[7] In Mann's opinion, only a federation of national States could justify a coining right.[8] The second opinion, concurring with economists like Hayek,[9] defends the 'societary' theory of money. Nussbaum wrote: 'the government … might be unable to force its issues upon the people … In conclusion we may say that in the phenomenon of money the attitude of society, as distinguished from state, is paramount'.[10] Nussbaum reminds us that as in Article 39 of the 1882 Italian Commercial Code 'reference was made to money that had "corso legale o commerciale" within the realm',[11] commercial tender could be understood as the customary circulation of money among businessmen.

[3] GF Knapp, *Staatliche Theorie des Geldes* (Leipzig, Duncker & Humblot, 1905).

[4] See J Carbonnier, *Droit civil*, vol. III (Paris, PUF, 2004) 16 ff.

[5] See T Ascarelli, *Obbligazioni pecuniarie*, 2nd edn, A Scialoja and G Branca (series eds), *Commentario del Codice Civile* (Bologna, Zanichelli-Foro italiano, 1971) 26.

[6] See FA Mann, *The Legal Aspect of Money*, 5th edn (Oxford, Clarendon Press, 1992) 14.

[7] Mann (n 6) 23. See also H Siekmann, 'Monetary Aspects of the Euro as Single European Currency – a German Perspective' in R Freitag and S Omlor (eds), *The Euro as Legal Tender. A Comparative Approach to a Uniform Concept* (Berlin, De Gruyter, 2020) 34.

[8] But concerning the transfer of sovereignty by eurozone Member States, see C Proctor, *Mann on the Legal Aspect of Money*, 6th edn (Oxford, Oxford University Press, 2005) 744 ff. Recently, Advocate General G Pitruzzella remarked: 'Moreover, as scholars of federal systems know, interference between the exercise of competences devolved to different levels of government or of overlapping of competences is common in multi-level governance systems, even where there is a clear distinction/separation of competences between the federal state and the other state units, according to "dual federalism" models, through constitutional catalogues that carefully distinguish between the competences of the federal state and those of the other state units' (para 46 of the Conclusions presented 29 September 2020, Joined Cases C-422/19 and C-423/19 *Johannes Dietrich* and *Norbert Häring v Hessischer Rundfunk* [2021] 2 CMLR 23).

[9] FA von Hayek had already expressed his support for the 'societary' theory of money, which he took up again in FA von Hayek, *The Nationalization of Money: An Analysis of the Theory and Practice of Concurrent Currencies*, Hobart paper special No.70 (London, Institute of Economic Affairs, 1976).

[10] See A Nussbaum, *Money in the Law National and International. A Comparative Study in the Borderline of Law and Economics* (Brooklyn, The Foundation Press, 1950) 27 ff.

[11] Nussbaum (n 10) 7. The Italian text reads: 'Se la moneta indicata in un contratto non ha *corso* legale o *commerciale* nel Regno, e se il corso non fu espresso, il pagamento può essere fatto con moneta del paese …'.

We must reconsider these theses in the light of developments in central bank digital money, at a particular moment in history[12] when jurists are focusing more of their attention on money.[13] Today, as paper money is becoming more and more residual as a means of exchange,[14] replaced not only by scriptural money, but also by electronic and digital forms, we can look favourably on Sáinz de Vicuña's revisionist proposal of the concept of an 'institutional theory of money', according to which money consists of a claim against a central bank as well as a credit balance of sight deposits held by people in commercial banks.[15] Some criticise this position, arguing that it would not comply with the provisions of the Treaty and underlying civil rights.[16]

III. European Union Monetary Law

As far as the rules of the Treaty are concerned, we must consider Articles 128[17] and 282(3). The first states that:

> 1. The European Central Bank shall have the exclusive right to authorise the issue of euro banknotes within the Union. The European Central Bank and the national central banks may issue such notes. The banknotes issued by the European Central Bank and the national central banks shall be the only such notes to have the status of legal tender within the Union.

In turn, the first paragraph of Article 16 of the Protocol on the ESCB and the ECB is worded as follows:

> In accordance with Article 128(1) of the [FEU Treaty], the Governing Council shall have the exclusive right to authorise the issue of euro banknotes within the Union. The [European Central Bank (ECB)] and the national central banks may issue such notes. The banknotes issued by the ECB and the national central banks shall be the only such notes to have the status of legal tender within the Union.

[12] In accordance with S Omlor, 'Geld und Währung als Digitalisate. Normative Kraft des Faktischen und Geldrechtsordnung' (2017) 72 *Juristenzeitung* 763.

[13] See studies in Freitag and Omlor (n 7); See also T Adrian and T Mancini-Griffoli, 'The rise of Digital Money' (2019) 19/01 *Fintech Notes* 1–15.

[14] On the role of cash in EU countries, see H Esselink and L Hernández, 'The use of cash by households in the euro area' (2017) 201 *Occasional Paper Series of the ECB* 1–68.

[15] A Sáinz de Vicuña, 'An Institutional Theory of Money' in M Giovanoli and D Devos (eds), *International Monetary and Financial Law: The Global Crisis* (Oxford, Oxford University Press, 2010) para 15.18. *Contra* Siekmann (n 7) 31 f.

[16] Siekmann (n 7) 39 ff. But the European Central Bank [*Report on a Digital Euro* (October 2020) 24] wrote: 'if the digital euro were to be issued as an instrument equivalent to a banknote, then the most expedient legal basis for its issuance would be Article 128 of the TFEU in conjunction with the first sentence of Article 16 of the Statute of the ESCB'.

[17] European Legal Tender Expert Group (ELTEG), *Report on the definition, scope and effects of legal tender of euro banknotes and coins* (Brussels, 21 January 2009) 2 f.

Article 182(1) of the Treaty states that only the European Central Bank (ECB), with the collaboration of the national central banks, is competent to print banknotes denominated in euro. Article 182(2) adds that national States are competent to mint the divisional currency denominated in euro within the limits set by the ECB. Only these banknotes and coins can and must be issued as euros in physical form as legal tender in the Eurozone. However, the Article says nothing to prohibit circulation and payments in euro in alternative forms: scriptural money, electronic money issued by EMIs and now probably central bank digital money as well.[18] It is no coincidence that in the transitional period immediately before the issue of banknotes, the euro only had a scriptural form. In fact, in that period, while on one hand,

> the parties surely had the right to exclude cash payment in the contract [on the other] the decision to pay in Euro during the transitional period necessarily meant that the payment has to be made by scriptural money. Stating the contrary and thus forcing the debtor to pay in a different currency from that fixed in the contract, would breach the basic principle 'No compulsion, no prohibition'.[19]

Significantly, Article 282(3) TFEU states that the ECB 'alone may authorise the issue of the euro', without any reference to banknotes and coins. This latter rule establishes the principle that the euro is the official unit of account of the Eurozone and that the ECB, in order to implement monetary policy, controls the quantity of issuance directly when it comes to material currency, and indirectly, eg through the official discount rate and the refinancing of private banks, when it comes to private money (scriptural and electronic; we will deal with central bank digital money later).[20]

The aforementioned Treaty rules do not prevent payments made in scriptural currency, electronic money, and moreover, do not prevent the complete equivalence of digital currency issued by the ECB with paper banknotes and coins,

[18] European Central Bank (n 16) 1–53. Advocate General G Pitruzzella (n 8) para 80, says that money (euro) 'exists both in physical form, expressed in banknotes and metallic coins (i.e., cash), and in written or electronic form (expressed, for example, in the balance of a bank account). Money, and therefore, in the eurozone, the euro, exists and circulates in economic life in various forms'.

[19] Recital 19 of the Council Regulation (EC) No 974/98 of 3 May 1998 on the introduction of the euro reads as follows: 'Whereas banknotes and coins denominated in the national currency units lose their status of legal tender at the latest six months after the end of the transitional period; whereas limitations on payments in notes and coins, established by Member States for public reasons, are not incompatible with the status of legal tender of euro banknotes and coins, provided that other lawful means for the settlement of monetary debts are available.' See V Santoro, 'L'Euro quale moneta scritturale' (2001) I *Banca Borsa e Titoli di Credito* 447 ff. See also Omlor (n 12) 754–63. Confirmation of what was stated in the text can be found in Commission Recommendation 98/287/CE, of 23 April 1998, concerning dual display of prices and other monetary amounts, of which para 4 and Article 2 states that the good practice articles should stimulate 'clear statement by dealers of accepting or not accepting payment in Euro during the transitional period; moreover a clear distinction between the monetary unit used to fix the price and the amount to pay on one hand and the real value on the other hand'.

[20] In any case, the European Central Bank (n 16) 25 opinion is that the digital euro can be treated as a banknote.

provided that such alternative currencies are denominated in euros. These equivalences are expressly recognised by Article 4(25) Directive 2015/2366/EU, where the European Legislator, listing funds that are the subject of payment services, states that

> 'funds' means banknotes and coins, scriptural money or electronic money as defined in point (2) of Article 2 of Directive 2009/110/EC.[21]

Thus we can conclude that fulfilment by means of scriptural or electronic payment (and in future, digital payment) of a 'sum of money' is valid and efficacious.[22] What should concern us is whether payments other than cash, eg those made through the transfer of bank deposits, are actually satisfactory for creditors, ie are legally correct in terms of quantity, time and place.[23]

IV. Digital Euro: A Monetary Policy Perspective

Monetary policy concerns the decisions taken by central banks to influence the cost and availability of money. A central bank uses a range of monetary policy tools to pursue its objectives.

Regarding the EU, the Treaty on the Functioning of the European Union (TFEU) contains no precise definition of 'monetary policy', but merely defines the objectives of monetary policy and the instruments available to the European System of Central Banks (ESCB) for the purpose of implementing that policy.[24] According to Article 3(1)(c) TFEU, the Union shall have exclusive competence in the area of monetary policy for the Member States whose currency is the euro.

Article 119(2) TFEU states that the activities of the Member States and the Union, ie

> the adoption of an economic policy which is based on the close coordination of Member States' economic policies, on the internal market and on the definition of common objectives, and conducted in accordance with the principle of an open market economy with free competition,

[21] Pitruzzella (n 8) para 76.

[22] In the opinion of R Wandhöfer, *The future of digital retail payments in Europe: A role for central bank issued crypto cash?*(2017) 24 'central bank money on the ledger is going to be an essential building block for the future of the fiat currency-based payments i.e. although the underlying technology may be new, the currency unit would not change'. Available at www.ecb.europa.eu. See, now, European Central Bank (n 16) 6.

[23] On the finalising of the payment and debtors' discharge in the intermediate payment, see V Santoro, 'Die schuldbefreiende Wirkung der Zahlung über Vermittler' (2007) 19 *Jahrbuch für Italienisches Recht* 162 ff.

[24] *Dietrich v Hessischer* (n 8) para 34; Pitruzzella (n 8) para 53. See also Case C-370/12 *Thomas Pringle v Government of Ireland and Others* [2013] 2 CMLR 2, para 53; Case C-62/14 *Peter Gauweiler and Others v Deutscher Bundestag* [2016] 1 CMLR 1, para 42; Case C-493/17 *Proceedings brought by Heinrich Weiss and Others* [2019] 2 CMLR 11, para 50.

are to include a single currency, the euro, and the definition and conduct of a single monetary policy and exchange-rate policy.

The primary objectives of the aforementioned policies are to maintain price stability and, without prejudice to this objective, to support general economic policies in the EU.[25] In particular, the aim of ECB monetary policy is to keep prices stable, ie to keep inflation below or close to 2 per cent in the medium term.

Finally, Article 127(2) TFEU provides that

> the concept of 'monetary policy' is not limited to its operational implementation (…) but also entails a regulatory dimension intended to guarantee the status of the euro as the single currency.[26]

The legal basis for the Eurosystem's issuance of a digital euro (ie, Articles 127(2), 128(1) or 133 TFEU; Articles 16, 17, 20 or 22 of the Statute of the ESCB) will depend on its design and the purpose for which it is issued.[27]

A part of the ECB's monetary policy strategy consists of defining and monitoring several monetary aggregates, which can reveal useful information on money and prices. ECB monetary analysis uses narrow (M1), 'intermediate' (M2) and broad monetary aggregates (M3). Monetary aggregates comprise monetary liabilities of monetary financial institutions (ie: central banks, deposit-taking corporations, credit institutions, money market funds, electronic money institutions) and central government (post office, treasury, etc). Each aggregate is composed of many different financial assets, from cash and banknotes to bank accounts, from savings deposits to electronic money. Every asset is money or can be converted into money in an easy, fast and non-costly way.

In the EU, money is generally issued by the ECB in the context of monetary policy, by way of crediting accounts held by banks.[28] The issuance of a digital euro could affect the transmission of monetary policy, as it fulfils the function of money.[29] The digital euro would be a new form of money, recorded as a

[25] *Dietrich v Hessischer* (n 8) para 37: 'the activities of the Member States and the European Union comprise three elements: a single currency (the euro), the definition and conduct of a single monetary policy, and the definition and conduct of a single exchange-rate policy'.

[26] *Dietrich v Hessischer* (n 8) para 38; Pitruzzella (n 8) para 70, remarked that: 'the European Union's exclusive competence in the area of monetary policy for the Member States whose currency is the euro within the meaning of Article 3(1)(c) TFEU must be understood as encompassing all the competences and powers necessary for the creation and proper functioning of the single currency, the euro, including a regulatory dimension relating to that single currency, which includes the definition and regulation of its status as legal tender'.

[27] See European Central Bank, *Report on a digital euro* (October 2020) 24. The ECB states that the variables should be: (a) a digital euro issued as an instrument of monetary policy, akin to central bank reserves, only accessible to central bank counterparties; (b) a digital euro available to households and other private entities through accounts held with the Eurosystem; (c) a digital euro issued as a settlement medium for specific types of payment, processed by a dedicated payment infrastructure only accessible to eligible participants; (d) a digital euro issued as an instrument equivalent to a banknote.

[28] Sáinz de Vicuña (n 15) 523.

[29] This is not the case for crypto assets, which do not fulfil the function of money. Crypto assets are not issued by central banks and are not currently used as means of payment. Therefore, they do not compete against cash and deposits in meeting the liquidity needs of the public. On crypto assets

liability on the ECB's balance sheet (like banknotes) and 'backed' by assets held by the ECB.[30]

There are many technical and organisational approaches to the introduction of the digital euro, and the effective impact on monetary policy could depend partially on which one is adopted.[31] The back-end infrastructure for the provision of a digital euro should in any case be controlled by the central bank, but it could be centralised (all transactions recorded in the ECB's ledger) or decentralised, where an end user could directly transfer bearer digital euro holdings to another end user, via distributed ledger technology (DLT)[32] protocols or by means of local storage.[33]

A centralised option with direct access by countless end users to central bank accounts would be technologically challenging and impose a heavy operational burden on the ECB. The decentralised option requires the ongoing assurance of central bank requirements at all times.

Although the ECB is not a regulated entity and regardless of the approach, to avoid reputational issues, maintain a high standard of consumer protection and ensure financial stability, a digital euro should assure the regulatory standards of payment instruments provided by the Payment Services Directive, but also by GDPR and the Anti-Money Laundering Directive.[34]

In both centralised and decentralised approaches, supervised intermediaries would be involved as gatekeepers[35] or as settlement agents on behalf of their clients, using the existing wholesale payment infrastructure.[36]

There is another important aspect of digital euro design to consider, namely the economic one. It concerns choices about who could hold a digital euro, whether a digital euro should bear interest, whether there should be limits on the amount of digital euros that can be held,[37] and whether a digital euro should be freely convertible into other forms of money or bank deposits.[38]

and monetary policy see ECB Crypto Assets Task Force, 'Crypto-Assets: Implications for financial stability, monetary policy, and payments and market infrastructures' (2019) 223 *ECB Occasional Paper Series*. There are different opinions regarding stablecoins. 'A hypothetical situation in which stablecoins become an "alternative store of value"… would have consequences for the transmission of monetary policy and other related issues'. See ECB Crypto Assets Task Force, 'Stablecoins: Implications for monetary policy, financial stability, market infrastructure and payments, and banking supervision in the euro area' (2020) 247 *ECB Occasional Paper Series* 19.

[30] For M McLeay, A Radia and R Thomas, 'Money creation in the modern economy' (2014) Q1 *Bank of England Quarterly Bulletin* 15, money is fundamentally a special kind of IOU (or promise to pay).

[31] See European Central Bank (n 27) 36 ff.

[32] ie a blockchain.

[33] ie prepaid cards.

[34] See European Central Bank (n 27) 20; Bank of England, *Central Bank Digital Currency Opportunities, challenges and design* (March 2020) 29 ff.

[35] In the case of a bearer digital euro, they could provide the physical devices and load funds on them.

[36] This is a hybrid option, where supervised intermediaries would provide payment services in digital euro to end users.

[37] For instance, an extensive use of the digital euro abroad could cause currency substitution in foreign jurisdictions. See European Central Bank (n 27) 29.

[38] See Bank of England (n 34) 11.

It is uncertain whether the digital euro might be a tool to strengthen monetary policy.[39] The ECB could directly influence the consumption and investment choices of households and companies through changes in the bank policy rate. On the other hand, there is a sort of trade-off between a potential benefit – a Central Bank Digital Currency (CBDC) would represent another channel for a central bank to support more effective transmission of monetary policy – and a potential risk, namely the disintermediation of the banking sector on banking provision.[40]

V. Digital Euro and Banks: A Dangerous Relationship

A digital euro might induce depositors to transform their commercial bank deposits into central bank liabilities, if the latter should prove to offer higher remuneration than the former.[41]

In the current negative interest rate environment, a digital euro bearing positive interest could induce a huge shift from bank deposits. Unlike banknotes, a digital euro would have no storage and insurance costs, so it is probable that even a non-interest-bearing digital euro could cause bank disintermediation.[42] If the public should switch some of their funds from deposits to CBDC, there could be potentially significant implications on the banking system, monetary policy and financial stability.[43]

[39] See European Central Bank (n 27) 13. J Meaning, B Dyson, J Barker and E Clayton, 'Broadening narrow money: monetary policy with a central bank digital currency' (2018) 724 *Bank of England Staff Working Paper* 30 wrote 'the impact [of a CBDC] on the monetary transmission mechanism is uncertain, but we believe the most likely consequence would be that CBDC would strengthen the monetary transmission mechanism, for a given change in policy instruments'.

[40] Bank of England (n 34) 34 correctly wrote 'CBDC would need to be carefully designed to ensure that the potential benefits for monetary and financial stability, as well as the wider benefits of introducing CBDC for the public, could be realised without jeopardising the Bank's objectives and the financial sector's ability to provide credit and other services to the wider economy'.

[41] According to Committee on Payments and Market Infrastructures Markets Committee, 'Central bank digital currencies' (2018) 11, 'CBDC accessible to individuals and designed as a non-interest bearing, retail payment instrument might primarily substitute for cash (eg token-based CBDC) and commercial bank deposits (eg account-based CBDC). CBDC that pays interest and is readily transferable would likely be attractive to professional financial market participants (eg cash pools and asset managers)'.

[42] See European Central Bank (n 27) 17. On bank disintermediation as a consequence of the introduction of a CBDC see also: M Kumhof and C Noone, 'Central bank digital currencies – design principles and balance sheet implications' (2018) 725 *Bank of England Staff Working Paper* 5 ff; T Mancini-Griffoli, MS Martinez Peria, I Agur, A Ari, J Kiff, A Popescu and C Rochon, 'Casting Light on Central Bank Digital Currency' (2018) International Monetary Fund Staff Discussion Note 21 ff. On the contrary, for D Andolfatto, 'Assessing the Impact of Central Bank Digital Currency on Private Banks' (2018) 26B *Federal Reserve Bank of St. Louis Working Paper*: 'CBDC need not have a negative impact on bank lending operations if the central bank follows an interest rate policy rule. (…) a well-designed CBDC is not likely to threaten financial stability'.

[43] In the early 1980s in Italy there was a significant drop in deposit demand, due to the introduction of an alternative financial investment, a form of short-term Treasury Bonds (BOT). Although BOTs were not means of payment, they were easily converted into cash and offered a higher interest rate than

Commercial bank deposits are an important part of the banking system's funding. If a successful digital euro should result in a lower volume of funding for commercial banks, they could react by reducing the volume of lending to the wider economy. Banks could also try to stabilise deposits by increasing their remuneration or replacing lost deposits with central bank borrowing or more expensive capital market-based funding.

A large-scale bank disintermediation would imply a potential drop in lending or an increase in the cost of credit to the public.[44] Moreover, during a systemic banking crisis, risk-free CBDC could become much more attractive than bank deposits: the run towards CBDC would amplify the effects of the crisis and financial stability could be undermined.[45]

The issuance of CBDC should therefore avoid the risk of excessive banking disintermediation and a worsening of banking crises.[46] According to some authors, CBDC would not necessarily lead to a contraction in bank funding if it is 'interest-paying, with an adjustable rate; distinct from, and not convertible to reserves; no explicit or implicit central bank guarantee of convertibility with deposits; issued only against eligible securities'.[47] Another proposed option is to differentiate remuneration based on the amounts of deposits held: a two-tier remuneration system with a lower interest rate above a certain threshold.[48]

Both hypotheses envisage limits on CBDC remuneration or on the quantity that can be held by the public, thus intervening on demand and prices and hampering the carrying out of monetary policy.[49]

There is no doubt that, in times of financial crisis, the issuance of CBDC can accelerate and make more widespread the flight from bank deposits. On the other hand, rather than limiting the holding of CBDC, it might be more efficient to strengthen the resolution frameworks, the depositor guarantee system and the central bank's capacity to act as a lender of last resort.

bank deposits. See G Vaciago and G Verga, 'Domanda di moneta e "disintermediazione" delle banche' (1982) 137 *Moneta e Credito* 59 ff.

[44] See R Juks, 'When a central bank digital currency meets private money: effects of an e-krona on banks' (2018) 3 *Sveriges Riksbank Economic Review* 79 ff; W Engert and B Fung, 'Central bank digital currencies: motivations and implications' (2017) 16 *Bank of Canada Staff Discussion Paper.*

[45] See Y Mersch, *Virtual or virtueless? The evolution of money in the digital age* (Lecture at the Official Monetary and Financial Institutions Forum, London, 8 February 2018).

[46] See U Bindseil, 'Tiered CBDC and the financial system' (2020) 2351 *ECB Working Paper Series* 17.

[47] M Kumhof and C Noone, 'Central bank digital currencies – design principles and balance sheet implications' (2018) 725 *Bank of England Staff WP* 36. A similar opinion is in O Bjerg, 'Breaking the Gilt Standard: The Problem of Parity in Kumhof and Noone's Design Principles for Central Bank Digital Currencies' (2018) *Copenhagen Business School Working Paper.*

[48] See F Panetta, '21st century cash: central banking, technological innovation and digital currency' in E Gnan and D Masciandaro (eds), *Do We Need Central Bank Digital Currency?* SUERF Conference Proceedings 2018/2 (Vienna, Larcier, 2018) 23 ff; Bindseil (n 46) 22.

[49] See Committee on Payments and Market Infrastructures Markets Committee (n 41) 17.

VI. What About Citizens' Rights?

Before proceeding further it should be noted that some scholars, especially in Germany, believe that the limitation of the use of cash is contrary to the European monetary order.[50] Two arguments have been made in this regard, with strong sociological rather than legal implications: (1) in European law there is a right to privacy guaranteed by anonymity in the transfer of cash, not by other forms of payment; (2) the use of cash is accessible to all local citizens, while the use of alternative payment instruments would require access to payment accounts or electronic platforms.

(1) The first statement is certainly true if we want to emphasise that European law guarantees the privacy of Union citizens,[51] but it does not seem to be supported by specific rules concerning cash in European monetary law. On the other hand, if the purpose is to guarantee privacy in money transfers, then the guarantee should hold regardless of which payment instrument the citizen freely chooses, including those covered by the secrecy imposed on banks and other intermediaries – a secrecy that certain market protagonists can and do maintain, as demonstrated by the decades-long experience with the Swiss banking system. But the absolute value of Swiss banking secrecy disappears due precisely to international agreements, demonstrating that International, European and individual State (including EU members) laws confirm that citizens' right to privacy must be balanced by careful evaluation of public interests in the transparency of money transfers (money laundering, terrorism, tax evasion); the question is how to apply the proportionality principle.

(2) As for the concern that the poor and (not so well educated) social classes[52] may suffer unjust inconvenience due to limitations on the use of cash, it seems excessive when it is acknowledged, as we do not hesitate to do, that cash cannot and must not be abolished but, on the contrary, must be accompanied by different forms of euro (scriptural, electronic and, in the future, digital) which are equally essential for the good economic and social functioning of our modern societies. Each of these forms of money has advantages and disadvantages,[53] and the possibility that under certain circumstances one form rather than another may need to be used contributes to the greater efficiency of the payment system as a whole.

Additionally, the European legislator has put in place specific actions for education and financial inclusion, in particular by providing access to basic accounts without fees.

[50] Siekmann (n 7) 40 ff. and the doctrine he cites in note 178. See also the problematic P Athanassiou, 'Impact of digital innovation on the processing of electronic payments and contracting: an overview of legal risks' (2017) 16 *ECB Legal Working Paper Series* 5 ff.

[51] See above, all of Article 8 of the Charter of Fundamental Rights of the European Union.

[52] Siekmann (n 7) 46 f.

[53] See European Legal Tender Expert Group (n 17) 6.

This excessive concern can mask a certain resignation to the fact that the disadvantaged social classes cannot get out of a condition in which they do not have access to a more sophisticated payment system, and must be kept in said condition. On the other hand, when it is pointed out that a significant percentage of the European population does not have access to bank accounts, it is not noted that this percentage includes a share of citizens who do not have access to a decent income; attention is thus shifted to bank accounts to avoid dealing with the problem of absolute poverty.

VII. The Function of Money

The jurist looks at money through a lens that distorts its image as it does not take into account what is most evident to economists, namely that bank deposits are equivalent to cash; once this is understood, digital currency is also seen as equivalent.[54]

Hayek has criticised this dystopian gaze among jurists who refer to the State conception of money,[55] and caustically points out that the Knapp approach led to the devaluation of the German mark to the tune of 1/1,000,000,000,000.[56] In truth, even in juridical terms it is not important to establish what money is, but to specify what its function is.[57] With regard to the essence, money is nothing more than a sign[58] to which the law attributes the virtue of freeing (discharging) the debtor through the transfer thereof: the sign therefore has the function of a means of exchange, and it is precisely this function that must be valued in legal terms.[59] Although central banknotes still bear the original imprint of debt securities containing the obligation of the issuing institution to pay a certain sum, this imprint has almost disappeared in euro banknotes except for the signature of the Governor.[60] No coercible legal obligation corresponds to these formulas, as the Germans realised in 1923 when the mark was drastically devalued and a wheelbarrow full of paper bills was required to buy bread.

On the other hand, while it is technically true that the central bank cannot fail in the sense that it is not subject to ordinary bankruptcy law,[61] it is not immune to

[54] Pitruzzella (n 8) para 76; V De Stasio and S Boatto, 'The Euro as Legal Tender from an Italian Perspective' in Freitag and Omlor (n 7) 53 ff.

[55] See Mann (n 6) and Knapp (n 3).

[56] von Hayek (n 9) ch 5.

[57] Proctor (n 8) 9 ff.

[58] Polanyi (n 2) [we read the Italian translation] explains that in ancient societies as well, money was often an abstract symbol represented by a word or a number.

[59] The other historical function of store of value has lost importance following the decision of the US Government of 15 August 1971 to suspend the convertibility of the dollar (international reserve currency) into gold.

[60] See Dalhuisen (n 1) 336 f.

[61] Siekmann (n 7) 48.

various forms of bankruptcy, usually liquidation according to the rules of public law.[62] On the other hand, since the essence of bankruptcy is the debtor's inability to repay his creditors at full value, this happens to a central bank when it is unable to control inflation. Historically, the case of the Reichsbank in 1923 is emblematic.

VIII. Cash Payment Limits

Restrictions on the use of cash can be established for reasons of public interest and compliance with the rules of fairness and good faith.

The first restriction is confirmed by the recent decision of the Court of Justice on 26 January 2021 according to which although national regulations

> the object or effect of which is to abolish, in law or in fact, cash in euro, in particular by calling into question the possibility, as a general rule, of discharging a payment obligation in cash, they do not in themselves enable a determination to be made as to whether a national rule that merely limits the use of cash for the purpose of discharging a statutorily imposed payment obligation would also be contrary to EU law.[63]

In this decision, the Court never questions the fact that euro banknotes must always retain a liberating effect, but establishes that there may be important exceptions when they are justified by 'public reasons' or 'reasons of public interest',[64] the concrete assessment of which is left up to national judges. The Court, however, then goes on to indicate what these reasons of public interest might be, and they range from crime fighting – eg anti-money laundering and anti-terrorism legislation[65] – but also (we believe) the fight against tax evasion.[66] Particularly significant is the fact that the public interest may well lie in ensuring the efficient organisation of payments in society, which is an objective of public order that certainly coincides with the interest of the contracting parties in an 'economically efficient contractual regulation'.[67]

[62] There have been recent cases in Zimbabwe (2010) and Tajikistan (2007); but in Italy we have the case of the Banca Romana (one of the six central banks operating in the country at the time) which, due to illegal circulation of 65 million lire and the duplication of paper bills in the amount of 40 million lire (enormous figures for the period), was liquidated and, in 1893, incorporated into the newly formed Bank of Italy.

[63] *Dietrich v Hessischer* (n 8) para 62.

[64] *Dietrich v Hessischer* (n 8) paras 65–78.

[65] Santoro (n 23) 161 f; T Bonneau, 'The concept of legal tender in France' in Freitag and Omlor (n 7) 85 f.

[66] Many eurozone countries forbid the use of cash for payment above relatively small sums: they include the most populous countries (France, Italy and Spain) except Germany, as well as Belgium, Greece, Portugal and Slovakia. In Estonia the limit is not on imports but on the number of banknotes and coins (no more than 50); in Finland entrepreneurs may not accept cash payments unless they declare them in advance. In Austria, the debtor, whether a consumer or a tenant, has the right to pay into an account designated by the creditor for the purpose: See S Perner, 'The Euro as Legal Tender from an Austrian Perspective' in Freitag and Omlor (n 7) 135 ff.

[67] S Arnold, 'The Euro in German (private) law – monetary obligations and the mutual dependence of public and private law' in Freitag and Omlor (n 7) 148 f.

However, the real exception concerns the application of the principles of fairness and good faith,[68] the scope of which is so great as to make one doubt whether non-cash payment is the exception rather than the rule.

To consider a few examples, cash payments of large sums are not in good faith because the security of the other party that you want to force to pay or receive cash is put at risk, and because you bear part of an improper and excessive cost of cashiers for counting. It is not in good faith to demand a cash payment in distance relationships as this forces the debtor in particular to risk sending the sums or (alternatively) to assume excessive insurance costs.[69] More generally, 'commercial' payments are not in good faith because they diverge from other business practices and are an obstacle to the construction of the single payments market, generating a disadvantage from a competitive point of view for companies from other countries or that are far from each other.

IX. Conclusions

Payment by means of scriptural, electronic and digital money is consistent with European law, specifically with both the functioning of the Single Market and the strengthening of the Monetary Union. Within the Single Market, the digital euro will allow better access, in comparison with cash and scriptural money, for consumers and businesses to digital goods and services across Europe. In fact, the Treaty freedoms require that all transfers must be costless in cases of purchase of goods or services and for the movement of capital or money by citizens within the EU area. The uniform regulation of the digital euro could overcome the different regulations and costs of cash payment among Member States. As regards the Monetary union, in order to compete on an equal basis with other subjects offering the same goods and services in the consumer's state, digital (as well as scriptural) payments (inter alia) through an intermediary in the payment systems must be compulsorily accepted by creditors. To this end, it is not sufficient that only a few operators accept this form of payment, because unless the rule is a general one,

[68] Arnold (n 67) 146 f.

[69] European Legal Tender Expert Group (n 17) 6, observes: 'At a first stage discussion, the Chair suggested four sets of objective reasons, all linked to the physical nature of cash (which, contrary to electronic means of payments, has to be transported and stored safely), according to which a retailer might validly refuse a cash payment. These reasons were the following: the security of people and of the business was at stake; the per unit value of the goods sold was so high that the retailer could face serious security/practical problems if all items were paid for in cash (e.g. car dealers); the shop was located in a remote area and there was no bank nearby allowing the retailer to deposit cash regularly; and, the purchase took place without any physical contact between the two parties to the contract (e.g. remote sales). It was not possible to reach an agreement on the issue because of the two different schools of thought described above: according to one school, contractual freedom can limit the public law provisions of legal tender, whereas according to the other one, contractual freedom cannot prevail over the public law principle of legal tender.'

debtors will not be confident due to information uncertainty regarding contract terms and to the risk of the creditor changing his mind, etc. In this sense, the digital euro will defeat the still-existing principle according to which only a cash payment is valid for discharging debts.

The issuance of digital euros poses a number of legal questions, beginning with the legal basis, which depends on both the intended design and the purpose of said issuance. As we believe that the digital euro must be issued as an instrument equivalent to banknotes (legal tender), the legal basis may be Article 128 TFEU in conjunction with the first sentence of Article 16 of the Statute of the ESCB.

8

The Approximation of National Banking Law in the European Banking Union

MARIA ELENA SALERNO

I. Introduction

A unified regulatory framework is the cornerstone of the construction of a true European single market. This does not mean that every market event needs to be centrally regulated, because full harmonisation is not feasible and perhaps not desirable. Rather, the suitable range of harmonised regulation should arise from a supervisory and regulatory effort across Europe that strikes a fair and satisfactory balance between integration and an unavoidable level of fragmentation due to the long-standing traditions and layered structures of national systems.[1]

Proceeding from this awareness, this chapter provides a critical analysis of the effectiveness of the Single Rulebook (SR) for the banking area in its current form. This analysis entails investigating the role that the regulatory function of the European Banking Authority (EBA) and the centralisation of supervisory and crisis management powers within the European Banking Union (EBU)[2] may have on the process of bringing national supervisory and regulatory frameworks into maximum harmonisation. The EBA and the integration mechanisms within the EBU act in concert to achieve this common and fundamental objective. However, since there is still a long way to go, some institutional changes might be useful to reduce national divergences by promoting the uniform implementation of the SR and its homogeneous application to banking intermediaries that benefit from the 'single European passport' (freedom of establishment and freedom to provide services).

[1] For legal and economic references concerning this regulatory effort, see ME Salerno, *Global Financial governance. The feasible future*, Collana di Diritto dell'Economia diretta da E Picozza and L Lener (Torino, Giappichelli, 2018) ch 1, *passim*.

[2] For the reasons underlying the creation of the EBU see the recent CV Gortsos, 'European Banking Union within the System Banking and Monetary Law' in MP Chiti and V Santoro (eds), *The Palgrave Handbook of European Banking Union Law* (Cham, Palgrave Macmillan, 2019) 21–23.

To set the scene, this chapter begins by outlining the legal basis of the EBU and the rationale for its creation (section II). It then goes on to analyse the institutional weaknesses of the EBA, and the two pillars of the EBU – the Single Supervisory Mechanism (SSM) and the Single Resolution Mechanism (SRM) – involved in promoting the maximum harmonisation process (section III and section IV). The aim of this analysis is to underline that the EBA and the two EBU integration mechanisms may carry out their respective regulatory and unificatory functions to increase the effectiveness of the SR (section V). The chapter concludes by laying out some potential institutional improvements that may assure broader consistency of national banking regulation, supervisory practices, and resolution procedures (section VI).

II. The Legal Basis of the European Banking Union

The need for a harmonised regulatory framework as a precondition for the building of the internal market for people, goods, capital, and services was formalised in the European Single Act of 1986, currently transposed in Title VII, Chapter 3 of the Treaty on the Functioning of the European Union (TFEU).[3] The approximation of national law, laid down in Article 114 TFEU, implies a transfer of regulatory competences from Member States to legislative European institutions (namely the European Commission – EC, the European Parliament – EP, and the Council). Under this provision, the achievement of regulatory convergence is based on the principles of 'minimum harmonisation' and 'mutual recognition' of national legislations. Since 2001, the attested flaw of these principles for the purpose of the internal market[4] has led to the adoption of Community financial-industry legislation according to the Lamfalussy regulatory process.[5] This law-making process is devoted to promoting greater convergence of Member State regulations towards the European regulatory framework (a broader harmonisation) through greater involvement in the centralised regulation process of national financial authorities charged with implementing and enforcing European regulation in their countries. The reason for this involvement is that while the production of financial law is centralised at European level, the (public) enforcement of European financial law continues to be managed on a national basis in compliance with the principle of 'home

[3] Consolidated versions of the TEU and the TFEU [2012] OJ C326/2012.

[4] The inadequacy of these principles became evident with the global financial crisis. See S Cappiello, 'Il meccanismo di adozione delle regole e il ruolo della European Banking Authority' (2016) 81 *Banca d'Italia – Quaderni di ricerca giuridica* 38–39.

[5] The Lamfalussy process introduces a four-level approach to European legislation. For more details see, also for references, Salerno (n 1) 161–64. More recently, see RM Lastra, 'Multilevel Governance in Banking Regulation' in Chiti and Santoro (n 2) 11–12.

country control' under which cross-border financial intermediaries are subject to licensing and prudential supervision by their own national competent authority (Title IV, Chapter 2 TFEU).

In this context, the EBU represents 'a further transfer of sovereign powers from the national to the supranational arena'[6] because, limited to the banking sector of the euro area, it introduces a centralised banking regulatory order and a centralised system of prudential supervision and crisis management as well. As has been efficaciously outlined,[7] its creation implies the identification in the EU financial supervisory architecture of two concentric circles: the external one includes all Member States and applies a decentralised model of financial supervision, based on the European System of Financial Supervision (ESFS) and the principle of 'home country control',[8] complemented by national resolution procedures; the internal one comprises the Member States of the euro zone alone (and non-euro zone countries that decide to participate voluntarily), and implements an EU-level structure for banking supervision and crisis management, revolving around the SSM and the SRM, respectively.

This single regulatory, supervisory, and resolution model adopted for the euro-zone banking area is conceived to ensure that banks are stronger and better supervised, and that potential insolvency problems are resolved more easily without using taxpayers' money. To this end, the EBU rests on three pillars, which are mandatory for all euro area Member States.[9] The first is the SSM,[10] under which, legitimised by Article 127 TFEU,[11] the European Central Bank (ECB) is directly responsible (by assuming the powers of both home and host supervisor) for supervising significant (ie, systemically important) credit institutions, and indirectly for less significant institutions, which remain subject to the principle of home country control. The second pillar is the SRM,[12] under which the Single Resolution Board (SRB), a new EU agency, assumes the resolution function of banks supported by a

[6] RM Lastra, *International Financial and Monetary Law*, 2nd edn (Oxford, Oxford University Press, 2015) 355. See also AH Türk, 'European Banking Union and Its Relation with European Union Institutions' in Chiti and Santoro (n 2) 41–64.

[7] M Mancini, 'Dalla vigilanza nazionale armonizzata alla Banking Union' (2013) 73 *Banca d'Italia – Quaderni di ricerca giuridica* 5. See also S Cassese, 'La nuova architettura finanziaria europea' in AA.VV., *Dal Testo unico bancario all'Unione bancaria: tecniche normative e allocazione dei poteri* (2014) 75 *Banca d'Italia – Quaderni di ricerca giuridica della Consulenza legale* 19–20.

[8] For details see, also for references, Salerno (n 1) 164–73.

[9] See, European Commission, 'Communication to the European Parliament and the Council – A Roadmap Towards a Banking Union' COM (2012) 510.

[10] Founded on: Council Regulation (EU) No 1024/2013 of 15 October 2013 (SSM Regulation) [2013] OJ L287/63.; Regulation (EU) No 468/2014 of the European Central Bank of 16 April 2014 (SSM Framework Regulation) [2014] OJ L141/1. For more details on the governance and functioning of the SSM, see Salerno (n 1) 175–79.

[11] For details see R D'Ambrosio 'Law and Practice of the Banking Union and of its governing Institutions (Cases and Materials)' (2020) 88 *Banca d'Italia – Quaderni di ricerca giuridica* 27–39.

[12] Created by Regulation (EU) No 806/2014 of the European Parliament and Council of 15 July 2014 [2014] OJ L225/1. For details on the SRM see O Capolino, 'The Single Resolution Mechanism: Authorities and Proceedings' in Chiti and Santoro (n 2) 247–70.

Single Resolution Fund (SRF). The third pillar, for the moment still handled at the national level,[13] is the Single Deposit Guarantee Scheme (SDGS).[14]

Both the supervisory and resolution mechanisms are grounded in a set of harmonised rules for the banks of all 27 Member States. These rules are epitomised by the banking SR which is designed, on the one hand, to prevent bank crises by increasing the minimum amount of capital for credit institutions (see Capital Requirements package – CR package),[15] and, on the other, to better address bank crises by providing a common framework to manage the recovery and resolution of non-viable credit institutions (see the Bank Recovery and Resolution Directive – BRRD)[16] and the operation of deposit guarantee schemes (see the Deposit Guarantee Scheme Directive – DGSD).[17] In addition, over the last eight years, the corpus of harmonised prudential rules for the banking sector has been widened to include further regulation, namely Anti Money Laundering Directives, Mortgage Credit Directive, Payment Services Directive, standardised Securitisation Regulation, and Wire Transfer Regulation, as well as their related Delegated and Implementing acts, RTS, ITS, Guidelines and Recommendations, and Q&As.[18]

III. The European Banking Authority: Mandate and Constitutional Weaknesses

The inclusion of the SSM for the banking sector (of the Eurozone) in the ESFS concerning all components of the EU financial market has led to the establishment of a very peculiar model of financial regulation and supervision where the banking supervisor is distinct from the banking regulator. Hence, recognition of the ECB as the centralised banking authority[19] does not affect the EBA specialised regulatory

[13] In November 2015, the Commission proposed to set up a European deposit insurance scheme (EDIS) for bank deposits in the euro area.

[14] For an overview of the European Banking Union, see R D'Ambrosio (ed), 'Scritti sull'Unione Bancaria' (2016) 81 *Banca d'Italia – Quaderni di ricerca giuridica della Consulenza legale*.

[15] The CR package comprises: Directive 2013/36/EU of the European Parliament and Council of 26 June 2013 (CRD IV) [2013] OJ L176/338, and Regulation (EU) No 575/2013 of the European Parliament and Council of 26 June 2013 (CRR) [2013] OJ L176/1.

[16] Directive 2014/59/EU of the European Parliament and Council of 15 May 2014; Directives 2001/24/EC, 2002/47/EC, 2004/25/EC, 2005/56/EC, 2007/36/EC, 2011/35/EU, 2012/30/EU and 2013/36/EU; and Regulations (EU) No 1093/2010 and (EU) No 648/2012, of the European Parliament and Council. For an overview of the contents of the BRRD see M Rispoli Farina and L Scipione, 'Recovery and Resolution Planning', in Chiti and Santoro (n 2) 271–98.

[17] Directive 2014/49/EU of the European Parliament and Council of 16 April 2014 on deposit guarantee schemes [2014] OJ L173/149. On this subject see C Brescia Morra, 'The Third Pillar of the Banking Union and its Trouble Implementation' in Chiti and Santoro (n 2) 393–407.

[18] See the Interactive Single Rulebook on the EBA website. For a full reconstruction of the evolution and contents of European banking law see A Brozzetti, *La legislazione bancaria europea. Le revisioni 2019–2020* (Milano, Giuffré, 2020).

[19] On the risk that the regulatory function of the EBC may impact the independence of the EBA see V Babis, 'The Single Rulebook and the European Banking Authority' (2018) 45 *University of Cambridge Faculty of Law Research Paper* 24–27.

tasks in relation to the EU as a whole.[20] At this point, a look at the EBA mandate and institutional features is in order to understand its fundamental role in the creation of the banking Single Rulebook and its consistent national implementation.

The micro-component of EU supervisory architecture was created with the specific aim of overcoming national financial-law fragmentation to create a true unified market for financial services. To this end, the EBA was granted the specialised function of creating, monitoring, and ensuring the proper implementation and application of EU banking law and regulation by Member States. In addition, its status as a network of national banking regulators and supervisors was expected to incentivise greater coordination and collaboration among national authorities, aimed at achieving uniformity in regulatory and supervisory practices.[21]

Specifically, according to its mandate, the EBA contributes to the creation of the SR through participation in levels two and three of the Lamfalussy procedure. At the second level, it has the right to draft technical and implementing standards, where Level one legislation so provides. At this stage, after EBA Board of Supervisors approval, to become binding, regulatory and implementing standards must be endorsed by the EC, subject to EP and Council scrutiny, and finally, must be issued and formalised as delegated acts of the EC (Articles 290 and 291 TFEU). Level two regulation is directly applicable in Member States, unlike level one Directives which require national transposition laws. At the third tier of the EU financial legislative process, the EBA is empowered to adopt a diversified series of acts that are non-binding for Member States, including guidelines and recommendations, on its own initiative or under specific level-one delegating provisions, that have an interpretative function and are treated on a comply-or-explain basis by national supervisors. Questions and Answers (Q&A) are a further interpretative tool available through the EBA web site, where the EBA answers questions posed by operators about the interpretation of level two rules.

In addition, the EBA has been granted other instruments that are not strictly regulatory, but that contribute to the effectiveness of the SR by exerting legal and reputational pressure on Member States to comply. So, to ensure supervisory convergence, the EBA is empowered to: conduct peer reviews, guarantee

[20] See Art 3(3) SSM Regulation. For the coordination of EBA and ECB tasks, see Regulation (EU) No 1022/2013 of the European Parliament and the Council of 22 October 2013 [2013] OJ L287/5. Concerning the horizontal distribution of regulatory competences between the ECB and the EBA see among others M Lamandini, DR Muñoz and JS Álvarez, 'Depicting the limits to the SSM's supervisory powers: The Role of Constitutional mandates and of Fundamental Rights' protection' (2015) 79 *Banca d'Italia – Quaderni di ricerca giuridica della Consulenza legale* 36–37; C Brescia Morra, 'From the Single Supervisory Mechanism to the Banking Union. The Role of the ECB and the EBA' (2014) 2 *LUISS Guido Carli, School of European Political Economy, Working Papers* in part. 8–11.

[21] ESA tasks are laid down in Arts 8 of Regulations establishing the EBA, ESMA, and EIOPA. For details, see E Ferran, 'Understanding the New Institutional Architecture Of EU Financial Market Supervision' and E Wymeersch, 'The European Financial Authorities or ESAs' both in E Wymeersch, KJ Hopt, G Ferrarini (eds), *Financial Regulation and Supervision. A Post-Crisis Analysis* (Oxford, Oxford University Press, 2012) 130–33, 232–35. V Troiano, 'The New Institutional Structure of EBA' (2013) 2 *Law and Economics Yearly Review* I 163–83.

supervisory disclosure, participate in supervisory colleges, provide training and staff exchange. Ultimately, EBA participation at the fourth level in support of the EC enforcement function may also further the uniform application of the SR. In fact, at this stage, the EBA has the legal means to highlight possible breaches of EU law by investigating its incorrect or insufficient application, taking decisions directed at individual competent authorities or financial institutions in emergency situations mediating to resolve disagreements between competent authorities in cross-border situations.

As regards its institutional features, the EBA has the legal powers and the formal status of EU agencies[22] institutionally separated from the EC and the Council. At the time of its conception, such a formal recognition induced the European legislature not to confer it binding regulatory functions and supervisory powers over individual intermediaries. The choice was the result of the then-prevalent, restrictive interpretation of the *Meroni* and *Romano* judgments,[23] according to which Article 114 TFEU (then Article 95 CEE Treaty), as the legal basis of the EBA creation,[24] was not solid enough to assign binding decision-making powers to European agencies not included in the Treaty. The same interpretation and caution regarding breaking the provisions of the Treaty led, a few years later, to the ECB being granted prudential supervision powers pursuant to Article 127(6) TFEU.[25] In any case, the EBA does not have the legitimacy and authority to impose upon Member States to comply with its decisions, because its decisions are not-legally-binding, not enforceable, and substantially anchored to the 'act or explain' mechanism[26] or to EC endorsement.

It is clear that the EBA lack of the legitimacy and authority and the consequently 'soft' nature of its regulatory production, alongside the minimum harmonisation of EU banking legislation and the existence of several options and discretion left to national authorities in its implementation, risks missing the SR target of

[22] For details about the institutional features of EU agencies see M Egeberg and J Trondal, 'Researching European Union Agencies: What Have We Learnt (and Where Do We Go from Here)?' (2017) 55(4) *JCMS: Journal of Common Market Studies* 675–90; E Chiti, 'Il "sistema delle agenzie europee" alla prova della valutazione' (2011) 5 *Giornale di diritto amministrativo* 557–60.

[23] Case 9/56 *Meroni v High Authority* ECLI:EU:C:1958:7 [1958] and Case 98/80 *Romano v INAMI* [1981] ECR 1241. On this subject see MP Chiti, 'L'organizzazione amministrativa comunitaria' in MP Chiti and G Greco (eds), *Trattato di diritto amministrativo europeo*, Tome I (Milan, Giuffré, 2007) 445–47; ACM Meuwese, J Schuurmans and W Voermans, 'Towards a European Administrative Procedure Act?' (2009) *Review of European Administrative Law* 3–35; M Chamon, 'The Empowerment of Agencies under the *Meroni* Doctrine and Article 114 TFEU: Comment on United Kingdom v Parliament and Council (Short-selling) and the Proposed Single Resolution Mechanism' (2014) 39(3) *European Law Review* 380–403.

[24] See CV Gortsos and K Lagaria, 'The European Supervisory Authorities (ESAs) as "direct" supervisors in the EU financial system' (2020) 57 *EBI Working Paper Series* 11–12.

[25] For a critical analysis of this choice see M Lamandini, 'Il diritto bancario dell'Unione' (2016) 81 *Banca d'Italia – Quaderni di ricerca giuridica* 23.

[26] GJ Schinasi, 'Financial-Stability Challenges in European Emerging-Market Countries' (2011) 5773 *Policy Research Working Papers* 19.

maximised harmonisation.[27] Moreover, at the EU level, this risk is augmented by the fact that the ESFS maintains prudential supervision at the national level in compliance with the principle of home country control, decentralising day-by-day supervision and retaining differences in European banking regulation is enforced in Member States.[28]

IV. The Impact of the European Banking Union on the Single Rulebook

National banking (prudential supervision and resolution) authorities participate in the governance system of the banking sector laid down for the EBU (SSM and SRM) and for the EU (ESFS, specifically the EBA) in ways that are more or less significant in relation to the various co-administrations and distribution of functions between central and peripheral organs. The adopted forms of co-administration follow a principle of progressive reduction of national powers in favour of their centralisation at the European level, and can be categorised in three ways.[29]

At one extreme (stronger national powers), national authorities are required to cooperate through their inclusion in colleges of supervisors and resolution colleges, respectively, by the CRD IV (Article 116) and the BRRD (Article 88). In this context, they hold a peer position based on a mechanism of co-decision wherein the EBA assumes a mediation role pursuant to Articles 19 and 21 Regulation (EU) 1093/2010.[30]

In a middle category, national authorities participate in the European rule-making process for the banking area through their membership on the board of supervisors and management board of the EBA. Notwithstanding the ESA reform adopted in 2019[31] to improve their impartiality and independence from national interests, national authorities continue to be actively involved in EBA governance and decisions because they are voting members of the board of supervisors, and the management board is made up 'of the Chairperson and six members of the Board of Supervisors, elected by and from among the voting members of the

[27] Lamandini (n 25) 19; Cappiello (n 4) 44–45; Babis (n 19) 10–15.

[28] The supervisory system in the EU continues to be a messy compromise between centripetal and centrifugal pressures See G Black, 'Restructuring Global and EU Financial Regulation: Character, Capacities, and Learning' in Wymeersch, Hopt and Ferrarini (n 21) 8–9.

[29] Lamandini (n 25) 26–27.

[30] For details on supervisory colleges see D Singh, *European Cross-Border Banking and Banking Supervision* (Oxford, Oxford University Press, 2020) 70–74. For legal analysis of European resolution colleges see A Gardella, 'La risoluzione dei gruppi finanziari cross-border nell'Unione Europea' (2016) 81 *Banca d'Italia – Quaderni di ricerca giuridica* 164–66.

[31] See Regulation (EU) No 2175/2019 of the European Parliament and of the Council of 18 December 2019 [2019] OJ L334/1.

Board of Supervisors'. In addition, the reform grants the Chairperson the right to vote, while the Executive Director, despite his or her important functions, participates in meetings of both internal bodies without the right to vote (Articles 40 and 45 Regulation (EU) 1093/2010).

At the other extreme (weaker national power), national authorities are involved in the EBU governance system according to an allocation of competences between the national and European levels which is not uniform across the SSM and the SRM. Within the SSM, national authorities assist the ECB in preparing, implementing, and enforcing supervisory acts relating to significant banks[32] and are subject to ECB direction or even replacement in supervision of less significant banks.[33] The ECB holds original exclusive competences under Article 4 Regulation (EU) 1024/2013 (SSM Regulation), in compliance with the specific micro and macro-prudential tasks legitimated by Article 127(6) TFEU. In addition, under Article 6 of the SSM Regulation, the ECB delegates national authorities in the SSM the responsibility to carry out these functions with respect to less significant banks (except for authorisation and withdrawal of authorisation, acquisition and disposal of qualifying holdings).[34] Within the SRM, national authorities are charged with the concrete execution of crisis-management plans decided at the centralised level (by the SRB, the EC, and the Council) (Article 29 Regulation (EU) 806/2014).[35] Notwithstanding the centralisation of resolution decisions, the original competences for banking crisis management are left to national authorities, except for specific cases where the SRB is allowed to claim these competences (Article 7 Regulation (EU) 806/2014 – SRM Regulation).[36]

For both the SSM and the SRM, the rationale for the adoption of the organisational solutions outlined above is based on the need to respect the principle of subsidiarity established by Article 5 TEU and the real conditions of the banking industry, which vary from country to country. Concerning this last point, going by the principle of 'one size does not fit all', many provisions of the CRD IV and the BRRD allow Member States to implement supervisory and resolution rules taking into account the dimension of the intermediary.

The description of relationships between European and national banking authorities within the centralised structures of the EBU may help us to understand

[32] For more insights see R D'Ambrosio, 'The involvement of the NCAs in the ECB's supervisory proceedings' (2020) 88 *Banca d'Italia – Quaderni di ricerca giuridica* 164–80.

[33] For details see R D'Ambrosio and S Montemaggi, 'Supervision of the less significant credit institutions' (2020) 88 *Banca d'Italia – Quaderni di ricerca giuridica* 204–16.

[34] For a critical analysis of the distribution of competences between the ECB and national supervisors see R D'Ambrosio 'Single Supervisory Mechanism: Organs and Procedures' in Chiti and Santoro (n 2) 160–65.

[35] Capolino (n 12) 252.

[36] For details about the allocation of decisional and executive tasks between the SRB and national resolution authorities see M Cossa, R D'ambrosio and A Vignini, 'The SRM: Allocation of tasks and powers between the SRB and the NRAs and organisational issues' (2020) 88 *Banca d'Italia – Quaderni di ricerca giuridica* 323–39.

their effective influence on the regulatory harmonisation process and thus on the real extent of the SR, at least its prudential supervision (CR Package) and resolution (BRRD) regulation parts.

Regarding prudential regulation, in cases of direct ECB supervision of significant credit institutions, harmonisation is ensured by the uniform application of the supervisory review and evaluation methodologies and criteria developed by the ECB. Conversely, there is the possibility of discrepancies among national supervisory processes in cases where the SSM includes the simultaneous participation of the ECB and national authorities.[37] First, supervisory review and evaluation methodologies and criteria developed by the ECB can become misaligned when they are applied by national competent authorities in cases of indirect ECB supervision of less significant credit institutions. In fact, in such cases, national supervisory authorities 'shall establish the frequency and intensity of the review and evaluation [...] having regard to the size, systemic importance, nature, scale and complexity of the activities of the institution concerned and taking into account the principle of proportionality'.[38]

Moreover, in cases of indirect supervision, the ECB delegates to national authorities decision-making power in supervisory matters (Article 6, para 4 SSM Regulation), which concretely risks undermining the rule-standardisation process. The European legislature itself is aware of this risk when, in the context of indirect supervision, '*for the purposes of ensuring the consistency of supervisory outcomes within the SSM*' or '*when necessary to ensure consistent application of high supervisory standards*', it empowers the ECB to: (a) issue regulations, guidelines or general instructions to national competent authorities; (b) decide to directly exercise all the relevant powers for one or more less significant credit institutions; (c) exercise oversight over the functioning of the system; (d) use its investigatory function towards less significant credit institutions; (e) request information from national competent authorities on the performance of tasks they carry out. Finally, consistency in the application of the SR may also be compromised in cases of granting and withdrawing of authorisation, acquisition and disposal of qualifying holdings, which fall under the exclusive competence of the ECB with respect to both significant and less significant banks. In such situations, the SSM Regulation (Articles 15 and 16) calls on national competent authorities to take a draft decision to propose to the ECB after assessing compliance with relevant national law which, in addition to the conditions set out by Union law, may currently provide for further conditions for authorisation and withdrawal of authorisation (Recital 21 SSM Regulation).[39]

[37] For details on relationships between the ECB and national competent authorities see R D'Ambrosio (n 11) 39–60.

[38] Art 97, para 4 of the CRD IV. On the principle of proportionality and its compliance with the aim of the Single Rulebook see B Joosen and M Leheman, 'Proportionality in the Single Rulebook' in Chiti and Santoro (n 2) 65–90, in part 71–73.

[39] Conversely, rules regarding acquisition and disposal of qualifying holdings arise from a maximum harmonisation directive (Directive 2007/44/EC).

Clearly the risk of inconsistency of national regulations increases within the SRM, where national authorities preserve their original competences, participate in the EU-level development of resolution plans, and implement decisions adopted by the SRB in accordance with the conditions established in national law (Article 29 SRM Regulation) that transposes BRRD.

V. Interaction between the European Banking Union and the European Banking Authority

From the above analysis we may deduce that, due to the particular structure of the current two pillars of the EBU (the SSM and the SRM) characterised by the co-existence of a centralised component (European) and a de-centralised component (national), the centralisation of supervisory and resolution powers within the EBU has limited prospects of solving the problem of regulatory harmonisation. This implies that in the institutional framework set up for the euro-zone banking sector, the role of the EBA continues to be crucial to achieving an effective European single market for credit institutions.[40]

More precisely, we are convinced that equality of competition among cross-border banking intermediaries within the EBU (and the EU as a whole) guaranteed by consistent and uniform national rules may be achieved through a unitary, organic effort by the EBA and the two mechanisms of the EBU. To this end, their institutional mandates – respectively, rulemaking and supervisory and resolution integration – can be considered complementary.[41] On the one hand, because European banking legislation adopted at level one of the Lamfalussy procedure continues to be characterised by minimal harmonisation (at least when it assumes Directive form), EBA regulation provides the common regulatory ground necessary to make SSM and SRM actions uniform and consistent within the EBU by helping to align areas of prudential regulation and resolution rules left to minimum harmonisation and thus to the discretion of national legislators. On the other hand, the EBA replacement of forms of regulatory and supervisory coordination and convergence of national banking authorities through the inclusion of national authorities in its governance and the establishment of colleges of supervisors and resolution authorities, along with mechanisms of centralised prudential supervision and crisis management, may foster harmonisation through unified and coherent application of the SR within the EBU.

[40] See C Brescia Morra (20) 10.

[41] S Cappiello, 'The interplay between the EBA and the Banking Union' (2015) 77 *EUI Working Papers* 4.

VI. *De Iure Condendo* Prospects for Further Harmonisation

The opportunity for a joint EBA/EBU effort aimed at assuring a truly level playing field for cross-border credit institutions should be increased through institutional changes to the EBA's role in constructing the SR and, consequently, to the integration mechanisms within the EBU. These changes might de facto have the effect of reinforcing the 'soft law' component of the SR to support the maximum harmonisation process at the basis of an effective EBU. They can be postulated thanks to the most recent interpretation of the *Meroni* and *Romano* jurisprudence.

Weaknesses in the construction of the EBA regulatory mandate also stem from its legal basis in Article 114 TFEU, and the complexity of both EBU pillars stems from its creators' need to give them a stronger legal basis than the provisions in Article 114 TFEU. In fact, at the time of the conception of the EBA, and later the EBU, the prevalent interpretation of this norm of the Treaty prevented European agencies not included in the Treaty from being assigned and/or delegated any competences, as this would have conflicted with a jurisprudence consistent enough to be considered 'doctrine', dating back to the *Meroni* and *Romano* judgments.[42] More recently, in a 22 January decision, 204 (C-270/12), concerning a dispute between the ESMA and the UK in the so-called 'short selling case',[43] the European Court of Justice has declared a set of principles that reshape the stringent interpretation of the *Meroni* and *Romano* doctrines.[44]

First, the Court states that the assignment of broad discretional powers to a European agency not included in the Treaty is neither a violation of any Treaty provision nor in conflict with the *Meroni* doctrine, if: (a) the agency is created by the EU, and (b) the European legislator fixes criteria and conditions delimiting the agency's area of action to prevent it from carrying out political functions. Secondly, in the opinion of the Court, following the reforms of Articles 263(1)

[42] For the most recent interpretations of the *Meroni* and *Romano* doctrines, see: MP Chiti, 'In the Aftermath of the Crisis. The EU Administrative System between Impediments and Momentum' (2015) 13 *EUI Law Working Papers* 311–33; N Moloney, 'European Banking Union: Assessing its risks and resilience' (2014) 51 *Common Market Law Review* 1609–10; M Scholten and M Van Rijsbergen, 'Erecting a New Delegation Doctrine in the EU upon the Meroni-Romano Remnants' (2014) 41 *Legal Issues of Economic Integration* 389–406; Lamandini (n 25) 23–24.

[43] For more on the ESMA case see: Case C-270/12 *United Kingdom of Great Britain and Northern Ireland v European Parliament and Council of the European Union (ESMA)* [2014] 2 CMLR 44; Opinion AG Jääskinen, Case C-270/12 *United Kingdom of Great Britain and Northern Ireland v European Parliament and Council of the European Union* [2012] ECLI:EU:C:2013:562. See: M Simoncini, 'Legal Boundaries of European Supervisory Authorities in the Financial Markets: Tensions in the Development of True Regulatory Agencies' (2015) 34(1) *Year Book of European Law* 319–50; MP Chiti, 'The European Banking Union in the Case Law of the Court of Justice of The European Union' in Chiti and Santoro (n 2) 105–34, in part 116–20.

[44] Lamandini (n 25) 23–24.

and 277 TFEU allowing an institution, body, office, or agency set up by the Union to adopt acts of general application, the conferral of such a power to a European agency does not conflict with the principles of the *Romano* judgment if said agency's incorporation act circumscribes this power to 'implementing' acts and precisely identifies these acts. Thirdly and most significantly, the Court declares that, under Articles 290 and 291 TFEU, the delegation by legislative act to the Commission of the power to adopt non-legislative acts of general application 'to supplement or amend certain non-essential elements of the legislative act' or the power to adopt implementing acts does not mean that solely the Commission may be granted delegated powers (as implicitly confirmed by Articles 263, 267, and 277 TFEU). Finally, the Court states that, under Article 114 TFEU, measures for national regulatory approximation concern not only law and regulation but also administrative actions, comprising those characterised by individual application. In addition, in the opinion of the Court, approximation measures need not necessarily be addressed to Member States alone.

In the light of the new judicial interpretation of the provisions of the Treaty, we can conclude that Article 114 may be a strong legal basis for the attribution of direct regulatory and supervisory powers to a European agency. Therefore, concerning our specific topic – the role of the EBA and the influence of integration mechanisms within the EBU on the maximum harmonisation process – we can deduce that while little can be done on the structural front, there is still room for improvement on the rulemaking side. Let me make this clear.

On the structural side, at this stage of the centralisation process, the conversion of the EBA into the Single (Supervisory, Resolution and Regulatory) Authority within the EBU is unthinkable and unfeasible, due to both political obstacles and questions of opportuneness and desirability in terms of cost-benefit analysis. On this point, we can only note with regret that the assignment of prudential supervision and resolution powers to the EBA could have precluded the complex structure based on the two current EBU pillars, the SSM and the SRM, and the too-complicated distribution of powers among European agencies (the ECB and the SRB) and national authorities.[45] In any case, we expect this solution, although unrealistic for the banking area, points the way forward for the European legislature with regard to the centralisation of supervisory powers in other financial market sectors, as borne out by the progressive granting to the ESMA of direct supervisory powers over specific financial entities (credit rating agencies; trade repositories; securitisation repositories; third-country central counterparties; critical benchmarks; data reporting service providers) in the process of construction the Capital Market Union.[46]

Conversely, concerning the rulemaking procedure, we are convinced that some improvements might be adopted for the banking sector as well. Beyond the 2019

[45] On criticisms of this complexity see Türk (n 6) 42–48.

[46] Gortsos and Lagaria (n 24) 12–14. For a detailed analysis of the progress towards a CMU see D Busch, 'The Future of EU Financial Law' (2021) 43 *EBI Working Paper Series*.

enhancement of the tools that the EBA can use at the third and fourth levels of the Lamfalussy procedure to promote supervisory convergence, the new reading of Articles 114, 290 and 291 TFEU should also have some effect at the second level of this procedure by legitimising the EBA, where Level one legislation so provides, to directly issue regulatory and implementing delegated acts that are binding for Member States. This legal solution might be able to speed up and simplify the rule-making procedure at the second level by removing inefficiencies and tensions connected to the involvement of three EU institutions (EC, EP, and the Council) and preserving technical measures from political influence by the EC. Moreover, it could help to clarify the allocation of principles and detailed rules at the first and second levels, which has not always been in the past coherent.[47] At the same time, to ensure a more EU-oriented approach in decision making, EBA governance should be made more independent from the interests of national authorities by including on the EBA executive board only qualified members not linked to member countries.

Finally, in addition to changes aimed at strengthening the EBA's regulatory function, further interventions on level one of the regulatory procedure and at EU-level regulating areas could contribute to furthering maximum harmonisation. Regarding level one of the Lamfalussy procedure, we would suggest greater use of the instrument of regulation, or at least of the maximum harmonisation Directive, in place of minimum harmonisation Directives. This should reduce the sort of discretional and optional regulation that hinders uniform cross-border prudential supervision and crisis management action by allowing Member States to find legal loopholes. As for the extension of harmonised areas, true equality of competition among banking intermediaries from different countries and effective supervisory and resolution actions would require expanding the SR beyond prudential regulation to include corporate law and insolvency law.[48]

VII. Conclusions

Starting with an analysis of the legal basis and the institutional weaknesses of the EBA and the EBU, this chapter has highlighted how the EBA and integration mechanisms (SSM and SRM) within the EBU can play a joint and interconnected role of mutual support to further the maximum harmonisation pursued through the production and especially the consistent and uniform implementation and application of the Single Banking Rulebook.

[47] Babis (n 19) 9–10.

[48] It is worth noting that with the implementation of the BRRD, resolution is included in national law as an alternative to national insolvency proceedings for managing bank crises. See Cappiello (n 4) 52; Capolino (n 12) 257–60; D Singh, 'European cross-border' (2020) 163–164.

The chapter concludes with some suggestions for the improvement and development of the harmonisation process, outlining the legitimate options of: (i) giving the EBA direct regulatory powers in setting up level-two technical norms; (ii) guaranteeing it greater independence in rulemaking; (iii) increasing the use of the legal instrument of regulation; and (iv) expanding centralised regulating areas. We hope that the European legislature moves in the direction we suggest in the near future.

9

The Banking Union in the Aftermath of the COVID-19 Pandemic: An Incentive to Finalise the Project?

MARCO BODELLINI

I. Introduction

The Banking Union is considered one of the most ambitious European projects since the creation of the single market and the single currency.[1] Its founding pillars are the centralisation of bank supervision and crisis management and the mutualisation of deposit insurance at European level. Through centralisation and mutualisation, the ultimate goal is to facilitate the integration and enhancement of the European banking system, while eradicating the vicious link between sovereign(s) and their national banking system(s).

The new institutional architecture is built upon the 'single rule book', a set of harmonised rules applying to credit institutions established in the EU. The most relevant pieces of legislation in this regard are the Capital Requirements Directive (CRD)[2] and Capital Requirements Regulation (CRR)[3] package, the Bank Recovery

[1] On Banking Union see *ex multis* N Moloney, 'European Banking Union: Assessing its Risks and resilience' (2014) 51 *Common Market Law Review* 1609–70; JH Binder, 'The Banking Union and the Governance of Credit Institutions: A Legal Perspective' (2015) 16 *European Business Organization Law Review* 467–90; BS Nielsen, 'Main Features of the European Banking Union' (2015) 26 *European Business Law Review* 805–22; M Nieto, 'Banking on Single Supervision in the Eurozone: Scepticism and a Reform Proposal' (2015) 16 *European Business Organization Law Review* 539–46; G Ferrarini, 'Single Supervision and the Governance of Banking Markets: Will the SSM Deliver the Expected Benefits?' (2015) 16 *European Business Organization Law* Review 513–37.

[2] Directive 2013/36/EU of the European Parliament and of the Council of 26 June 2013 on access to the activity of credit institutions and the prudential supervision of credit institutions and investment firms, amending Directive 2002/87/EC and repealing Directives 2006/48/EC and 2006/49/EC [2013] OJ L176/338.

[3] Regulation (EU) No 575/2013 of the European Parliament and of the Council of 26 June 2013 on prudential requirements for credit institutions and investment firms and amending Regulation (EU) No 648/2012 [2013] OJ L176/1.

and Resolution Directive (BRRD)[4] and the Deposit Guarantee Schemes Directive (DGSD).[5]

Yet, eight years after the establishment of its first component, the Single Supervisory Mechanism (SSM),[6] the project is still incomplete and some important parts are missing. While centralisation of bank supervision has been fully accomplished with the involvement of the European Central Bank (ECB) overseeing the SSM, crisis management functions have been assigned to a new European agency, the Single Resolution Board (SRB), the central authority of the Single Resolution Mechanism (SRM).[7] However, the SRB is only in charge of the resolution of institutions under its remit, to be executed by the NRAs.[8] This means that failing or likely to fail (FOLF)[9] credit institutions that do not meet the public interest assessment (PIA)[10] for being submitted to resolution will be placed into insolvency proceedings under national laws,[11] which are not harmonised at European level and are

[4] Directive 2014/59/EU of the European Parliament and of the Council of 15 May 2014 establishing a framework for the recovery and resolution of credit institutions and investment firms [2014] OJ L173/190.

[5] Directive 2014/49/EU of the European Parliament and of the Council of 16 April 2014 on deposit guarantee schemes [2014] OJ L173/149.

[6] The legal foundations of the SSM are Council Regulation (EU) No 1024/2013 of 15 October 2013 conferring specific tasks on the European Central Bank concerning policies relating to the prudential supervision of credit institutions [2013] OJ L287/63, and Regulation (EU) No 468/2014 of the European Central Bank of 16 April 2014 establishing the framework for cooperation within the Single Supervisory Mechanism between the European Central Bank and national competent authorities and with national designated authorities (SSM Framework Regulation) [2014] OJ L141/1.

[7] The legal basis of the SRM is Regulation (EU) No 806/2014 of the European Parliament and of the Council of 15 July 2014 establishing uniform rules and a uniform procedure for the resolution of credit institutions and certain investment firms in the framework of a Single Resolution Mechanism and a Single Resolution Fund and amending Regulation (EU) No 1093/2010 [2014] OJ L225/1.

[8] According to Art 2(1)(1) of the BRRD: 'resolution means the application of a resolution tool or a tool referred to in Article 37(9) in order to achieve one or more of the resolution objectives referred to in Article 31(2)'.

[9] According to Art 32 para 4 of the Directive 2014/59/EU: 'an institution shall be deemed to be failing or likely to fail in one or more of the following circumstances: (a) the institution infringes or there are objective elements to support a determination that the institution will, in the near future, infringe the requirements for continuing authorisation in a way that would justify the withdrawal of the authorisation by the competent authority including but not limited to because the institution has incurred or is likely to incur losses that will deplete all or a significant amount of its own funds; (b) the assets of the institution are or there are objective elements to support a determination that the assets of the institution will, in the near future, be less than its liabilities; (c) the institution is or there are objective elements to support a determination that the institution will, in the near future, be unable to pay its debts or other liabilities as they fall due; (d) extraordinary public financial support is required except [in a few cases]'.

[10] See M Bodellini, 'Impediments to resolvability: critical issues and challenges ahead' (2019) 5 *Open Review of Management, Banking and Finance* 48, where it is underlined that the PIA aims at ascertaining whether the resolution of a failing or likely to fail institution is considered to be needed in the public interest.

[11] According to Art 32 of the BRRD: 'Member States shall ensure that resolution authorities shall take a resolution action in relation to an institution referred to in point (a) of Article 1(1) only if the resolution authority considers that all of the following conditions are met: (a) the determination that the institution is failing or is likely to fail has been made by the competent authority, after consulting the resolution authority or; subject to the conditions laid down in paragraph 2, by the resolution authority after consulting the competent authority; (b) having regard to timing and other relevant circumstances, there is no reasonable prospect that any alternative private sector measures, including measures by an IPS, or supervisory action, including early intervention measures or the write down or conversion of

administered by the domestic (either administrative or judicial) authorities of the jurisdiction concerned.[12] In a similar vein, mutualisation of deposit insurance through the establishment of the European Deposit Insurance Scheme (EDIS) has not yet been implemented, due to differing positions and views among Member States, therefore deposit insurance exists only at national level on the grounds of various domestic provisions transposing the DGSD.

Still, the incompleteness of the Banking Union means that the reliability of credit institutions, and thus the safety of deposits, still depend largely on the public finances of the Member State(s) where they are based. This also means that the objective of removing the vicious link between sovereign(s) and national banking sector(s) has not yet been achieved, and will not be achieved until a fully-fledged mutualised EDIS becomes operational and bank insolvency regimes are harmonised.

This critical situation is likely to be further exacerbated by the impact of the economic crisis provoked by COVID-19, which is expected to affect credit institutions (and the financial system in general) once the massive relief measures implemented by Member States come to an end. In light of these concerns, Member States should try to make the most out of the current COVID-19 crisis and endeavour to strike a meaningful political compromise to bring about completion of the Banking Union. This can be achieved through harmonisation of bank insolvency proceedings, looking at the experience of those Member States which have long had special regimes in place for bank crisis management, and the establishment of a fully-fledged EDIS that is not only in charge of depositor pay-outs, but also tasked with implementing preventive and alternative measures.[13]

Taking a forward-looking approach, this chapter will focus on the future of the Banking Union in the aftermath of the COVID-19 crisis. After a discussion concerning the institutional architecture of the Banking Union and the rationale(s) behind this ambitious project, this chapter will look at the impact of the COVID-19 crisis on credit institutions and at the relief measures adopted to date by Member States to keep the economy afloat and credit institutions alive, and will conclude with some policy considerations.

II. The Establishment of the Banking Union

The Banking Union is a key component of the Economic and Monetary Union. It was created as a response to the Global Financial Crisis (GFC) of 2007–08 and

relevant capital instruments and eligible liabilities in accordance with Article 59(2) taken in respect of the institution, would prevent the failure of the institution within a reasonable timeframe; (c) a resolution action is necessary in the public interest pursuant to paragraph 5'.

[12] See M Bodellini, 'The Optional Measures of Deposit Guarantee Schemes: Towards a New Bank Crisis Management Paradigm?' (2021) 13 *European Journal of Legal Studies* 341.

[13] See M Bodellini, 'Alternative forms of deposit insurance and the quest for European harmonized deposit guarantee scheme-centred special administrative regimes to handle troubled banks' (2020) 25 *Uniform Law Review* 212.

the ensuing Euro Area sovereign debt crisis of 2010–12 to ensure that the banking sector in participating countries (and the wider EU) is stable, safe and reliable, thus contributing to financial stability. The Banking Union is intended to make the banking system more robust and able to withstand future financial crises, allow the resolution of non-viable banks without using taxpayers' money and with minimal impact on the real economy, and reduce market fragmentation thanks to harmonised rules.

Every Euro Area Member State is part of the Banking Union, while non-Euro Area EU Member States can join the Banking Union by entering into close cooperation with the ECB. This is the case of Bulgaria and Croatia, which joined the Banking Union in 2020.

According to the original project, the three pillars of the Banking Union were meant to be: (1) the SSM, (2) the SRM, and (3) the EDIS. The SSM is the new system of banking supervision that comprises the ECB and national supervisors, known as national competent authorities (NCAs), of the participating countries. The SRM is the new system of bank crisis management that comprises the SRB and the national resolution authorities (NRAs) of the participating countries. The EDIS is the proposed centralised deposit guarantee scheme financed by banks established in the participating countries, intended to provide equivalent protection to every depositor regardless of bank location. However, a political agreement on the creation of the EDIS has not yet been reached.

With the creation of a new system of supervision based on close cooperation between the ECB and NCAs, the goal is to ensure consistent supervision of every bank in the Banking Union and tackle the issue of supervisory forbearance ontologically embedded in domestic supervision.

In the new framework, the ECB supervises the banking sector from a European perspective by establishing a common approach, taking harmonised actions and corrective measures and ensuring the consistent application of regulations and policies. This means that the ECB, in cooperation with NCAs, is responsible for ensuring that banking supervision is effective and consistent across the Banking Union. In practical terms, the ECB has the authority to: (a) conduct supervisory reviews, on-site inspections and investigations, (b) grant or withdraw banking licences; (c) assess banks' acquisition and disposal of qualifying holdings, (d) ensure compliance with EU prudential rules, (e) set higher capital requirements (buffers) to counter any financial risks.

To make the system more effective, credit institutions have been grouped into two categories: significant institutions and less significant institutions.[14]

[14] The criteria to qualify institutions as significant are: (a) total value of assets exceeding EUR 30 billion; (b) economic importance for the specific country or the EU economy as a whole; (c) total value of assets exceeding EUR 5 billion and ratio of cross-border assets/liabilities in more than one other participating Member State to total assets/liabilities above 20%; (d) institution has requested or received funding from the European Stability Mechanism or the European Financial Stability Facility; (e) an institution can also be considered significant if it is one of the three most significant banks established in a particular country.

The former (over 100 institutions holding almost 82 per cent of banking assets in the participating countries) are directly supervised by the ECB, while the latter continue to be supervised by their NCAs in close cooperation with the ECB, which can decide at any time to draw them under its direct remit to ensure that supervisory standards are applied consistently.

The involvement of the ECB as the main prudential supervisor for significant credit institutions has certainly decreased the risk of forbearance, which was embedded in the previous national supervision-system. Nevertheless, the goal of further integrating the European banking sector has not been achieved. Integration and consolidation of the banking sector still take place largely at the national level, due in part to some protectionist approaches aimed at discouraging cross-border mergers and take-overs. This in turn makes it complicated to remove the interdependence between banks and sovereigns.

The SRM is a system of cooperation between the SRB and participating countries' NRAs, whose main purpose is to ensure the efficient resolution of FOLF banks with minimal cost to taxpayers and to the real economy. The SRB supervises the system and has been given powers allowing it to execute – in close cooperation with NRAs – bank resolution over a weekend. A Single Resolution Fund (SRF), financed by contributions from banks, has been created to pay for resolution measures. The scope of application of the SRM reflects that of the SSM, and the criteria for the distribution of tasks between the SRB and NRAs are also rather similar, with the former in charge of handling crises involving significant and cross-border institutions, and the latter in charge of less significant institutions.

The creation of the SRM is closely connected with the adoption of the BRRD, which, by implementing the Financial Stability Board Key Attributes of Effective Resolution Regimes for Financial Institutions,[15] has introduced a new administrative procedure, called resolution, to handle a bank crisis when a number of requirements are met.[16]

Still, the lack of a harmonised regime for bank insolvency remains a major issue, further exacerbated by the fact that the majority of banks, in the event they are FOLF, will likely be subject to liquidation and not to resolution.[17]

III. The COVID-19 Crisis and its Impact on Credit Institutions

The crisis provoked by the COVID-19 pandemic differs intrinsically from the global financial crisis (GFC) of 2007–09. Whereas the GFC was a crisis arising

[15] Financial Stability Board, 'Key Attributes of Effective Resolution Regimes for Financial Institutions' (2014) *passim*.

[16] See Art 32 para 4 of Directive 2014/59/EU.

[17] See Bodellini (n 13) 212.

from the financial system which then dramatically affected the real economy, the current one is an economic crisis primarily caused by the lockdown and other containment and social distancing measures implemented in almost every country in the world.[18] Such measures, aimed at slowing down the propagation of the virus, have affected both demand and supply of goods and services, with only a few economic activities and sectors (eg e-commerce and internet services) benefiting from the new situation.[19]

Yet, despite its economic nature, the COVID-19 crisis is expected to hit the banking system as well. Due to the numerous strong interconnections between the banking sector and the real economy, it is just matter of time before the former will be negatively impacted.[20] Intuitively, enterprises that have been struggling over the last months due to full or partial lockdowns and the drastic drop in the demand for their services and goods might soon start defaulting on repaying their loans to credit institutions. Once unemployment support programmes activated by several governments end, households with members who have lost their jobs could become unable to repay mortgages and credit lines, once again passing their (in)solvency issues on to the banking sector. This situation, replicated on a large scale, will initially lead to many business failures, and will then strike the banking system, potentially triggering a financial crisis.[21]

Moreover, in such an environment, banks will find it increasingly difficult to lend money, due to the sharp deterioration of many of their borrowers' risk profiles.[22] This might in turn exacerbate the current economic crisis, prolonging its duration.[23] But even worse, banks might end up with an excess of non-performing loans in their balance sheets.[24] The increase in non-performing loans is considered particularly threatening because many banks had not yet managed to offload previously accumulated stocks of such assets when the pandemic began

[18] See GW Ringe, 'COVID-19 and European banks: no time for lawyers' in C Gortsos and GW Ringe (eds), *Pandemic Crisis and Financial Stability* (Frankfurt, European Banking Institute, 2020) 43.

[19] See C Hadjiemmanuil, 'European economic governance and the pandemic: Fiscal crisis management under a flawed policy process' in Gortsos and Ringe (n 18) 175.

[20] See M Bodellini and P Lintner, 'The impact of the Covid-19 pandemic on credit institutions and the importance of effective bank crisis management regimes' (2020) 9 *Law and Economics Yearly Review* 182.

[21] See M Draghi, 'We face a war against coronavirus and must mobilise accordingly' *Financial Times* (25 March 2020), where the former President of the European Central Bank argues that the pandemic has already provoked a spiral of economic consequences that will inevitably lead to a serious recession, with the risk of it then 'morphing into a prolonged depression, made deeper by a plethora of defaults leaving irreversible damage'.

[22] See LS Morais, 'The EU fiscal response to the COVID-19 crisis and the Banking sector: risks and opportunities' in Gortsos and Ringe (n 18) 300.

[23] See C Brescia Morra, 'Lending activity in the time of coronavirus' in Gortsos and Ringe (n 18) 392.

[24] E Avgouleas, R Ayadi, M Bodellini, B Casu, WP De Groen and G Ferri, 'Non-performing loans – new risks and policies? What factors drive the performance of national asset management companies?' (2021) *Study Requested by the ECON committee*, PE 651.386, 1–40.

in February/March 2020.[25] And now, cleaning up their balance sheets in current market conditions might prove to be extremely challenging.[26]

All these criticalities are further exacerbated by the low profitability that has characterised the commercial banking business model in recent years, particularly in Europe.[27] Commercial banks' low profitability is the result of a combination of different factors, including interest rates having been close to zero (or even negative) for quite some time, and an excess of capacity attributable in many countries to too many branches and staff, which proportionally increases operating costs. The ability to begin making profits again will thus be pivotal for the banking industry to recover from the crisis and make the economy rebound.[28]

In such a dark scenario, the good news is that banks are, on average, much better capitalised than they were during the global financial crisis of 2007–09. Indeed, because of the legislative and regulatory initiatives adopted in the aftermath of that crisis with a view to making banks stronger and more resilient, they are required to hold a much higher level of capital, consisting mainly of more loss-absorbing items.[29] Incidentally, these higher levels of capital have already enabled supervisors to temporarily lower banks' buffers thereby allowing them to continue extending loans to borrowers.[30]

In the face of the severity of the current crisis, regulators and supervisors have already reacted by adopting a plethora of rules primarily aimed at permitting banks

[25] C Gortsos, 'The application of the EU banking resolution framework amidst the pandemic crisis' in Gortsos and Ringe (n 18) 367, correctly points out that the rate of non-performing loans during the last years has, on average, significantly decreased due mainly to the introduction of the Council Action Plan of July 2017 on Non-Performing Loans and the accommodating macroeconomic conditions. However, the existing stock of NPLs resulting from the global financial crisis or the subsequent fiscal crisis in the Euro Area still varies significantly among Member States.

[26] The increase in non-performing loans in banks' balance sheets is closely observed by supervisors, and it has been reported that the European Central Bank has been assessing the possibility of creating a Euro-Area bad bank to manage huge portfolios of non-performing assets; see M Arnold and J Espinoza, 'ECB pushes for Euro Zone bad bank to clean up soured loans' *Financial Times* (19 April 2020).

[27] See I Aldasoro, I Fender, B Hardy and N Tarashev, 'Effects of Covid-19 on the banking sector: the market's assessment' (2020) 12 *BIS Bulletin* 5.

[28] See Bodellini and Lintner (n 20) 182.

[29] See M Bodellini, 'The long "journey" of banks from Basel I to Basel IV: has the banking system become more sound and resilient than it used to be?' (2019) 20 *ERA Forum passim*; see also International Monetary Fund, 'Global Financial Stability Report, October 2018: A Decade after the Global Financial Crisis: Are We Safer?' (2018) www.elibrary.imf.org/view/IMF082/25319978148437559 4/25319-9781484375594/ch02.xml; see Financial Stability Board, 'Implementation and Effects of the G20 Financial Regulatory Reforms' 3rd Annual Report (2017) www.fsb.org/wp-content/uploads/P030717-2.pdf.

[30] See European Central Bank, 'ECB Banking Supervision provides temporary capital and operational relief in reaction to coronavirus' Press Release (12 March 2020) www.bankingsupervision.europa.eu/press/pr/date/2020/html/ssm.pr200312-43351ac3ac.en.html. On 16 April 2020, the European Central Bank also temporarily relaxed the capital requirements for market risk, see European Central Bank, 'ECB Banking Supervision provides temporary relief for capital requirements for market risk' Press Release (16 April 2020) www.bankingsupervision.europa.eu/press/pr/date/2020/html/ssm.pr200416~ecf270bca8.en.html.

to continue lending and thus keep the economy afloat.[31] Accordingly, a number of measures have been implemented, the most notable of which concern: (a) lowering capital buffers, (b) favourable prudential treatments for non-performing loans in terms of less loss provisioning required, (c) new rules on legislative and non-legislative moratoria on loan repayments, (d) flexible application of the IFRS 9 international accounting rules, (e) suspension of dividends distribution, share buy-backs and bonuses, (f) relaxion of State aid limitations.[32]

With regard to capital requirements, on 12 March 2020, the ECB announced the relaxation of some prudential rules for significant banks under its direct supervisory remit. Such measures aim to exempt those institutions from a number of capital requirements.[33] The first capital buffer to be relaxed was the capital conservation buffer (CCB), which is a non-risk-weighted capital requirement, previously set at 2.5 per cent, application of which depends on assessment of the total risk exposure amount. The main effect arising from this measure is that a growing portfolio of loans and/or – as will likely be the case in the current situation – an increase in the risk-weighted density of a portfolio will spare the institution from being required to hold additional capital. Accordingly, banks should have more leeway in extending loans.

Additionally, with regard to Pillar 2 requirements, (ie, the additional capital surcharge imposed by supervisors), the ECB decided that even less loss-absorbing instruments, such as Tier2 instruments, can be considered fit for the purpose. As a result, banks will no longer be obliged to issue CET1 instruments to raise this additional amount of capital, on the grounds that in the current market situation this could prove exceedingly difficult.

Concerning non-performing loans, in April 2020, the Basel Committee on Banking Supervision (BCBS) published a document entitled 'Measures to reflect the impact of Covid-19', arguing that the risk-reducing effects of the various extraordinary support measures adopted in many jurisdictions, particularly government guarantees and different payment moratoria, should be taken into consideration in calculating risk-weighted assets and thereby capital requirements. Accordingly, the BCBS clarified that in determining the credit risk for loans benefiting from sovereign guarantees, the relevant sovereign risk weight should be used.[34]

[31] These measures add on to the massive monetary policy interventions that central banks have been implementing in order to maintain price stability and, sometimes, financial stability as well; the European Central Bank, for example, launched a huge assets purchase programme, called the Pandemic Emergency Purchase Programme (PEPP), which covers private and public sector securities. Significantly, PEPP treats the capital key of national central banks in a more flexible manner, allowing the European Central Bank, through the National Central Banks, to target assistance to countries where the need is greatest.

[32] See D Busch, 'Is the European Union going to help us overcome the COVID-19 crisis?' in Gortsos and Ringe (n 18) 29.

[33] See B Joosen, 'Balancing macro and micro-prudential powers in the SSM during the COVID-19 crisis' in Gortsos and Ringe (n 18) 344.

[34] See Brescia Morra (n 23) 397–98.

Furthermore, the BCBS, recalling that the Basel framework requests higher capital requirements for loans that are categorised as 'past due' or 'defaulted', has agreed that payment moratorium periods relating to the COVID-19 pandemic can be disregarded by banks when counting the days to categorise their non-performing loans.

Consequently, the European Banking Authority (EBA) has issued new specific guidelines 'on legislative and non-legislative moratoria on loan repayments in the light of the Covid-19 crisis',[35] which have been followed by national measures introducing moratoria on payments of credit obligations, and by a package adopted on 28 April 2020 by the European Commission.[36] The EBA Guidelines are particularly important since they set out the criteria to be met for payment moratoria in order to avoid triggering forbearance classification.[37] However, it has been observed that although the flexibility given to credit institutions to extend the period for the classification of loans as non-performing is justified in light of the need to support the economy, such a move may nonetheless cause huge problems after the lapse of the moratorium period.[38]

With regard to accounting rules, the BCBS has also urged banks to take advantage of the transitional regime relating to the IFRS 9, given that it was introduced with the aim of mitigating the impact of unexpected events on regulatory capital.[39]

The ECB has also adopted some measures concerning the application of accounting rules, requiring banks to avoid pro-cyclical assumptions in their expected credit loss estimates under the IFRS 9.[40] Such measures are necessary in particular to address the tensions arising from new levels of credit risk and potential credit losses.[41]

Regarding the suspension of dividends distribution, share buy-backs and bonuses, the EBA's Statement of 12 March 2020 pointed to the need to follow prudent policies,[42] and accordingly most national supervisors have expressed

[35] See European Banking Authority, 'Guidelines on legislative and non-legislative moratoria on loan repayments in the light of the Covid-19 crisis' (2 April 2020).

[36] See European Commission, 'Commission Interpretative Communication on the application of the accounting and prudential frameworks to facilitate EU bank lending' COM (2020) 169 final.

[37] See Morais (n 22) 300.

[38] See Gortsos, 'The application' (n 25) 368, who argues that the extent of these problems will be different among Member States, depending on the strength and duration of the current and upcoming recession, as well as among credit institutions, depending on the composition of their portfolio of loans.

[39] See Brescia Morra (n 23) 398, who argues that the European Union its implementation requires a recast of Regulation EU No. 575/2013 (CRR).

[40] See European Central Bank, 'ECB Banking Supervision provides further flexibility to banks in reaction to coronavirus' EBA/GL/2020/02 (2020) www.bankingsupervision.europa.eu/press/pr/date/2020/html/ssm.pr200320-4cdbbcf466.en.html.

[41] See Morais (n 22) 301.

[42] See European Banking Authority, 'EBA Statement on actions to mitigate the impact of COVID-19 on the EU banking sector' Press Release (12 March 2020) www.eba.europa.eu/sites/default/documents/files/document_library/General%20Pages/Coronavirus/EBA%20Statement%20on%20Coronavirus.pdf.

general expectations to either limit or suspend any decisions in this regard.[43] These measures were reaffirmed by the EBA's Statement of 31 March 2020.[44] But the ECB Recommendation issued on 27 March 2020 was especially crucial.[45] Indeed, the ECB urged every significant bank under its direct supervision to suspend all dividends distribution and share buybacks at least until October 2020, and requested that NCAs adopt analogous measures concerning less significant banks.[46]

Moreover, the Commission has relaxed the rules on the provision of State aid in order to more effectively cope with the economic emergency resulting from the COVID-19 pandemic. The Commission has adopted a 'Temporary Framework for State aid measures to support the economy in the current Covid-19 outbreak',[47] which also deals with precautionary recapitalisation.[48] According to the new framework, if credit institutions need extraordinary public financial support in the form of a liquidity, recapitalisation or impaired asset measure due to the COVID-19 outbreak, and the measure meets the conditions under Article 32(4), point (d) (i), (ii) or (iii) BRRD, the credit institution receiving such extraordinary public financial support will not be deemed FOLF.[49] If such measures address problems linked to COVID-19, they fall under point (45) of the 2013 Banking Communication, which sets out an exception to the requirement of burden sharing by shareholders and subordinated creditors. Such an exception is of particular significance as it empowers the Commission to exclude the application of the burden-sharing mechanism when it would endanger financial stability or lead to disproportionate results. Thus, despite the use of public resources, the burden-sharing mechanism,

[43] See A Sciarrone Alibrandi and C Frigeni, 'Restrictions on Shareholder's Distribution in the COVID-19 Crisis: Insights on Corporate Purposes' in Gortsos and Ringe (n 18) 433.

[44] See European Banking Authority, 'Statement on dividends distribution, share buybacks and variable remuneration' Press release (31 March 2020) www.eba.europa.eu/coronavirus.

[45] See European Central Bank, 'Recommendation of the European Central Bank of 27 March 2020 on dividend distributions during the COVID-19 pandemic and repealing Recommendation ECB/2020/1' [2020] OJ C102/1 I.

[46] A similar decision has been made also by the UK Prudential Regulation Authority (PRA), that, having urged the seven largest UK lenders (ie, the systemically important deposit-takers, namely HSBC, Nationwide, Santander, Standard Chartered Bank, Barclays, RBS, Lloyds Banking Group) not to distribute dividends, see Prudential Regulation Authority, 'Letters from Sam Woods to UK deposit takers on dividend payments, share buybacks and cash bonuses' (31 March 2020) www.bankofengland.co.uk/prudential-regulation/letter/2020/letter-from-sam-woods-to-uk-deposit-takers-on-dividend-payments-share-buybacks-and-cash-bonuses; the PRA has then published a statement where it publicly welcomed the choice of the latter to suspend dividends distribution and shares buyback until the end of 2020, see Prudential Regulation Authority, 'Statement on deposit takers' approach to dividend payments, share buybacks and cash bonuses in response to Covid-19' (31 March 2020) www.bankofengland.co.uk/prudential-regulation/publication/2020/pra-statement-on-deposit-takers-approach-to-dividend-payments-share buybacks-and-cash-bonuses.

[47] See European Commission, 'Communication from the Commission, Temporary Framework for State aid measures to support the economy in the current Covid-19 outbreak' [2020] OJ C91/1 I *passim*.

[48] On this, see C Gortsos, M Siri and M Bodellini, 'A proposal for a temporarily amended version of precautionary recapitalisation under the Single Resolution Mechanism Regulation involving the European Stability Mechanism' (2020) 73 *EBI Working Paper Series*.

[49] See European Commission (n 47) para 7.

affecting both shareholders and subordinated creditors, does not necessarily have to be applied.[50]

The Temporary Framework, therefore, might potentially pave the way for an increased number of precautionary recapitalisations to be conducted through the use of public money. It would mean that both shareholders and subordinated creditors could be exempted from the application of the burden-sharing requirement where the COVID-19 pandemic has brought about the need for such a measure.[51] Accordingly, the purchase of NPLs in the context of a precautionary recapitalisation with a view to effectively tackling the increase in bad assets caused by the COVID-19 pandemic is expressly discussed by the Commission in its December 2020 Action Plan.[52] This aspect is relevant since the COVID-19 crisis is expected to lead to a significant surge in the stock of NPLs that credit institutions will be required to manage over time. For these institutions to be able to successfully lower the amount of NPLs in their balance sheets, some sort of public intervention might be needed.[53] And in this regard, the Commission has explained the requirements that must be met in order for public intervention to be authorised as legitimate State aid with a view to clearing stocks of NPLs from bank balance sheets.

Clearly, all these measures are beneficial, as they have so far enabled banks to carry out their vital function of supporting the economy through lending. They have also allowed for the postponement of NPL recognition and consequent surge. Nonetheless, it is unlikely that they will be able in and of themselves to resolve the enormous problems that credit institutions (and the economic system as a whole) face. They are also meant to be temporary, so they will be lifted at some point, leaving credit institutions to contend with the expected economic downturn. This situation should thus be regarded as an incentive to accomplish the finalisation of the original Banking Union project.

IV. Concluding Remarks

Some years after its presentation and the establishment of its initial components, the Banking Union project still merits a positive assessment as a policy initiative. However, in order to deliver on the original goals, the Banking Union project must be completed through the creation of a fully-fledged EDIS. Additionally, the harmonisation of bank insolvency regimes will be key in light of the fact that the majority of EU banks, in the event that they are FOLF, will likely be liquidated under national laws rather than resolved. Currently, there are discrepancies between the

[50] See Avgouleas et al (n 24) 1–40.
[51] See Bodellini and Lintner (n 20) 209.
[52] See European Commission, 'Communication from the Commission to the European Parliament, the Council and the European Central Bank, Tackling non-performing loans in the aftermath of the COVID-19 pandemic' (Brussels, 16 December 2020) COM(2020) 822 final, 3.
[53] See Avgouleas et al (n 24).

resolution regime and the State aid framework concerning the provision of public support that may incentivise national bank insolvency over resolution. With a view to avoiding distortions, such incentives should be removed by aligning the requirements for the provision of public support in both regimes.

Against this background, the COVID-19 crisis – despite its catastrophic impact on the economy (and on society at large) – should be considered an opportunity and leveraged with a view to reaching a political agreement on the establishment of the EDIS and the harmonisation of national bank insolvency regimes. In this regard, in early 2021 the Commission launched a consultation to gather feedback on the revision of the Crisis Management and Deposit Insurance regime.[54] The ECB and the SRB, participating in the Commission's consultation, have already pointed to the importance of setting up a fully-fledged EDIS and harmonising national bank insolvency regimes.[55] This is certainly the right moment to take the final step and complete the original project. After all, only through these legislative actions can a real Banking Union be established to the benefit of the banking sector and, ultimately, the European people.

[54] See European Commission, 'Targeted Consultation Review of the Crisis Management and Deposit Insurance Framework' (2021) https://ec.europa.eu/info/consultations/finance-2021-crisis-management-deposit-insurance-review-targeted_en.

[55] See European Central Bank, 'ECB contribution to the European Commission's targeted consultation on the review of the crisis management and deposit insurance framework' (2021) www.ecb.europa.eu/pub/pdf/other/ecb.consultation_on_crisis_management_deposit_insurance_202105~98c4301b09.en.pdf; see Single Resolution Board, 'SRB replies to consultation on Review of the Crisis Management and Deposit Insurance Framework' (2021) www.srb.europa.eu/en/system/files?file=media/document/2021-04-20_srb_replies_consultation_cmdi_review.pdf.

PART II

The Energy of Credit and Capital

10

The Progressively Increasing Relevance of Commercial Partnerships' Monetary Capital in Early Modern Europe

LUISA BRUNORI

I. Introduction

Legal history says much about the construction of a community's identity and the structures that underpin the development of a society as a whole. This is particularly true of the European legal experience.[1] Indeed, in his inaugural lecture of the European Chair at the *Collège de France*, legal historian Alain Wijffels explicitly asked: 'Does European law have a history? Does it need one?' He answered by citing Braudel's[2] concept of 'the very long duration of a civilisation … which became fully recognisable during the first centuries of the second millennium of the Christian era' and which had forged a mode of operation known as *ius commune*.[3] Hence Wijffels asserted that it was 'conceptually impossible' to consider Europe as a legal *tabula rasa*.[4]

These considerations are particularly stimulating for business law, the evolution of which reveals long-term dynamics that have invested the whole of Europe,

[1] P Grossi, *L'Europa del diritto* (Bari, Lateraza, 2009); A Padoa Schioppa, *Storia del diritto in Europa*, (Bologna, il Mulino, 2007); AM Hespanha, *A Cultura Jurídica Europeia – Síntese de um Milénio* (Lisboa, Almedina, 2002); JL Halpérin, *Histoire des droits en Europe de 1750 à nos jours* (Paris, Flammarion, 2005); R Lesaffer, *European Legal History: A Cultural and Political Perspective* (Cambridge, Cambridge University Press, 2009); H Pihlajamäki, MD Dubber and M Godfrey (eds), *The Oxford Handbook of European Legal History* (Oxford, Oxford University Press, 2018); T Duve, 'European Legal History – Concepts, Methods, Challenges' in T Duve (ed), *Entanglements in Legal History: Conceptual Approaches, Global Perspectives on Legal History* (Frankfurt am Main, Max Planck Institute for European Legal History, 2014) 29–66; M Stolleis, 'Europäische Rechtsgeschichte, immer noch ein Projekt?' (2009) 1 *Clio@Themis*.

[2] F Braudel, *Les mémoires de la Méditerranée* (Paris, Editions de Fallois, 1998).

[3] A Wijffels, *Le droit européen a-t-il un histoire ? En a-t-il besoin ?* (Paris, Collège de France, 2017) 72–73.

[4] Wijffels (n 3) 74.

leaving a consistent mark that has considerably influenced the development of contemporary legal cultures.[5] As Wijffels so effectively puts it:

> the very fluidity of business in international trade networks makes trade a vehicle for propagating procedures and rules that can be invoked by agents belonging to different legal traditions. It is in this sense that business law in Europe has often been at the forefront of the trans-regional spread of widely shared legal practices.[6]

European historiography has recently taken a new approach to the history of business law, based on new epistemological pillars and viewing Europe as a 'legal ecosystem' that must be considered in its entirety in the historical analysis.[7] It is clear that juxtapositions, comparisons and confrontations are not sufficient to explain the evolution of a business law that entails European-wide homogeneity, has no equivalent in other branches of law, and even today remains the most uniform in the European legal area. Consequently, the history of business law is rapidly detaching itself from its municipal or national anchorage to unfold in the European space that forged its very characteristics, and the 'historical a-nationality' of business law[8] can be asserted. This is why comparative law is not sufficient: it fails to account for the fact that the formation of business law cannot be dealt with in terms of a sum of nations, since commercial norms and practices have been shaped not by parallel national forces, but by converging a-national forces within Europe.[9] These converging forces, in terms of practices and rules in commercial law, have created the many pieces that together construct a European community and identity.

Without any pretence of exhaustiveness, the aim here is to examine one of the most effective vectors of this legal homogeneity in Europe at one of the most critical moments in the construction of European identity, the sixteenth century – a

[5] It may be significant that in the argumentation Wijffels proposed in *Le droit européen*, the two historical case-studies given as illustrations are both drawn from the history of business law, see pp 37–53; L Brunori, 'History of business law: a European history?' (2018) 15 *Glossae – European Journal of Legal History*; L Brunori, A Masferrer and A Wijffels, 'Beyond particular traditions: Comparative Legal History' (2018) 15 *Glossae – European Journal of Legal History* preface; B Clavero Salvador, 'Historia como derecho: La libertad mercantil' in C Petit (ed), *Del ius mercatorum al derecho mercantile* (Madrid, Marcial Pons, 1997) 383–96.

[6] Wijffels (n 3) 51.

[7] L Brunori, O Descamps and X Prévost, *Pour une histoire européenne du droit des affaires: comparaisons méthodologiques et bilans historiographiques*, Études d'histoire du droit et des idées politiques n° 27 (Toulouse, Presses de l'Université Toulouse 1 Capitole, 2020); see also www.phedraproject.wordpress.com/.

[8] F Osman, *Les principes généraux de la lex mercatoria: contribution à l'étude d'un ordre juridique anational* (Paris, Librairie Générale de Droit et de Jurisprudence, 1992).

[9] P Bonacini and N Sarti (eds), *Diritto particolare e modelli universali nella giurisdizione mercantile: secoli XIV-XVI* (Bologna, Bononia University Press, 2008); D De Ruysscher, 'L'acculturation juridique des coutumes commerciales à Anvers. L'exemple de la lettre de change (XVIe-XVIIe siècle)' in in B Coppein, F Stevens and L Waelkens (eds), *Modernisme, tradition et acculturation juridique. Actes des Journées internationales de la Société d'Histoire du Droit 2008* (Brussels, Koninklijke Vlaamse Academie van België voor Wetenschappen en Kunsten, 2011) 151–60.

time when Europe, although shaken by religious wars, was seeing the impact of a mercantile dimension in unprecedented expansion.[10]

II. From *Intuitus Personae* to *Intuitus Pecuniae*

The unparalleled acceleration of economic and market changes in the sixteenth and seventeenth centuries produced a radical evolution of the nature of commercial partnerships, of which today's commercial corporations are direct consequences. Defined as 'the legal instrument of capitalist development',[11] the commercial partnership was a key element in the transition that led to the socio-economic and legal structures of contemporary society.

Between the sixteenth and seventeenth centuries, the structure of trade partnerships was transformed in the wake of changes in the economy as the market became proto-global.[12] This evolution involved the transition from partnerships characterised by the legal significance of the subjective element of each partner's individuality (*intuitus personae*) to capital companies[13] in which the predominant legal importance is attributed to the size of the company's assets, namely money (liquid assets), which became an independent focal point for the imputation of legal effects (*intuitus pecuniae*).[14] This was a fundamental and extremely complex transition, the legal dynamics of which stretched across many European countries.[15]

These considerations lead to a question that interconnects with the concept of monetary capital as an object of economic and social behaviour permeating

[10] M Fusaro, C Heywood and MS Omri (eds), *Trade and Cultural Exchange in the Early Modern Mediterranean: Braudel's Maritime Legacy* (London, Bloomsbury Publishing, 2010); B Yun Casalilla, 'Localism, global history and transnational history. A reflection from the historian of early modern Europe' (2007) 127 *Historisk Tidskrift* 88–98.

[11] A Lefebvre-Teillard, 'La révolution: une période décisive pour les sociétés par actions' (1989) 107 *Revue des sociétés* 345–58.

[12] EM García Guerra and G De Luca (eds), *Il mercato del credito in età moderna. Reti e operatori finanziari nello spazio europeo* (Milan, Franco Angeli, 2010); A Crespo Solana, 'The Iberian Peninsula in the First Global Trade. Geostrategy and Mercantile Network interests (XV to XVIII centuries)' in F Mayor Zaragoza (ed), *Global Trade before Globalization (VIII–XVIII)* (Madrid, Fundación Cultura de Paz, 2007) 103–27; H Chaunu and P Chaunu, 'Économie atlantique, économie-monde (1504–1650)' (1953) 1 *Cahiers d'histoire mondiale* 91–104; AG Hopkins (ed), *Globalization in World History* (New York, W. W. Norton & Company, 2003).

[13] To avoid an anachronistic use of the term 'joint-stock company' or 'corporation', I will use the term 'capital company' for this general category, as opposed to the individual-partnership category in which the focus is on the members' identities.

[14] F Braudel, *La dynamique du capitalisme* (Paris, Flammarion, 1985); J Gentil da Silva, 'Les sociétés commerciales, la fructification du capital et la dynamique sociale, XVIème–XVIIème siècle' (1969) 2 *Anuario de Historia Económica y Social* 117–90; R Harris, 'The institutional dynamics of Early Modern Eurasian Trade. The Commenda and the Corporation' (2009) 71 *Journal of Economic Behaviour and Organisation* 606–22.

[15] S Hierro Anibarro, *El orígen de la sociedad anónima en España: la evolución del asiento de avería y el proyecto de compañías de comercio de Olivares: 1521–1633* (Madrid, Tecnos, 1998).

the long-term legal evolution of Europe as an area of dynamic relations between private individuals. To use the terms introduced in the previous paragraph, how can we verify the metamorphosis of commercial structures from an *intuitu personae* partnership model into an *intuitu pecuniae* model, ie, from personal partnerships into capital companies? What are the indicators of such a metamorphosis and to what extent did they contribute to the convergent development of legal instruments in Europe?

The medieval partnership was certainly a contract or agreement between persons, based on the parties' *consensus* and *affectio*, ie on essentially subjective elements of the company's personal constituent aspects.[16] This is one of the most important legacies left by Roman law to medieval law, with the direct consequence of the legal significance of the partners' personal identities.[17] The '*qui societatem contrahit certam personam sibi eligit*' principle (Institutes of Justinian 3.25.5) expresses the *intuitus personae* rule. It meant that, for a person contracting a partnership with another person, the specificity of the other party was of fundamental importance, because capacity and honesty were essential considerations in entering into partnership. This implies that consideration of the partner's person, or *intuitus personae*, governed all aspects of the partnership and shaped its governing legal mechanisms. These mechanisms can be summarised as follows: the duration of the partnership, to last no longer than its partners' lifetime; the dissolution of the partnership if one of the members renounced or had to drop out (ie, for reasons of incapacity); the need to stipulate a new partnership contract between the remaining partners; the impossibility of transmitting the status of a partner to a third person; the need for a new stipulation to allow a new member to join (an amendment was not sufficient); the fact that the partnership's capital could not be viewed as an entity separate from the partners' assets; the inseparability of the identity of the partnership from the partners' identities as persons; the lack of differentiation between the partners' personal liability and the company's liabilities (no limited liability).

Certainly, some forms of associations existed among merchants in the medieval world in which the personal element receded as the importance of the financing provided increased. They included the various forms of *commenda* and *compagnia*

[16] V Simon, '*L'affectio societatis*. Étude historique sur l'élément intentionnel du contrat de société' (2016) 2 *Revue des contrats* 343–52; V Cuisinier, *L'affectio societatis* (Paris, Litec, 2008).

[17] V Arangio-Ruiz, *La Società in diritto romano* (Naples, Jovene, 1950); E Contino, '*Societas* e famiglia nel pensiero di Baldo degli Ubaldi' (2009) LXXXII *Rivista di Storia del Diritto Italiano* 19–92; L Gutierrez-Masson, *Del 'consortium' a la 'societas'* (Madrid, Universidad Complutense, 1989); KM Hingst, *Die societas leonina in der europäischen Privatrechtsgeschichte, Der Weg vom Typenzwang zur Vertragsfreiheit am Beispiel der Geschichte der Löwengesellschaft vom römischen Recht bis in die Gegenwart* (Berlin, Duncker & Humblot, 2003); R Mehr, '*Societas' und 'Universitas': römischrechtliche Institute im Unternehmensgesellschaftsrecht vor 1800* (Wien, Böhlau-Verlag, 2008); FS Meissel, '*Societas*': *Struktur und Typenvielfalt des römischen Gesellschaftsvertrages* (Frankfurt am Main, Peter Lang, 2004); M Talamanca, 'Società in generale. Diritto Romano' in *Enciclopedia del Diritto*, XXXVII, 816–86; R Zimmermann, *The Law of Obligations: Roman Foundations of the Civilian Tradition* (Johannesburg, Clarendon Press, 1996).

that developed especially in central-northern Italy at the end of the Middle Ages, in which one of the partners mainly financed the company without taking part in its activities, while the other contributed through his work and the practical management of the business activity.[18] But it is important to remember that the existence of a partner who only provided financing, and the unequivocal identification of the capital he contributed, do not mean that *intuitus personae* did not play a role. On the contrary, we can assert that, despite these forms of differentiation between partners, their identities still remained a determinant factor in the legal mechanisms underlying partnerships, especially where partnership duration and membership transferability were concerned.

Fundamental changes began to occur at the start of the fourteenth century, resulting from the 'great explorations' that led to new transatlantic economic relationships and encouraged the rapid growth of large business concerns. A new economy emerged on a hitherto unknown scale over a relatively short period.[19] Aside from the considerable risks incurred when sailing across the Atlantic, this new economic context created new conditions regarding the need for financial support, calling for partners who did not necessarily have to be professional merchants, but rather financial backers whose identities were wholly irrelevant to the success of the company: *socii stantes* who participated solely through financial contributions without taking part in the material management of the partnership.

Ultimately, partners became interchangeable and the *intuitus personae* principle gradually became less relevant. From then onwards, partnerships were more strongly identified in terms of capital than of partners as individuals.[20] In this

[18] G Astuti, *Origini e svolgimento storico della commenda fino al secolo XIII* (Torino, Bottega d'Erasmo, 1933); M Berti, 'Commende e redditività di commende nella Pisa della prima metà del Trecento (da documenti inediti)', *Studi Federigo Melis* vol II (Florence, Giannini, 1978) 53–145; Harris, 'The institutional dynamics' (2009); HS Hunt, *The Medieval Super-Companies. A Study of the Peruzzi Company of Florence* (Cambridge, Cambridge University Press, 1994); J Martínez-Gijón, 'La comenda en el Derecho español. II, la comenda mercantil', *Anuario de Historia del Derecho Español (1966)* (Madrid, Boletín Oficial del Esado, 1966) 379–456; G Nigro, 'Francesco and the Datini company of Florence in the commercial trading system' in G Nigro (ed), *Francesco di Marco Datini. The Man and the Merchant* (Florence, Firenze University Press, 2010) 229–48; JH Pryor, 'The Origins of the Commenda Contract' (1977) 52 Speculum 5–37; U Santarelli, *Mercanti e società fra mercanti* (Turin, Giappichelli, 1992).

[19] E Crailsheim, *The Spanish Connection: French and Flemish Merchant Networks in Seville (1570–1650)* (Köln-Weimer, Böhlau Verlag, 2016); G De Carlos Boutet (ed), *España y América un océano de negocios. Quinto centenario de la Casa de la Contratación (1503–2003)* (Madrid, Sociedad Estatal Quinto Centenario, 2003); JH Elliot, *Spain, Europe and the Wider World (1500–1800)* (New Haven, Yale University Press, 2009); AB Fernández Castro, 'A Transnational Empire Built on Law: The case of the Commercial Jurisprudence of the House of Trade of Seville (1583–1598)', in Duve (ed), *Entanglements in Legal History* (n 1) 187–212; E Martiré, 'El marco jurídico del tráfico con las Indias españolas' in Petit (ed), *Del ius mercatorum* (n 5) 229–35; F Melis, *Il commercio transatlantico di una compagnia fiorentina stabilita a Siviglia a pochi anni dalle imprese di Cortés e Pizarro* (Zaragoza, Institución Fernando el Católico, 1954); E Vilar Vilar, 'Los Europeos en el Comercio Americano: Sevilla como Plataforma' in *Latin America and the Atlantic world (1500–1850). Essays in honor of Horst Pietschmann: Lateinamerikanische Forschungen 33* (Böhlau, Köln, 2005) 279–96.

[20] JF Padgett and PD McLean, 'Organizational Invention and Elite Transformation. The Birth of Partnership Systems in Renaissance Florence' (2006) 111 *American Journal of Sociology* 1463–568.

context, limited liability began to take shape. The idea of liability being limited to the amount of the capital contribution attracted non-commercial capital and non-commercial partners,[21] and the value of the partners' skills had less and less bearing: merchants needed money, not people. Giving special status to investing partners who were only interested in profit by limiting their liability was a considerable innovation – all the more so when we consider that this construction was the forerunner of future capital companies, which raised the question of the legal personality of a partnership. The progressive introduction of limited liability techniques and the emergence of the partnership's legal personality are intertwined. Once share capital is separated from that of shareholders in economic or legal relationships with third parties (the principle of limited liability), it follows that the concept of the autonomy of the company's legal personality from that of shareholders can crystallise.

III. The Mechanics of the Legal Transition

The transition from one model to another was not immediate, and required daring experiments in mercantile practice. Even a cursory look at archives reveals that the sixteenth and seventeenth centuries were truly the transition period in which commercial partnerships gradually adapted to the new needs of trade. It was an empirical adaptation, involving attempts and experiments that anticipated the doctrine and compensated for the lack of an adequate normative system. Whereas sixteenth-century theologians and jurists continued to construe the *societas* in the philosophical terms of Aristotle, Cicero and Thomas Aquinas, as a form of friendship (*amicitia*)[22] or brotherhood (*fraternitas*),[23] the merchants of the time were gradually losing interest in the reliability of the partner's person while becoming more interested in the reliability (ie, consistence and solvency) of the partner's assets. This new trend was reflected in the new legal forms of commercial companies set up through commercial practices for pragmatic purposes – practical experiments, dictated by the requirements of the new proto-global trade, that were only later translated into a systematic legal framework. The constraints and potentialities of business practice had to address the weaknesses of the partnership, and thus the personalistic partnership model was transformed into a capital company model.

[21] G Ripert, *Aspects juridiques du capitalisme moderne* (Paris, Librairie Générale de Droit et de Jurisprudence, 1946).

[22] W Decock, 'The Catholic Spirit of Capitalism? Contrasting Views on Profit-Making Through Capital Investment in the Age of Reformations' in W Decock, JJ Ballor, M Germann and L Waelkens (eds), *Law and Religion, The Legal Teachings of the Protestant and Catholic Reformations* (Göttingen, Vandenhoeck & Ruprecht, 2014) 22–43.

[23] L Brunori, 'Late Scholasticism and Commercial Partnership: Persons and Capitals in the Sixteenth and Seventeenth Centuries' in D De Ruysscher, S Dauchy, A Cordes and H. Pihlajamäki (eds), *The Company in Law and Practice: Did Size Matter ? Middle Ages-Nineteenth Century* (Leiden, Brill, 2017) 42–69.

To analyse precisely how the behaviour of European merchants changed due to the changing role of money capital, we must first state the questions in analytical terms: what factors and strategies changed the partnership by giving unprecedented relevance to the role of money? How did this change develop in European countries? How did the practice change the legal mechanisms commercial companies were based upon? How did the most important business law instruments that still exist today take shape?

Notaries certainly played a key role in shaping those new models, and contributed to their homogenisation at European level through the European circulation of notarial forms.[24] Obviously, this transition did not happen abruptly, nor did it develop in a single, unitary way. However, we can identify some essential elements that marked the transition from personal partnership to share capital company, which can be seen as part of the convergent construction of a European legal model. The essential markers of the transition from an *intuitus personae*-based to an *intuitus pecuniae*-based partnership mirror the characteristics of medieval partnerships to some degree: the presence of *socii stantes*, ie exclusively financial contributions, in which the partner participated in the company only with liquid assets, without any participation in the management of the company; a progressively longer duration of the partnership, specifically beyond the partners' lifetime, and the continuation of the company with the deceased partner's heirs (a possibility that was not considered in medieval practice); an extension of the capacity to join a partnership; the possibility of transferring partner status via *actus inter vivos* or *mortis causa* (with or without the other partners' consent); limited liability; the prohibition of any competition seen as harmful to the company rather than relying on an act in violation of *fraternitas* drawn up between the partners (the forms of the compensation provided would be significant); the development of trademarks and the protection of the partnership's identity; the development of accounting techniques which reveal the existence of a partnership's capital through more sophisticated book-keeping than in the Middle Ages.

But why were these elements so essential to the transition from partnership to corporation? To answer this question and those posed above, we must take a closer look at these elements.

A. *Socii Stantes*

Although capitalist partners, ie partners who only provided a financial contribution, were already present in various medieval forms of *commendas*, the practice increased significantly beginning in the sixteenth century. In the new sphere of

[24] V Piergiovanni (ed), *Tra Siviglia e Genova: notaio, documento e commercio nell'eta' colombiana* (Milano, Giuffrè, 1994); B Van Hofstraeten, 'Historiographical Opportunities of Notarized Partnership Agreements Recorded in the Early Modern Low Countries' in H Pihlajamäki, A Cordes, S Dauchy and D De Ruysscher (eds), *Understanding the Sources of Commercial law* (Leiden, Brill, 2018).

transatlantic trade in particular, no one was willing to gamble all their wealth in very risky overseas ventures, but many wanted to take part in the exploitation of newly discovered resources by joining partnerships in which risks and costs, as well as profits, were shared among all of the partners. The capitalist partner who participated in the profits without working for or taking part in the administration of the partnership was known as a *socius stans*.[25] The presence of the *socius stans* is emblematic of the progressive importance of money as an autonomous factor within partnerships, and as an imputation centre for the attribution of legal effects on its own.[26]

B. Progressively Extended Partnership Duration

i. Over Three Years

The autonomous and predominant role of money in the structuring of partnerships has a direct impact on the duration of the company, and is one of the factors that determined the progressive lengthening of the duration of partnerships. The duration depends, first and foremost, on the partners' will, as they can determine the date of its dissolution. Medieval trade partnerships normally had a three-year duration, which was rather short. This aspect is very much linked to the role played by *intuitus personae*: the more decisive the partner's identity, the shorter the duration of the partnership. In fact, the brevity of the duration made it possible to get rid of members with whom personal relationships had deteriorated, and to avoid remaining bound to people one no longer trusted or with whom one was no longer comfortable. Conversely, the less important the shareholder's identity became, the less important it was to be able to get rid of a partner quickly. What was crucial, on the other hand, was to ensure that capital remained within the partnership for as long as possible. Maintaining the stability of monetary capital over time also meant trying to keep the partnership going beyond the death of a member. This, however, posed problems from the legal/technical point of view.

[25] E Soria Mesa, 'Conversos, comerciantes y regidores: el origen mercantil de la élite local granadina (ss. XVI-XVIII)' in JJ Iglesias Rodríguez, RM Pérez García and MF Fernández Chaves (eds), *Comercio y cultura en la Edad Moderna*, Vol 2 (Sevilla, Universidad de Sevilla, 2015) 185–202; A Merchant Rivera, 'Participation of Women in the Notarial Public Deed of the 16th Century. From the Constriction of the Marital Licence to the Fullness of Widowhood' (2017) 11(13) *European Scientific Journal*; C Sanz Ayán, 'Negocio, dinero y mujer. Empresarias en la primera Época Moderna (S. XVI-XVII)' (2019) 216(2) *Boletín de la Real Academia de la Historia* 149–69.

[26] A Amend-Traut, 'The Productivity of Capital with (Silent) Participation in Trading Companies. Controversies' in L Brunori, S Dauchy, O Descamps and X Prévost (eds), *Le droit face à l'économie sans travail: finance, spéculation et investissements de l'Antiquité à nos jours* (Paris, 2019) 135–149; X Lamikiz, 'Social capital, networks and trust in early modern long distance trade' in MH Sànchez and K Kaps (eds), *Merchants and Trade Networks in the Atlantic and the Mediterranean* (London, Routledge, 2017) 39–61.

In Roman and medieval law, partnerships did not carry on with a deceased member's heirs, even if explicitly stipulated in an agreement between members.[27] In the early sixteenth century, practice (and scholars as well) began to lean towards the continuation of partnerships with deceased partners' heirs. In fact, in spite of the rule inherited from Roman law according to which each new member's entry into a partnership required its *novatio*, preventive *pro haeredibus* agreements (either in the articles of association or by separate instrument) aimed at continuing partnerships with deceased members' heirs were fairly frequent in practice and were implicitly allowed by the existing legal framework (*Las Partidas*, for instance).[28] Again, a tendency to consider partnerships as entities independent of their physical partners can be viewed as a 'depersonalisation' of partnerships to the advantage of an increasingly autonomous role of monetary capital, which survived and was active independently from the partners' persons.

C. Extending the Capacity of the Parties

The importance of the personal element naturally leads us to an in-depth examination of the subjective aspects of the contractors, among which capacity is of particular importance. The issue of the capacity to enter into a commercial partnership must be differentiated from the more general question of the capacity to act. The capacity to be a partner originally assumed the exercise of an activity that could be considered commercial *latu sensu*, and therefore the specific capacity to do business must be considered. This means that, apart from ordinary rules on the capacity to commit to contracts (which still applied), certain categories of people were banned from performing commercial activities, like clerics, officers or aristocrats. This restriction was subsequently considerably relaxed.

Throughout the sixteenth century, we can observe a gradual erosion of the capacity to be a partner. This is highly significant because, on the one hand, it was assumed that being a member of a partnership no longer necessarily implied the concrete exercise of an activity (exclusively financial participation had become

[27] '*Hæredes vero mortui non permanet, etiamsi in pactum id fuisset deductum*' (J de Lugo y Quiroga, *De Iustitia et de Iure* [Lyon, Petrus Prost, 1642], in accordance with the principle established in the *Corpus iuris civilis* and confirmed by the Glossators). However, Roman law and *ius commune* already acknowledged that in some cases it would have been counterproductive to consider this type of agreement invalid, for instance in cases of partnerships created in the general interest (like the *societas publicanorum* for collecting taxes), where the partnership had to be continued with the heir *ob favorem publicum*. Nevertheless, even in these cases, the personal qualities of the new member were still very important because the partnership went on '*dummodo hæres idoneus sit societati*', a positive assessment of the personal qualities of the member being indispensable.

[28] L Brunori, 'Tendances et continuité de l'activité commerciale européenne au *Siglo de Oro*: nouveaux apports à l'étude des contrats de société commerciale d'après des documents inédits de l'*Archivos de Protocolos* de Séville' in A Mages (ed), *Les fondements historiques du droit européen des affaires*, Études d'histoire du droit et des idées politiques n° 29 (Toulouse, Presses de l'Université Toulouse 1 Capitole, 2021) 45–81.

generally accepted), and on the other hand, the gradual phasing out of capacity rules concerning the partners' person status attests to the progressive loss of importance of the partners' personal qualities and the increasing importance given to the quality of their money contribution.

D. The Transfer of Partner Status Via *Acta Inter Vivos* or *Mortis Causa*

Colonial trading companies (East India Companies and French privileged companies) that began to develop during the seventeenth century are the emblem of a paradigmatic shift towards the free transferability of membership through the instrument of the stock-market.[29] Although the literature has shown that the public limited company model was not yet in place at the end of the eighteenth century, we can observe that throughout Europe the transition had already begun in the sixteenth century, through the gradual detachment from an *intuitus personae*-based structure in which any modification had to be accepted by the pre-existing members, to a free-transfer-of-partner-status model.[30] These changes in commercial structures gave much greater importance to the stability of capital/money than to the partners' identities, which made it logical to tend towards the free transferability of purely financier partners. This transition was obviously gradual.

In cases of transfer of partner status by *acta inter vivos*, the partners' behaviour was illustrative; there was verification of whether explicit consent or refusal had been expressed, whether a prior agreement had already been provided for this purpose, and whether the partnership had actually accepted the transfer of membership by continuing the company's business activity with the new shareholder (for conclusive acts) in contrast with the application of the *intuitus personae* rule.[31]

Archives also reveal examples of *mortis causa* transfers by testament. These cases are particularly interesting because the *intuitus personae* rule theoretically denies *mortis causa* partner-status transfers, since the other partners' consent would be required for any change in the composition of the partnership: in theory, the testator cannot make decisions by testament, overriding or superseding the will of the other members who have the right to choose the identity of the person who will join the partnership. But archives are full of cases in which partnerships did indeed continue, implementing the willingness clause, via explicit consent or

[29] S Gialdroni, *East India Company. Una storia giuridica (1600–1708)* (Bologna, il Mulino, 2011).

[30] A Amend-Traut, *Legal Structure of Early Enterprises – from Commenda-like Arrangements to Chartered Joint-Stock Companies (Early Modern Period)*, in *The Company in Law and Practice: Did Size Matter? (Middle Ages-Nineteenth Century)* (2017) 63–82.

[31] B Van Hofstraeten, 'Private Partnerships in Seventeenth-Century Maastricht' in B Van Hofstraeten and W Decock (eds), *Companies and Company law in Late Medieval and Early Modern Europe* (Leuven, Peters, 2016) 115–48.

tacit acceptance expressed by continuing the company's business activity with a new shareholder.[32]

E. Limited Liability

The structuring of limited liability is one of the most interesting steps in the development of companies. There is no doubt that the conceptualisation of the separation of shareholders' assets from the company's assets developed gradually, but identifying this process in practice is extremely challenging. In the sixteenth century, mechanisms began to appear to substantially limit liability, especially for the *socii stantes*:[33]

i. The pacta de salva sorte reddenda

Following the expansion of the market due to the first period of globalisation, many people became involved in partnerships by contributing to a company's capital as an investment. Given the undeniably increased risk of economic operations these types of investors (*socii stantes*, described above) usually guaranteed the security of their investments not only through insurance (which was becoming widespread at the time) but also through various agreements with *socii tractantes (operator partners)*, who, under these agreements, bore all or some of the capital risk. The *contractus trinus* is a very important example of this type of pact.[34] It is clear that the aim here is the protection of capital, which takes on autonomous legal significance, independent from the partner's identity, which has no relevance within this legal mechanism.[35]

ii. Management, expenses and losses

On the basis of Roman law, even though companies had no external relevance and partners consequently acted in their own names, partners had to be reimbursed for expenses incurred in the *causa negotiorum societatis*. Normally, expenses and

[32] M Basas Fernández, 'Contratos de compañías mercantiles castellanas del siglo XVI' (1960) 78 *Revista de Derecho Mercantil* 375–412; L Brunori, 'Tendances'.

[33] D de Ruysscher, 'Innovating Financial Law in the Early Modern Netherlands and Europe: Transfers of Commercial Paper and Recourse Liability in Legislation and Ius Commune (Sixteenth-Eighteenth Centuries)' (2011) 19 *European Journal of Private Law* 505–18.

[34] The *contractus trinus* was in fact a set of three contracts. The basis was a partnership contract between a financing partner who contributed capital and an operator-partner who contributed through his work. Two other contracts were drawn up along with the partnership contract: a *contractus assecurationis capitalis* to insure the backer's capital risk, and a *contractus de lucro certo pro incerto* in which the financing partner sold his share of the profits in return for a fixed annuity.

[35] C Petit Calvo, 'Ignorancias y otras historias, o sea, reponsabilidades limitadas' (1990) 60 *Anuario de historia del derecho español* 497–508.

losses due to *causa negotiorum societatis* had to be borne jointly by *socii stantes* as well, even if they were not involved in the management of the partnership. Conceding the need to deal with the vagueness of the concept of '*causa negotiorum societatis*', we can assume that while the distinction between *tractans* and *stans* partners was gradually emerging, the distinction between the partners' personal debts and those of the partnership was also becoming clearer.[36] To prove this hypothesis, it will be necessary to determine whether the differentiation between reimbursable expenses made in the interest of a partnership and the partner's personal expenses gradually developed into the idea of the company's assets being independent, en route to recognition of the partnership's own artificial identity.

F. Accounting Methods

Accounting books will be a very important source for examination with regard to the above hypothesis.[37] They may provide clues concerning a new key element in understanding the evolution of partnerships: the new governance of partnerships, with potential tension between administrators and managers on the one hand and capital providers on the other.[38] It is important to note that the gradual increase in the use of the double-entry accounting method invented by Luca Pacioli in 1480 helped to establish the partnership as an independent legal entity. The progressive refinement of accounting techniques simultaneously contributed to a refinement of the distinction between partners' own and company's assets, with the consequent emergence of the company as a separate entity from the partners.[39]

IV. Conclusions

At the beginning of the Early Modern era, the monetary capital of commercial partnerships began to take on a profoundly different role than in previous centuries. The socio-economic behaviour of merchants throughout Europe adapted to this substantial change. What ensued was a profound modification in the juridical structure of partnerships themselves, in which the monetary element acquired autonomy and shaped their organisation, profoundly altering their essence, which

[36] D de Ruysscher, 'A Business Trust for Partnerships? Early Conceptions of Company-Related Assets (Later Sixteenth-Early Seventeenth Century)' in Van Hofstraeten and Decock (n 31) 9–27.

[37] H Pihlajamäki, A Cordes, S Dauchy and D de Ruysscher, *Understanding the Sources of Early Modern and Modern Commercial Law. Courts, Statutes, Contracts, and Legal Scholarship* (Leiden, Brill, 2018).

[38] F Melis (ed), *Mercaderes italianos en España. Siglos XIV-XVI. Investigaciones sobre su correspondencia y su contabilidad* (Sevilla, Publicaciones de la Universidad de Sevilla, 1976).

[39] M Lacombe-Saboly, 'Pratiques comptables et associations entre marchands aux XVIe et XVIIe siècle: une étude en Midi toulousain' (1998) 4 *Comptabilité-Contrôle-Audit* 5–24.

shifted from an association of persons to a pooling of monetary resources. The tendency to standardise these traits at European level consolidated the behaviour and legal standards of the European merchant community.

We can clearly perceive that European business law is implemented above all through practice. Practitioners were very often at the origin of the process of construction of the original mechanisms of financing, investment and speculation which still govern European business law in the twenty-first century. The great discoveries of an expanding New World in part explain the upheaval that practice generated in the new economic-legal system, investing the whole of Europe. From the modern era onwards, the use of capital financing, insurance, foreign exchange and countless other types of speculative contracts became common throughout Europe. These practices were simply contractual experiments carried out by individuals, which gradually coalesced to develop a business law that had increasingly uniform features across Europe.

Moreover, we cannot forget that throughout its construction process, business law in Europe has been conceived in terms of doctrine. Legal scholars have taken up empirical material and given it abstract and paradigmatic value. In particular, they have sought to design a structured system of law, offering original ideas in the pursuit of coherence and consistency in a landscape of complex and extremely creative practice. The countless intellectual centres scattered throughout Europe and linked since the Middle Ages by the frequent exchange of ideas and the drafting of theoretical treatises contributed greatly to the homogenisation of the system of commercial law in Europe.[40] This led to the construction of a community united not only by common interests and practices but also by a common cultural foundation.[41]

[40] L Brunori 'Pédagogie et internationalisme des professeurs de la Seconde Scolastique – XVIe XVIIe siècle', in M Cavina (ed), *L'insegnamento del diritto (secoli XII-XX)-L'enseignement du droit (XII e-XX e siècle)* (Bologna, il Mulino, 2019).

[41] W Decock, *Theologians and contract law: the moral transformation of the Ius Commune (ca. 1500–1650)* (Leiden, Martinus Nijhoff, 2013); C Petit, *Historia del Derecho Mercantil* (Madrid, Marcial Pons, 2019); R Savelli, 'Modèles juridiques et culture marchande entre 16e et 17e siècles' in F Angelini and D Roche (eds), *Cultures et formation négociantes dans l'Europe moderne* (Paris, EHESS, 1995) 403–15.

11

Towards European Venture Capital? A Proposal for More State Involvement in Venture Capital to Foster Inclusive and Green Growth and European Community

JOHANNES LENHARD AND LEO REES

I. Introduction

In early 2021, much happened in European startup land. The European Innovation Council, the first pan-European direct-investment vehicle, was launched in early March;[1] not coincidentally, the EU Startup Nation Standard, a best-practice sharing framework to enable the ecosystem to grow smoothly, launched the same month. Similarly, many state-level initiatives are explicitly aimed at fostering a stronger entrepreneurial ecosystem post-COVID-19; from Germany's 10bn Future Fund announced in December[2] to the UK's equivalent, originally structured as a COVID-19-relief vehicle but extended into an ongoing investment fund.[3] In short, there are many live initiatives to get Europe up to speed on entrepreneurship, with support from the State.

All of this comes at a time when – as the editors of this volume set out in their introduction – Europe has been facing a plethora of general and specific challenges from the subprime crisis following 2008 and COVID-19 to Brexit and the rise of nationalism. The contributions in this book ask how the European community can on the one hand tackle these challenges together but on the other hand move

[1] European Innovation Council (EIC), *European Innovation Council (EIC) Fund Investment Committee* (2021) https://ec.europa.eu/research/eic/pdf/ec_eic_fund-investement-committee.pdf.

[2] M Partington, 'Germany launches €10bn "Future Fund" for startups. But will it go far enough?' (*Sifted*, 12 December 2020) www.sifted.eu/articles/germany-future-fund-startups/.

[3] UK Government, 'Future Fund launches today' (*Gov.UK*, 20 May 2020) www.gov.uk/government/news/future-fund-launches-today.

forward towards a more inclusive, sustainable economy and alliance. Specifically, what role can money, different kinds of capital, play in this development?

In this chapter, we take this query into the ecosystem(s) where venture capitalists (VCs), limited partners (the asset owners behind the VCs) and startup founders rule. There is significant optimism attached to the potential of tech financing and entrepreneurship. Since the rocket-like success of technology companies coming out of Silicon Valley; we expect startups fuelled by venture capital not only to produce world-changing innovation (solving our biggest problems from better healthcare to cleaner air and more environmentally friendly food) but also employment and economic growth more generally. And we know that they can deliver:[4] historical examples from the US include semiconductors (eg, Sun Microsystems) and the iPhone. We are starting to see revolutionary innovation come from Europe too – Graphcore working on world-leading AI chips and Lilium on the forefront of electric vertical take-off and landing vehicles are just two examples.

However, what is often misunderstood, or at least seen in tension with entrepreneurship, is the role of the State in startup financing and policy making. We will therefore sketch the history of what we know about the crucial role the US State and its agencies played in bringing to life Silicon Valley and Route 128, before looking specifically at Europe.

Based on almost two dozen original interviews with policy makers, academics, entrepreneurs, limited partners and venture capital investors from a variety of European States, this chapter touches on three main questions: should the EU (or its Member States) invest more? How can the right European startup ecosystem be fostered? How can some of the EU's core strengths be used in this direction? Our main learnings strengthen, concretise and link existing opinions. First, while capital is needed, it should likely be funnelled through fund-of-fund structures (such as the European Investment Fund (EIF)) and come with incentives, rules and guidelines to target future-proofing industries (eg, climate tech) with patient capital. However, success metrics need to be set, measured and go beyond financial returns in all programmes. Secondly, building European institutions to be resilient for the long-term, and using the EU's procurement power will be as crucial a part of ecosystem construction. Thirdly, policy making, regulation and investments should be harmonised: support for upstream investment and downstream policy influence should be complimentary, as should work at the EU vs Member State level.

To provide historical context, in the following section we will analyse some of the core learnings from the often-admired American VC ecosystem before diving into our three-partite analysis afterwards.

[4] W Gornall and I Strebulaev, 'The Economic Impact of Venture Capital: Evidence from Public Companies' (2015) 3360 *Stanford Graduate School of Business Working Paper* www.gsb.stanford.edu/faculty-research/working-papers/economic-impact-venture-capital-evidence-public-companies.

II. Historic Learnings – The Role of the State in Financing and Enabling Innovation in the US

Two recent accounts have comprehensively traced the historical origins of the venture capital industry in the US. Both books are written by historians at Harvard[5] and Washington[6] respectively and strongly agree on one thing: startups and the VC funders behind them would not be able to enjoy the major successes we celebrate them for without the involvement of the State. The bottom line is that the State – in various iterations and forms – played a crucial role in fostering both VC directly and technological change more broadly.

In his history of American venture capital, Harvard historian Tom Nicholas is very clear about the crucial role of government since the first attempts at privately financing new (technology) startups in the 1950s. Perhaps the first instance of direct government *investment* in startups dates back to the Small Business Investment Company programme in the late 1950s (running to this day). It is one of the largest fund-of-funds in the US and has provided more than $67 billion of capital to more than 160,000 companies, channelled through over 2,000 VC, PE and other types of funds. Its explicit aim from the beginning was to 'increase the pool of investment capital available to small businesses' leveraging the 'full faith and credit of the US government'.[7] The role of the State in the birth of the ecosystem went beyond investment and money, however. Certain kinds of (de)*regulation* were crucial for VC to grow. The Employee Retirement Income Security Act of 1974 (ERISA)[8] created a new era of VC investment; particularly with the clarification of the 'prudent man rule' in 1979. This Act gave American pension funds the freedom to invest in VCs. Gompers and Lerner[9] argue that ERISA (together with subsequent capital gains tax cuts[10]) significantly increased the supply of money available from VC funds, widening the pool of companies supported and the risks taken.

However, perhaps even more significantly than opening new sources of investment, was the role of government policy in fostering a startup and technology ecosystem. In her history of Silicon Valley, Margaret O'Mara traces its unprecedented success back not only to 'free markets, the individual entrepreneur, and the miracles of a wholly new economy' but 'big-government programmes that political leaders … and many tech leaders viewed with suspicion'.[11] Government

[5] T Nicholas, *VC: An American History* (Boston, Harvard University Press, 2019).

[6] M O'Mara, *The Code – Silicon Valley and the Remaking of America* (New York, Penguin Random House, 2019).

[7] Office of Investment and Innovation, *SBIC Program Overview* (2018) www.sba.gov/sites/default/files/2019-02/2018SBICProgramOverview.pdf.

[8] Pub.L. 93–406, 88 Stat. 829, enacted 2 September 1974, codified in part at Title 29 of the United States Code, ch. 18.

[9] PA Gompers and J Lerner, 'What Drives Venture Capital Fundraising' (1999) 6906 *NBER working paper* www.nber.org/system/files/working_papers/w6906/w6906.pdf.

[10] See O'Mara (n 6) 167 ff.

[11] ibid 5.

money – often channelled through the military-industrial-complex around the Department of Defense or NASA (founded in 1958) – did not only provide the trillions necessary for basic research (funded at places like Stanford but before that on the East coast); it also took away the 'market risk' for entrepreneurs by being a 'buyer of first resort'.[12] Fairchild Semiconductor, one of the first silicon chip makers (which ended up giving the whole region its name) was originally almost fully funded by government contracts; the 'decentralized, privatized, fast-moving public contracting environment encouraged entrepreneurship', was critical, according to O'Mara.[13] And throughout Silicon Valley's ascent 'defense [procurement] remained the big-government engine hidden under the hood of the Valley's shiny new entrepreneurial sports car'.[14]

As economist Mariana Mazzucato,[15] a pronounced sceptic of the libertarian (and ahistoric) tendencies of Silicon Valley, proudly repeats again and again: the personal computer, the internet (or ARPANET as the network between a handful of university computers was originally called), the iPhone, lithium batteries – these path-breaking technology innovations are as much products of *government* efforts (and money) as of private sector actors. As she put it in her 2017 *The Value of Everything*: 'governments, along with the many institutions and traditions of a society, are the womb in which markets are nourished'.[16] Turning to the future and particularly focusing on the recovery from COVID-19 as well as the big challenges ahead – climate change and the environmental disaster more broadly – Mazzucato proposes in her latest book that governments must step up again. She argues that 'government … cannot limit itself to reactively fixing markets, but must explicitly co-shape markets to deliver the outcomes society needs'[17] because 'only government has the capacity to steer the transformation on the scale needed'.[18]

Obviously, there is no need to dismiss the crucial role of the private 'innovators' and the necessary inspiration and initiative of individuals and markets as a core ingredient for the success of tech startups (and VC funding). However, the discourse has over the last decade shifted dangerously in the direction of libertarian market-fundamentalists who (wrongly and conveniently for themselves) forget the State's role in history. Many entrepreneurs – Jobs, Musk, Zuckerberg, Bezos and the like – have gained cult status together with their companies; and in turn the cult of the entrepreneur (and their investors) has become a

[12] WH Janeway, *Doing Capitalism in the Innovation Economy: Markets, Speculation and the State* (Cambridge, Cambridge University Press, 2018).

[13] O'Mara (n 6) 53.

[14] ibid 260.

[15] M Mazzucato, *The Entrepreneurial State – Debunking public vs. private sector myths* (London, Penguin, 2013); M Mazzucato, *The Value of Everything – Making and Taking in the Global Economy* (London, Allen Lane, 2017); M Mazzucato, *Mission Economy: A Moonshot Guide to Changing Capitalism* (London, Allen Lane, 2021).

[16] Mazzucato, *The Value of Everything* (n 15) 268.

[17] Mazzucato, *Mission Economy* (n 15) 21.

[18] ibid 23.

quintessential feature in contemporary society,[19] with arguably concerning consequences (eg, labelling precarious gig workers as entrepreneurs).[20] The State's full role in the ecosystem – as investor, ecosystem-builder, regulator and market-maker – is often not acknowledged.

Turning to Europe and picking up from the above history and learnings, we started our research feeling suspicious towards calls for European Elon Musks as saviours for our startup-ecosystem,[21] and the creation of European Tech Giants.[22] Similarly, simply copying the US DARPA-model into Europe,[23] is mostly not specific enough and crucially does not take into account the core strengths and specificities of the European circumstances. In this chapter, rather than comprehensively trying to assess the evolving European landscape of the State-VC-startup-complex, we are focusing on devising principles on how experts believe this nexus should look like going forward. Naturally, wherever applicable, we will include references to existing programmes and entities – from the European Investment Fund to the newly launched European Innovation Council as well as regulatory initiatives – but wherever possible we try to offer a principle-led approach, rather than a direct critique of these institutions.

III. A Note on Method

The research we conducted for this chapter consists of 21 semi-structured interviews both authors led between January 2021 and March 2021. The group of interviewees consisted of policy makers, academics, entrepreneurs, limited partners (in State funds as well as private fund-of-funds) and venture capital investors. We interviewed a mix of participants from Germany (4), France (3), the Nordics (4), the UK (6), North America (2) and the Benelux countries (2), the majority of whom were men (70 per cent). Before the interview which lasted between 30 and 60 minutes, all participants gave verbal consent to being interviewed and for the data being used for research publications. We assured every participant anonymity to protect their identity and views and enable a frank conversation without compromising relationships at work or otherwise. Throughout the chapter, we

[19] I Gershon, *Down and Out in the New Economy: How People Find (or Don't Find) Work Today* (Chicago, The University of Chicago Press, 2017).

[20] AJ Ravenelle, *Hustle and Gig – Struggling and Surviving in the Sharing Economy* (Oakland, University of California Press, 2019).

[21] M Mawad and M Palmer, 'Five ways to get Europe its own Elon Musk' (*Sifted*, 11 November 2020) www.sifted.eu/articles/elon-musk-challengers-europe/.

[22] M Johnson, 'EU needs to think bigger to develop tech champions' *Financial Times* (15 October 2020) www.ft.com/content/32de6543-ef13-4352-9358-bf45c3ea7624.

[23] D Marin, 'Europe Needs a DARPA' (*Project Syndicate*, 6 February 2021) www.project-syndicate.org/commentary/germany-europe-need-government-technology-research-agency-by-dalia-marin-2020-02?barrier=accesspaylog.

will refer to informants accordingly with a pseudonym as well as a categorising descriptor (eg, VC investor in Germany) when quoting specifically or paraphrasing.

The research for this chapter is part of a bigger research project at the Max Planck Cambridge Centre for Ethics, Economy and Social Change led by Dr Johannes Lenhard on what he calls the 'ethics of venture capital'; it hence falls under the ethical approval this project has received from the Ethics Board of the Department of Anthropology at the University of Cambridge. As part of the 'Ethics of VC' project, this chapter's insight, while being explicitly devised from the specific interviews, also benefits from the contextual understanding of the 400+ interviews Lenhard conducted with VCs and LPs since 2017 between the US and Europe. The chapter also benefits from a strong contextual view on the technology policy world from Leo Rees. Rees contributes important expertise from his work as a technology fellow at the UK think tank Onward, and is an experienced consultant to players at each stage of the technology and innovation ecosystem, from big tech to start ups, VCs and the UK Government.

IV. Should States (or the EU) Invest More into Startups?

'Governments are incompetent to choose companies but also sectors that should be fostered; so [I am] unsure about the government picking winners [beyond] market distortions that are intentional [...] governments are not good at foreseeing the future.' Brian,[24] a seasoned VC investor in the UK, very openly expressed his disdain for governments getting involved as a direct investor ('choosing companies') and even as an ecosystem maker. He was not alone, several interviewees expressed concern that direct investment vehicles like the European Innovation Council (announced shortly before time of writing) would cannibalise the existing VC market.

This assessment of governments being incapable and incompetent was not only an opinion voiced repeatedly in our interviews but mirrors a long-standing academic critique. In an early contribution, Florida and Smith, for instance, warn of government involvement in venture capital and startup activity: 'government is ill-equipped to perform the role of venture capitalist'[25] as a direct investor. They are pointing to the bad track record of the Small Business Investment company (SBICs) in the US (only a third of supported companies survives for more than a decade) and the inability for State-run programmes to achieve comparable financial returns and exits compared to privately run VCs. The opinion of government's 'incompetence' as a VC investor mentioned by Brian above has been echoed in

[24] All names of individuals and organisations are anonymised to protect our informants' identities.

[25] R Florida and DF Smith, 'Keep the Government Out of Venture Capital' (1993) 9(4) *Issues in Science and Technology* 62.

more recent studies. In his groundbreaking 2009 book, Lerner provides a host of evidence on the impact (or lack thereof) of boosting entrepreneurship in France between the 1980s and 2000s (eg, failure to fund a 'French Silicon Valley in Brittany').[26] Lerner also points at problems with 'capture' (ie, industry 'grabbing' the direct/indirect subsidies the government hands out, eg in the form of investments). One of the examples he gives comes from Australia, where the Australian Building on Information Technology Strengths (BITS) programme from the early 2000s was trying to use incubators and accelerators funded by the government to channel money into tech startups;[27] the problem was that most of the funding went into the administration and running of the incubators (ie, they became bureaucratic and sunk costs) rather than fuelling startup growth.

The conclusion of most experts, however, is not that the government should stay out of financing startups completely. In fact, States can bring real value to the world of venture capital, which is also the consensus among our interviewees. A recent study by Brander et al[28] of cross-country data (from US and Europe to Asia) including 5,000 funds (with about 10 per cent of those funds having received at least some government money) found that government sponsored VCs (GVCs) have an important role to play. When they are part of the investment mix (ie, invest together with private funders) portfolio companies tend to outperform companies which only received private investment (measured in terms of likelihood of exit/IPO and overall funding received). A study by Guerini and Quas[29] with a specific focus on Europe examining the effect of GVCs on company performance confirmed these findings. They explain the potential for an overall positive effect with reference to the potential to 'screen and certify' startups and crowding-in private capital. Specifically, they found that a company which received VC through a vehicle which is (at least partially) funded by government money is three times more likely to attract private capital subsequently. Government co-investments (ie, always together with and following private investors in the same funding round) in the UK (as part of the ongoing angel co-investment fund) further confirmed the potential for government money to attract private money – and more generally to close existing funding gaps.[30]

[26] J Lerner, *Boulevard of Broken Dreams – Why Public Efforts to Boost Entrepreneurship and Venture Capital have failed, and what to do about it* (Princeton, Princeton University Press, 2009) 74 ff; VCs exist (economically speaking) to reduce such information uncertainties, ie they are a specific type of investor equipped with the right kind of network and expertise to overcome the kind of 'incompetence' described here. Long-standing research has proven this attribute of VCs (see R Amit and J Brander, 'Why do Venture Capital firms exist? Theory and Canadian evidence' (1998) 9026(97) *Journal of Business Venturing* 441–66.

[27] Lerner (n 26) 84 f.

[28] JA Brander, Q Du and T Hellmann, 'The Effects of Government-Sponsored Venture Capital: International Evidence' (2015) 19 *Review of Finance* 571–618.

[29] M Guerini and A Quas, 'Governmental venture capital in Europe: Screening and certification' (2016) 31(2) *Journal of Business Venturing* 175–95.

[30] RO Baldock and C Mason, 'The role of government co-investment funds in the supply of entrepreneurial finance: An assessment of the early operation of the UK angel co-investment fund' 35(3) *Environment and Planning C: Government and Policy* 434–56.

The above evidence suggests that government money can be *good* money for VCs and startups, even if cynicism remains over direct investment. What this means concretely in Europe, is that the best way to address the 'innovation funding gap'[31] and bolster global competitiveness is to focus on making the venture capital market efficient.[32] In short, Europe should double down on its role as an indirect investor and an LP. Europe already has a successful history of being an LP with the European Investment Fund's[33] VC programme which has grown into the biggest (cornerstone) LP for VCs since its inception in 1994.[34]

That's not to say that this is a panacea. A recent assessment of the EU's VC intervention by the European Court of Auditors[35] found significant flaws in its current operation. From the lack of a comprehensive investment strategy[36] to missing impact measurement[37] and confusion around the variety of instruments,[38] the auditors propose re-focusing the EU and EIF VC activities. Their main recommendations are to put evaluations in place following the design of a comprehensive strategy (giving certainty to where the money should go geographically, into which sectors and with what goals)[39] and a streamlining of programmes in the hands of the EIF.

From our primary data, we want to supplement these recommendations with three concrete proposals as to where some of the strategy and evaluation in particular can be strengthened, for the benefit of the European ecosystem as a whole: first, focus on future-proofing European industries, secondly, enable a long-term time horizon (for some instruments) and thirdly, impose success metrics beyond just financial returns.

A. Focus on Future-proofing European Industries

The aforementioned 2019 audit of the EU's VC activities explicitly found that the market need (eg, for investment) was mostly not measured and specified ex-ante

[31] T Tyková, M Borell and TA Kroencke, 'Potential of Venture Capital in the European Union' (2012) *Study requested by the European Parliament, Directorate General for Internal Policies Policy Department A: Economic and Scientific Policy Industry, Research and Energy*, IP/A/ITRE/ST/2011-11, PE 475.088, www.europarl.europa.eu/RegData/etudes/etudes/join/2012/475088/IPOL-ITRE_ET(2012)475088_EN.pdf.

[32] ibid 15.

[33] European Investment Fund, 'EIF – Who We Are' (*EIF*, accessed 4 March 2021) www.eif.org/who_we_are/index.htm.

[34] H Kraemer-Eis, A Botsari, S Gvetadze and F Lang, 'EIF VC Survey 2018 – Fund managers' perception of EIF's value added' (2018) 51 *EIF Working Paper* www.eif.org/news_centre/publications/EIF_Working_Paper_2018_51.htm.

[35] European Court of Auditors, 'Centrally managed EU interventions for venture capital: in need of more direction' (2019) 17 *Special Report*; see p 13 for an overview.

[36] ibid 23.

[37] ibid 21.

[38] ibid 32.

[39] ibid 42 ff.

for many of the initiatives. Alongside the absence of a clear investment strategy, the money did not necessarily end up where it could make the biggest impact (eg, in less developed VC markets or specific high-growth/high-risk sectors of the economy).[40] Many of our interviewees spoke similarly about the lack of vision and leadership in the European VC ecosystem more generally, and proposed *focused* government interventions and incentives. Hannah, a VC in a German fund, stated:

> We need more money in deep tech, in business models that are not that VC-compatible; they might need longer development periods, a different perspective on things ... there is a market failure here that needs to be taken up by the state indeed!.

Hannah explicitly mentions deep tech as a market opportunity (and many industry reports confirm this; Dealroom announced 2021 to be the 'year of deep tech').[41] Others talked about clean tech or health and bio tech as other areas where VC money in Europe is often lacking but where there are big (technological and innovation-driven) opportunities. These are all areas which have (with the exception of a brief and mostly disastrous first cleantech boom in the 2000s) been underfunded by European VCs, which often require more (initial) investment and at times a longer-term investment horizon (see below for more on this subject).

A recent study by the European Investment Bank[42] concluded that more funding for what they call key enabling technologies (KETs) – from nanotech and advanced materials, to photonics, and advanced manufacturing systems, what often is classed as 'deep tech' – in Europe was desperately needed, particularly growth capital and financing for companies without significant revenue.[43] Similar issues – a scale-up funding gap, the lack of patient capital, missing focus on the sector – have been diagnosed in a 2020 World Economic Forum report[44] focused on European growth companies in sustainability, green tech and climate tech. While 'European innovation look[s] primed for unprecedented growth [...] given Europe's legacy of industrial excellence', without support, companies face the 'danger of succumbing to the funding "valley of death"'.[45]

In reality, such 'ecosystem gaps' have been addressed with a government-sponsored fund-of-fund models or blended finance (grants and equity investments) approaches in other geographies since the 1990s. For example, in

[40] European Court of Auditors (n 35) 18–23.

[41] Dealroom, *2021: The year of Deep Tech* (*dealroom.co*, 2021).

[42] S Gigler, 'Financing the Deep Tech Revolution: How investors assess risks' (2018) European Investment Bank Report, www.eib.org/attachments/pj/study_on_financing_the_deep_tech_revolution_en.pdf.

[43] ibid 6.

[44] World Economic Forum, 'Bridging the Gap in European Scale-up Funding: The Green Imperative in an Unprecedented Time' (2020) *Community Paper*, in collaboration with KPMG, www3.weforum.org/docs/WEF_Bridging_the_Gap_in_European_Scale_up_Funding_2020.pdf.

[45] ibid 3.

2017, Jordan (supported by the World Bank) set up its Innovative Startup and SME Fund (ISSF) with roughly USD 100m to invest in VC funds (and directly in startups). Modelled on successful examples from around the world – such as Israel's Yozma fund (launched in 1993) or Singapore's Early Stage Venture Fund (ESVF) – the goal was to foster entrepreneurship financially (crowding in private money) but also to build up the (governance, regulatory and administrative) ecosystem. Overall, the government's involvement in this project went as far as the co-design of the programme and putting in place the policy (initiatives, for example around GP/LP legal fund structuring). Meanwhile, the day-to-day of the investment decision making is left to a private fund manager with a 15-year time horizon. What is special is that the ISSF has a mandate to invest in 'lagging regions, underserved sectors and underserved groups such as youth and women entrepreneurs', and seems to be achieving against its mandate.

Setting a clear agenda seems possible and an earlier McKinsey and WEF report[46] makes clear suggestions in this direction for Europe. First, the authors suggest that a pan-European initiative needs to leverage key industrial strengths of Europe (from healthcare to advanced manufacturing) to develop deep tech innovations in (local) sandboxes; this could lead to a strong influx of money into key European technology sectors by bridging a risky funding gap in the market. Secondly, they also explicitly suggest focusing on bringing more diversity into the ecosystem (eg, by reserving government funding for female entrepreneurs or GPs[47]) to build up the existing talent pool that has driven prosperity.

There have been some encouraging signs to set and scale up such agendas. The Danish Growth Fund, for instance, invests equity and provides loans and guarantees for SMEs in collaboration with private partners with a strong focus on 'deep tech'. An early assessment has shown that the DGF 'attracts additional investments, which would not otherwise have been made and there is no sign of DGFs investment crowding out private investments'.[48] Further positive outcomes include capacity building in VC fund managers as well as the development of a sustainable ecosystem through its indirect (FoF) investments. Similarly, Germany recently announced a dedicated deep tech fund (under the High Tech Gründerfond brand) and France set aside 300m for VCs to distribute specifically for climate investments.[49]

[46] World Economic Forum, 'Innovate Europe Competing for Global Innovation Leadership' (2019) *Insight Report*, in collaboration with McKinsey & Company, www3.weforum.org/docs/WEF_Innovate_Europe_Report_2019.pdf?utm_source=Nicolas.

[47] ibid 28.

[48] G Murray and M Cowling, 'Evaluation of the Danish Growth Fund Evaluation of activities, 2010–2012' (2014) 6, https://ore.exeter.ac.uk/repository/handle/10871/14883.

[49] Maddyness, 'L'État prévoit 300 millions d'euros pour financer les GreenTech' (*Maddyness*, 23 February 2021) www.maddyness.com/2021/02/23/plan-numerique-environnement-300-millions-greentech/.

B. Make Long-term Investments (and Set the Right Incentives for Others to Do So)

A Danish policy maker with a focus on and background in the VC world put it very simply in an interview with us: the government should 'enable deals that wouldn't have been possible otherwise'. What we heard repeatedly is not only that certain sectors with specific strategic importance and opportunity were underfunded but also that certain kinds of funding aren't available: patient or longer-term capital.

While the usual VC funding life cycle within the existing GP-LP structure follows a standard timeline of 10+/-2 years, a variety of investments, specifically in the bio tech and deep tech space (see above) require a longer-term horizon. Given the risk profile connected with the illiquidity of the investments (LPs are not able to flexibly withdraw money from VC funds before the fund life cycle ends) commercial LPs – fund-of-funds, endowments and foundations – are mostly not keen to extend this timeline. There is a clear gap which the government could fill. One UK-based VC investors put it to us in the following way:

> Governments could afford to put money down and not have it returned for 50 years; I have been shocked that Google never did this – one of the most frustrating conversations was with the Google X lot. They have to invest capital within 10 years, too. If Google doesn't do it – who else does: sovereign wealth funds. But they are only warming up to alternative assets ... I wonder whether the government could be a good funder of proprietary deep tech from their home nation ... investments that don't have to be returned within a long time frame.

This opinion on the viability of investing in crucial (and very high-risk/high-cost) deep tech experiments with government money is mirrored in the aforementioned EIB report: 'KETs projects, perhaps more than other segments, demand "patient" capital and we need to find innovative ways to finance them'.[50] How can the EU step in here (and ideally attract and incentivise private capital to follow)?

One part of a potential solution goes beyond the financing itself and into the wider regulatory and procurement ecosystem (see below), a different kind of (fund-of-)fund structure can also contribute to the development of this type of investment. We can see inspiration for this already active on the continent. In the UK, British Patient Capital was established in June 2018 with £2.5bn of government money as part of the British Business Bank (established explicitly to replace the EIF funding with the UK's exit from the EU). It explicitly focuses on 'a long-term patient capital strategy' (crowding in private capital such as pension funds into this asset class)[51] with a mandate to also invest in *evergreen* funds. Several

[50] Gigler (n 42) 3.
[51] See also World Economic Forum (n 44) 16.

evergreen VC funds have been announced in the last two years, from Draper Esprit in the UK, to Crista Galli in Denmark and 2050 in France; they are concerned with (mostly) advancing deep tech endeavours (tackling problems from health to climate) and use a rolling fund structure without a fixed payout period to be able to make longer-term investments. Another one of our interviewees, herself a senior official in a State-fund, called this approach – which she believed was something the State should engage in – the *marathon approach:*

> With the marathon approach, you would have one [VC] fund that takes you from pre-seed to exit [...] and you are looking at 25-30 years [...] this should complement the relay approach we are [closer to now] where a series of 10+2s funds invest in pre-seed/seed/A/B/+ [where] each is focusing on a unique aspect of growth in those particular phases who hand off to each other that works as a system to create patient sources of capital.

C. Make VCs Report (and Measure Them) on Returns and Social Benefit Metrics

Most assessments and reports conclude similarly: governments so far have a poor track record with setting the right targets and implementing useful (successful) metrics for VC investors. Going back to the European Court of Auditors' 2019 report, impact measurements of earlier EU VC interventions were 'insufficient' (eg, reporting simply on the number of funds supported and money spent); they lament that data collection was not pre-planned at setup, leading to a strong reliance on (ex-post) qualitative interviews over quantitative data.[52] Also, insufficient targets with regard to any meaningful outcome (including 'high returns')[53] were set. One of our interviewees, a former partner in a European State-sponsored VC, confirmed these criticisms from his experience:

> If you have a supervisory board that is state-led you have the problem that they set these specific [budget] guidelines but beyond that – they don't look whether the business is future proof, sustainable; if the basic numbers are okay they don't look at anything, they don't really do metrics well – that would take work and their incentives aren't aligned with that kind of work.

A starting point of how to finance innovation better would be to set clear and meaningful return metrics with every fund-of-fund investment in a VC fund. Best practice among LPs in the industry is to set a target for its VCs, such as '3x net money returns at the end of the fund life cycle'.[54] Additional metrics

[52] European Court of Auditors (n 35) 21.
[53] ibid 29.
[54] W Mead, 'Why Your Investor Might Pass On Your Next Fund – An LP's perspective on benchmarking in venture capital' (*Medium*, 20 April 2016) www.medium.com/sapphire-ventures-perspectives/why-your-investor-might-pass-on-your-next-fund-884dfc34f8d0.

around economic impact could be raised including jobs created, contribution to European GDP and the so-called leverage ratio, ie private capital attracted or crowded in. The World Bank sets goals in this way for its VC (and other) investments (eg, five times the amount of private capital invested as WB/state money). First steps have also been taken in recent European activities in this direction; the newly established European Innovation Council (EIC) in its vision paper is aiming for a leverage ratio of 1:3-1:5 of its own vs private VCs money in its investments (European Commission, 2020:10).

But building on our proposals above – funnelling money into future-proofing industries and enabling long-term investments – social benefit or impact metrics beyond financial or economic returns need to be thought through and implemented. Crucially, they should match metrics used to measure desired policy outcomes to ensure alignment between 'upstream' investment and 'downstream' market demand. Encouragingly, the Vision Roadmap also cites the ability for portfolio companies to contribute to the UN's sustainable development goals as targets. However, from speaking to several people close to the EIC, it's clear that precise social or policy outcomes are not a formal part of their investment thesis, and are instead an aspiration. As one German investor told us, non-financial metrics and KPIs are 'something [they] are looking into at this point; [they are] interested in measuring carbon/climate impact [and how the] EU GDP [grows] significantly [...] we can hopefully start measuring that at a later point'. Following up from recent EU legislation around SFDR,[55] one starting point for their fund-of-fund (and direct) investments would be strict due diligence, goal setting and reporting on ESG factors. Metrics such as the diversity of VC's own team (as well as its portfolio and boards) as well as carbon footprints (Scope 1-3) would be a starting point. Given European VC's big issues around a lack of diversity,[56] putting pressure on funds as an anchor investor such as the EIF would address a clear market failure. Other commentators[57] have recently called for even more far reaching 'sustainability metrics' including the emissions reduction potential.

Overall, however, we believe governmental or pan-European organisations should not only impose financial and non-financial metrics to ensure the success of their VC-investment programmes; they are also, given their strong position as LPs, already in a unique position to shift investment emphasis, best practice around ESG and to collect industry wide-data.

[55] SFDR stands for Sustainable Finance Disclosure Regulation; it is a reporting framework limited to 'sustainable investors' that was put in place in March 2021.

[56] Diversity VC, 'Diversity in UK Venture Capital 2019' (2019) https://diversity.vc/diversity-in-uk-venture-capital-2019/.

[57] D Visevic, 'Investors love data. So why not dig into sustainability metrics?' (*Sifted*, 18 February 2021) www.sifted.eu/articles/sustainability-metrics-vc/.

V. How Can We Build a European VC Ecosystem, Beyond Investments?

> If you want the ecosystem to grow you have to de-bottleneck simultaneously in different pinch points – that is ecosystem theory.
>
> Betty, policy and research lead, European State LP

Our interviews suggested that the State has a clear role in promoting a strong tech ecosystem beyond direct and LP investing. While LP investing as we have seen is established territory – the EIF has acted as a fund-of-funds via VCs for years,[58] and national equivalents like the British Business Bank pour more money into venture capital annually[59] – other parts of the ecosystem-making are less explored.

As Mazzucato[60] has previously identified, our research unearthed cynicism that Europe was as effective as it could be in taking a coherent approach, in particular ensuring that 'upstream' incentives (eg, the State providing capital as an LP) matched 'downstream' support (eg, procuring services and providing subsidies to promote market uptake). One former senior EU policy maker commented:

> Tinkering at the edges isn't enough; Europe needs to do more to use all of the tools at its disposal, from policy to procurement, to drive a strong ecosystem.

An holistic approach is particularly important for seeding markets that are strategically important for Europe, but are currently underserved by private investment. This is normally because they have one or more of the characteristics: they are innovation intensive, with long pay-off times, and difficult paths to commercialisation, often exceeding the 10+2 year return window of most VCs and at prohibitively high cost initially (see also section I(B) above). Another of our interviewees, a veteran European investor, represents the investor perspective on the same problem well: '[some of the DeepTech investments] I made as an angel 12 years ago haven't reached fruition. As investors generally can't see beyond 10 years, and policy is more reactionary, why would I make that bet again today?'

We propose that policy makers have a key role to play in addressing these challenges – again beyond investment – by giving certainty that allows for longer bets, and making markets with non-obvious financial inducements more attractive to enter into.[61]

[58] Tyková, Borell and Kroencke (n 31).

[59] British Business Bank, *UK Venture Capital – Financial Returns 2020* (2020) www.british-business-bank.co.uk/wp-content/uploads/2020/11/BBB-VC-Returns-Report-2020-FINAL-1.pdf.

[60] Mazzucato, *The Entrepreneurial State* (n 15).

[61] D Popp, J Pless, I Haščič and N Johnstone, 'Innovation and Entrepreneurship in the Energy Sector' (2020). 27145 *NBER Working Paper* www.nber.org/system/files/working_papers/w27145/w27145.pdf.

A. Introduce Full System Policy Making with Holistic Goals

State-set incentives and subsidies have been crucial for seeding markets for vital technologies. Europe's climate journey provides a fantastic example of what is possible. In 1990, Finland was the first country in the world to introduce a carbon tax. Since then, 16 European countries have followed suit, implementing carbon taxes that range from less than €1 per metric ton of carbon emissions in Ukraine and Poland to over €100 in Sweden.[62] At the time of writing, the EU carbon price had hit a record high of over €45 a ton.[63]

Alongside putting a valuation on the externality of carbon, so that the market could price it in, the second secret to Europe's (relative) success was aggressive decarbonisation policies. This pushed the demand-side and procurement markets towards low carbon options, bootstrapping and galvanising investment yet further. In this vein it is encouraging to see the European Commission denoting €1tn within the Green Deal,[64] and an explicit recognition in the European Innovation Council's initial grants of the Green Deal (even if not based on specific metrics as discussed above).[65] However, a recent report by CleanTech for Europe analysing the state of European cleantech has suggested there is still room to improve conditions for VCs.[66] While the EU attracts 23 per cent of global seed capital for cleantech, that number falls to 6.9 per cent of global growth equity capital (compared with 54.3 per cent going to North America). The report finds that 'this lack of scale-up capital is a consequence of a demand-side challenge for EU cleantech innovation: there are not enough EU wide demand signals for adoption of green products and solutions'.

It is this 'full system' policy making – focusing on both the supply and demand side – that drives real change. As Europe works to iterate its climate ecosystem, the next step is to use policy to put a price on other challenges the market can respond to: health outcomes, welfare and equality. Inspiration on the indicators that drive progress against these challenges can be found in the UN's Sustainable Development Goals.

[62] The World Bank, 'Carbon Pricing Dashboard' (*World Bank*, 2021) https://carbonpricingdashboard.worldbank.org/.

[63] N Chestey, 'EU carbon price hits record high above 45 euros a tonne' (*Reuters*, 20 April 2021) www.reuters.com/business/energy/eu-carbon-price-hits-record-high-above-45-euros-tonne-2021-04-20/.

[64] European Commission, 'The Just Transition Mechanism: making sure no one is left behind' (*ec.europa.eu*, 2019) www.ec.europa.eu/info/strategy/priorities-2019-2024/european-green-deal/actions-being-taken-eu/just-transition-mechanism_en.

[65] European Commission, 'EASME – Executive Agency for SMEs' (*ec.europa.eu*, 2020) https://wayback.archive-it.org/12090/20210412123959/https://ec.europa.eu/easme/en/.

[66] Cleantech Group, *Seizing the EU's man on the moon moment* (2020) www.cleantechforeurope.com/download-report.

B. Supplement with Long-Term, Trustworthy Institutions

Converting policy goals into metrics that the market can respond to, and aligning upstream and downstream policy making is a start, but is insufficient on its own to engender investor confidence for hard-to-reach sectors. The EU27 is an endlessly changing patchwork of governments all with political cycles that are often too short lived to provide certainty for long-term change. Even at the supra-national level of the EU institutions themselves, change comes every four to five years.

By contrast, the average biotech company takes four years to build a prototype and create a marketable product (before any revenue generation).[67] This is a good illustration of the long pay off times that innovation intensive businesses require. The combination of that long lead-in time with the regulatory whims of policy making means private investors are unlikely to stake their capital to solve hard challenges.

One venture capitalist and former policy maker we spoke to remarked that

> navigating government and policy is a really specialist skill set that carries its own language, why would most investors gamble [their portfolio], playing on a pitch they can't control?

Alongside rebooting the adversarial culture of entrepreneurs vs regulation (see section VI below), the answer is to mitigate the risk of unpredictable policy making as an unwelcome and unfamiliar externality for investors. This requires the establishment of long-term, trustworthy institutions that can set the direction of travel for investors outside of political cycles.

Good inspiration for institutional success can be found from the UK's Committee on Climate Change. In 2008, the UK Government established the non-departmental public body, the Committee on Climate Change (CCC). The CCC's role as defined in their statutes is twofold:[68] first, to conduct independent analysis into climate change science, economics and policy; secondly, to provide independent advice on setting and meeting carbon budgets including by projections of possible decarbonisation pathways.

Vesting certainty of tackling climate change with an institution outside of the politics of government has acted as a powerful incentive for UK politicians to stay the course on reaching net zero. Partially as a result of this strong, long-term policy direction, the UK has decarbonised its electricity grid faster than any other major economy over the last decade.[69] The data shows a corresponding knock-on

[67] Boston Consulting Group, *The Dawn of the Deep Tech Ecosystem. BCG Henderson Institute* (2019) http://media-publications.bcg.com/BCG-The-Dawn-of-the-Deep-Tech-Ecosystem-Mar-2019.pdf.

[68] Climate Change Committee, 'About the Climate Change Committee' (*The CCC*, 2021) www.theccc.org.uk/about/.

[69] The Economist, 'How Britain decarbonised faster than any other rich country' (*The Economist*, 15 February 2021) www.economist.com/britain/2021/02/15/how-britain-decarbonised-faster-than-any-other-rich-country.

effect for VC appetite too. In contrast with the EU figures given above, the UK has attracted 4.8 per cent of global growth equity for cleantech,[70] over two-thirds the amount attracted by the entire EU27. This is a powerful lesson: Europe must see enticing demand side policy and institutional certainty as two of its key levers to crowd in VC.

C. Leverage Procurement

Every year, over 250,000 public authorities in the EU spend around 14 per cent of GDP (c.€2 trillion per year) on the purchase of services, works and supplies (European Commission, 2021c). That puts the annual pan-European procurement budget at 200x the total budget of the European Innovation Council for the period 2021–27.

Multiple interviewees spoke of procurement as the most underused tool in Europe's armoury. As mentioned in the first part of this paper, the US Government's role as a procurer of technology from Silicon Valley was critical to the development of the ecosystem. Procurement underpinned all stages of a technology being developed and tested; then supported it through commercialisation and competitiveness. Madelin has argued strongly that innovative procurement should offer companies a bridge across Europe's 'Valley of Death'.[71]

There is limited aggregated data on procurement, and particular its impact on benefiting companies. That said, Atomico's State of European Tech report[72] gives a flavour of the landscape, and shows a mixed picture. Year-on-year, startups' share of the total annual contract value for public healthcare procurement has increased markedly in some European economies (in the UK 51 per cent to 60 per cent, in Germany 67 per cent to 69 per cent, in the Netherlands 39 per cent to 77 per cent). Elsewhere, SME share has dropped (in France 52 per cent to 46 per cent, in Italy 52 per cent to 46 per cent, in Portugal 54 per cent to 44 per cent).

However, interviewees felt that Europe was falling short of its potential. One former senior policy maker commented that: 'for the most part, procurement contracts do not cater for innovative solutions, but are biased towards those that are delivered by traditional organisations with a track record'.

Interviewees felt Europe faced three problems in procuring effectively. First, that procurement needs to be used more flexibly, to consider the potential upside of procuring from higher-risk but more innovative companies and not just the downside of greater uncertainty. Secondly, that it should take a strategic approach to using procurement to build ecosystems that deliver innovations of strategic

[70] Cleantech Group (n 66).

[71] R Madelin and D Ringrose, *Opportunity now: Europe's mission to innovate* (Luxembourg, The Publications Office of the European Union, 2016).

[72] Atomico, 'The State of European Tech 2020' (2020) https://2020.stateofeuropeantech.com/chapter/state-european-tech-2020/.

importance where it has the potential to lead globally – per the KETs.[73] Thirdly, from demographics that are traditionally underserved by the market.

This is no secret to policy makers. The European Commission has identified this as a longstanding issue in its own strategy:[74]

> [Procurement] can enable investment in the real economy and stimulate demand to increase competitiveness based on innovation and digitalisation … It can also support the transition to a resource-efficient, energy-efficient and circular economy … and foster sustainable economic development and more equal, inclusive societies.

Similarly, its Start Up Nation Standard[75] demands that 'there are no legal or administrative impediments that would put startups /scaleups at a disadvantage compared to other participants in innovation procurement opportunities. Public buyers and procurement services are officially encouraged to procure innovations from startups'.

More recently, rhetoric from Internal Markets Commissioner Thierry Breton and Europe's recent digital strategy (*Shaping Europe's Digital Future*) have placed heavy emphasis on using State support to build European tech champions.[76] The question is how. In our conversations, several interviewees remarked that procurement was the only way to achieve this – emulating the Chinese model. A leading European venture capitalist, for instance, described what a European spin on this process could look like:

> First, you open up the market by regulatory reform, tax cuts or 'buy European' procurement and invite entrepreneurs to compete. Second you wait until competition determines the winner. Finally, you support the winner with huge investment and exercise of soft power to compete globally.

As many have pointed out, including the Centre for European Reform,[77] this kind of intervention is a double-edged sword. Some investors felt that using State apparatus to drive scale and growth to homegrown tech shows Europe is a good place for VCs to do business, and opens up an enormous demand-side market. However, others felt that too much manipulation of procurement would upset a perceived level playing field, as prone to count investors out as in. A policy expert on startups summarised the concern nicely in an interview with us: 'it's difficult to put Europe-first [approach] without putting off non-Europeans'.

What is clear, however, is that when it comes to boosting innovative businesses using procurement, Europe can do more. Currently it risks over-indexing on keeping traditional 'European Champions' on life support with its procurement

[73] Gigler (n 42).

[74] European Commission, 'Communication From the Commission To the European Parliament, the Council, the European Economic and Social Committee and the Committee of the Regions – Making Public Procurement work in and for Europe' COM (2017) 572 final.

[75] European Commission, 'Declaration on the EU Startup Nations Standard of Excellence' (2021).

[76] Johnson (n 22).

[77] J Springford, 'Insight Should the EU develop "European champions" to fend off Chinese competition?' (*The 17 SDGs* [*United Nations*] 2021) sdgs.un.org/goals.

process, and failing to use its strongest asset to help startups over the 'Valley of Death'. A stronger State-led demand side market would bolster VC appetite in regulated markets.

VI. How Can We Use Europe's Natural Cultural Strengths and Reputation as a Regulator to its Advantage?

> Europe is culturally rich, but not united when it comes to innovation and technology. That is holding us back.
>
> Partner, head of research, European top-tier VC

So far, this chapter has considered the role of investment, procurement power and accompanying policy at the State's (and union's) disposal to drive an effective ecosystem and lead venture capital to 'good' outcomes. But as history shows, the quantifiable elements of a strong ecosystem are only half the story: Silicon Valley's secret sauce is as much cultural as it is economic and political.

In contrast to Silicon Valley, Europe is an overlapping mesh of different norms, policies, languages and cultures. The majority of people we spoke to felt that this was both an advantage and a disadvantage. The same investor who provided the opening statement for this section commented 'creativity comes from diversity of thought, and in that way, Europe is well equipped', but later observed '[unlike the US] entrepreneurs and investors [in Europe] have to scale a business to 27 different marketplaces'. This sums up the predicament Europe faces: how to reap the benefits of a diverse range of perspectives and skills, including traditional local strengths – eg financial services in the UK; manufacturing in Germany etc – while mitigating the downsides of a fragmented marketplace that can be hard to navigate.

The challenge is significant: European policy makers need to overcome a trust gap among investors and entrepreneurs. Atomico's State of European Tech report 2020 found that 23 per cent of venture capitalists and 19 per cent of founders thought the concerns of startups and scale-ups were being heard by policy makers, compared with 34 per cent and 36 per cent respectively who thought they weren't. The European Court of Auditors suggests several causes that may induce a lack of trust, not least that the Commission's current approach 'clearly favours the most developed venture capital markets, leading to a concentration of investments, which does not contribute fully towards a pan-European venture capital market'.[78]

To tackle this, our conversations on culture, and resultant findings, centred around discussion on how to build a more unified identity for the EU that can act

[78] European Court of Auditors (n 35) 42.

as a 'shop window' for global investors and entrepreneurs, but without destroying local ecosystems

A. Creating a Cohesive and Cultural Identity for European Tech …

The EU is widely known as a leading global regulator. In recent years it has taken the first step in regulating data privacy through the General Data Protection Regulation (GDPR)[79] and Artificial Intelligence through its AI Strategy.[80] Next on the list are novel competition and content rules for the digital sector in the form of the Digital Markets Act and Digital Services Act.[81] Several interviewees observed this approach to regulating 'blank spaces' is at odds with promoting a well-funded and healthy ecosystem, and can often act as a turn off to investors. One European investor commented that the European tech sector is 'best known for its red tape rather than its innovative companies'. As many academics have pointed out[82] it's certainly true that one of the keys to Silicon Valley's success was its lack of rules (and decreasing regulation as discussed above). To many people we spoke to, the EU's identity as a regulator is therefore at odds with the myth of what allows entrepreneurs and startups to thrive: a bloc more interested in exporting global norms and creating obstacles than allowing innovation to run free.

However, others felt that its focus on rule-making was its true strength: 'innovation in hard areas, like climate, like health require strong rules and clear long-term governance. Europe is good at coming up with rules, and that should be good for investors and entrepreneurs [in these areas]'. This chimes with the views of Mazzucato[83] and others that the State should act as a 'market maker' rather than regulator, and that the next wave of innovation will require close concordance between regulators and entrepreneurs as technology increasingly starts to penetrate regulated spaces.[84]

[79] Regulation (EU) 2016/679 of the European Parliament and of the Council, of 27 April 2016, on the protection of natural persons with regard to the processing of personal data and on the free movement of such data, and repealing Directive 95/46/EC (General Data Protection Regulation) [2016] OJ L 119/1.

[80] European Commission, 'Europe fit for the Digital Age: Commission proposes new rules and actions for excellence and trust in Artificial Intelligence' (*ec.europa.eu*, 2021) www.ec.europa.eu/commission/presscorner/detail/en/ip_21_1682.

[81] European Commission, 'The Digital Services Act package' (*ec.europa.eu*, 2021) http://digital-strategy.ec.europa.eu/en/policies/digital-services-act-package.

[82] See for instance O'Mara (n 6).

[83] Mazzucato (n 15).

[84] See eg E Burfield and JD Harrison, *Regulatory Hacking: A Playbook for Startups* (London, Penguin, 2018).

Correspondingly, facing existential threats from future pandemics, climate change and the political fallout of inequality, many (see eg the writings of Marc Andressen[85] and Tim O'Reily[86]) have argued that we are at a pivotal point where the role of the entrepreneur will cease to be building consumer products, and start solving 'hard to reach' and regulated challenges. Solving these challenges requires certain policy and institutional maturity, both of which Europe is well set up for. As a European VC partner and former policy maker Nicolas Colin has observed:[87]

> Up to this point, the US has been a clear winner of the first part of the race (growing successful tech companies), but it didn't seem really interested in tackling the challenge of institutional innovation … As for Europe, well, it's the exact opposite. So far we have failed at growing successful tech companies with a clear shot at dominating their market at the global level. On the other hand, many people in Europe are interested in the second half of the race: building new institutions so that the Entrepreneurial Age is more inclusive and more sustainable. Many of us are working hard on catching up in the first half, in hopes that maybe after that we'll be able to start working on the second half with the right tools.

To take advantage of this shift, the EU should play a leading role in reframing the relationship between regulation and innovation, to one of cooperation rather than adversarialism in the areas where it has competency and can provide long-term signals to the market, like climate, transport, financial services and data-driven innovation. Crucially, many respondents felt this means it should stop talking out of both sides of its mouth: simultaneously talking up the harms of technology, while professing a desire to see the European startup sector flourish. As one member of the startup ecosystem told us: 'it's easier to see the notion of digital sovereignty as a threat rather than a help'.

B. But Avoid Destroying Local Ecosystems

Most interviewees pointed out that the majority of innovation did not take place at a pan-European level but in the clusters that have organically developed across the continent. Many feared that action at an EU level could be hugely damaging to these nascent ecosystems. This tension, between the desire for regulatory harmonisation and over-regulation from the top down, is one that is keenly felt by start and scale-ups.

[85] M Andreessen, 'It's Time To Build' (*a16z podcast*, 18 April 2020) http://future.a16z.com/podcasts/its-time-to-build/.

[86] T O'Reilly, 'The End of Silicon Valley as We Know It?' (*O'Reilly blog*, 11 March 2021) www.oreilly.com/radar/the-end-of-silicon-valley-as-we-know-it/.

[87] N Colin, 'How Governments Can Deal With the K-Shaped Recovery' (*European Straits*, 25 February 2021) https://europeanstraits.substack.com/p/how-governments-can-deal-with-the?utm_source=url.

For example, Atomico's State of European Tech report shows that regulatory fragmentation is the most pressing concern felt by companies of <10 employees (48 per cent); 11-100 employees (50 per cent); and >100 employees (55 per cent) limiting the growth of European start and scale-ups compared with their American and Chinese counterparts, ahead of funding limitations and public procurement requirements. However, many people we spoke to also expressed concern for building one size fits all rulesets. One of the European investors we interviewed summarised the optimal balance: '[it should be] up to the EU to enact tough rules to provide startups with a level playing field, make it easier to scale up across borders, [then leave it] to local players to make an ecosystem'. In other words, the EU should foster the framing environment and long-term certainty where it can, but the culture for the hubs should come from localities.

VII. Conclusions

What we learnt from our interviews, from recent events and contextual reports and pieces of research is nothing new but still surprising for many: Europe should *not* try to emulate the American model of the military industrial complex which led to the success of Silicon Valley. There should be a new, distinctly European, way to build a strong VC and innovation ecosystem. This will require European States to leave some of their reservations behind when it comes to order and risk-mitigation. As one senior European policy official told us: 'we have to create a license for dirt and for mess in order to enable innovativeness to get access to tax payers money'. Inefficiencies – and lost money – is the nature of the game in venture capital. To date, Europe has been bold as regards its policy making of innovative sectors, and is rightly respected as a global leader. It should now ensure its strategic prioritisation and boldness in policy making is emulated in its support for startups and venture euros.

This will require long-term thinking in terms of big missions (eg, to tackle climate change or deep tech challenges) and requires a more unified culture and ecosystem within which to achieve them. To crowd-in private capital, continued investment and capital is needed – both funnelled through existing fund-of-fund structures like the EIF or State-level vehicles like KfW or BBB and as a market-maker with procurement-money. Europe has made steady progress in this regard.

But this is not enough on its own. European institutions and States should embrace their strengths in order to foster a unique European VC ecosystem: setting conditions, standards, rules, regulations and the right incentives. In particular, we need clear targets for strategic success and impact measurement for the State to track progress (eg, return targets, GDP contribution, jobs created, regional growth) and non-financial metrics that the market willingly factors in (eg, incentives to reduce carbon, and build strong health and equality (DEI) outcomes).

The levers to do this require a 'whole system approach', we need to use policy and money in tandem *rather* than against each other.

Our recommendations to achieve this are:

1. Europe should largely steer clear of direct investment, but look to leverage and build on its position as an LP to direct capital towards better economic and social outcomes aligned with its policy goals.
2. Europe should create institutions and sources of patient capital that outstrip existing investment and political timelines. This certainty should provide confidence for entrepreneurs and investors thinking long, in 'hard to reach', regulated and strategically important sectors like climate, biotech and health.
3. Harmonised rulesets, procurement potential and cultural difference should be considered strengths to be harnessed rather than weaknesses to be covered up. Europe needs to lean into its reputation of norm setting to become a market maker.

12

Building an EU Venture Capital Market: What About Corporate Law?

CASIMIRO A NIGRO AND ALPEREN A GÖZLÜGÖL

I. Introduction

Venture capital (VC) has developed a solid reputation for seeding firms that disrupt market equilibria and consumer habits, making profound contributions to job creation and economic growth.

Policy makers around the globe have consequently been striving to create vibrant VC markets. The last 30 years of European policy initiatives and regulatory measures are a case in point. These initiatives have focused chiefly on stimulating VC supply by means of public interventions and by facilitating capital raising across borders.

As recent scholarship has pointed out, however, the development of a VC market also requires a flexible corporate law, so that venture capitalists and entrepreneurs can address market failures that stand in the way of financing innovative projects and tailor their investments to the specific exigencies of the VC business model.

This prompts an inquiry into whether European policy makers have considered the role of corporate law in their attempts to build a VC market. It seems that they did not. Despite the EU's engagement with corporate law in general and with improving the legal framework for small and medium firms, including startups, policy making at the European level has largely ignored the role that corporate law can, depending on its relative rigidity or flexibility, play in hindering or supporting VC investments. The reason for this seems to lie in their narrow approach to policy making in the area. Disregarding the role of corporate law and the importance of institutional complementarity in building a VC market, European policy makers' approach to VC-related discussion may prove problematic, as it can lead to the adoption of inadequate policy recipes.

This chapter unfolds as follows. Section II briefly describes the VC business model. Section III provides an overview of issues that venture capitalists and entrepreneurs have to deal with as they negotiate the terms of their contract, referencing the contractual terms that are of common use in the US to address them. Section IV explains why corporate law matters for VC investments. Section V summarises the main actions that the EU has undertaken to encourage VC investments. Section VI reviews these actions and demonstrates that the EU seems to have thus far missed crucial aspects of the relevance of corporate law in stimulating VC investments. Section VII concludes.

II. The VC World

Innovative entrepreneurship is the main driver of long-term, sustainable macro-economic growth.[1]

Severe frictions in the market for entrepreneurial finance, however, generate allocative inefficiencies. After exhausting their limited resources, many innovative firms are left to languish in 'Death Valley' as they slowly fade away.[2]

While banks have ameliorated this funding shortage to some extent and new technologies may also do so,[3] empirical research concludes that the financing of innovative firms has generally been the prerogative of VC.[4]

The VC industry consists of financial intermediaries specialising in providing financial and non-financial support to early stage, high-tech firms with significant growth potential in order to generate value within a relatively short timeframe.[5]

Each financial intermediary incorporates one or more investment funds, which take on the form of a limited liability partnership (or functionally equivalent organisational scheme). The intermediary itself takes the position of general partner through a formally independent legal entity with limited liability, whilst the fund investors – ranging from pension funds, insurance companies, foundations, and family offices, to high-net-worth individuals – assume the position of limited partners.[6]

[1] See R Solow, 'A Contribution to the Theory of Economic Growth' (1956) 70 *Quarterly Journal of Economics* 65–94.

[2] See J Lerner, 'The Governance of New Firms: A Functional Perspective' in NR Lamoreaux and KL Sokoloff (eds), *Financing Innovation in the United States – 1870 to Present* (Cambridge MA, MIT Press, 2007) 405–32, 406.

[3] For the important role of banks in stimulating innovation, see R Cole, DJ Cumming and D Li, 'Do Banks or VCs Spur Small Firm Growth?' (2016) 41 *Journal of International Financial Markets, Institutions and Money* 60–72. For the emerging data regarding the role of new technologies, particularly through the so-called 'crowdfunding' (in its various forms), see F Hervé and A Schwienbacher, 'Crowdfunding and Innovation' (2018) 32 *Journal of Economic Surveys* 1514–30.

[4] See also for further references, PA Gompers and J Lerner, 'The Venture Capital Revolution' (2001) 15 *Journal of Economic Perspectives* 145–68; and J Lerner and R Nanda, 'Venture Capital's Role in Financing Innovation: What We Know and How Much We still Need to Learn' (2020) 34 *Journal of Economic Perspectives* 237–61.

[5] See eg B Zider, 'How Venture Capital Works' (1998) 76 *Harvard Business Review* 131–39, 132; and WA Sahlman, 'The Structure and Governance of Venture-capital Organizations' (1990) 27 *Journal of Financial Economics* 473–521.

[6] See eg Zider (n 5) 133.

The separation of control and ownership inherent in the adoption of the limited liability partnership paves the way for opportunism, which in turn calls for a complex private ordering-based response. Contracts in this area therefore include, among others, covenants of various types, co-investment schemes, compensation arrangements, distribution provisions,[7] and, perhaps most importantly, a term setting fixed date for the mandatory dissolution of each VC fund, so that its lifespan will generally run from 8 to 10 years.[8]

This term 'de facto' implies a review period during which VC fund investors decide whether to re-entrust their capital with the same VC fund manager or to reallocate it towards a new one or even another asset class. At that crucial time, the performance of the VC fund's managers is subject to the market's assessment, which will be a fundamental determinant of the next capital raising campaign. VC fund managers who want to survive in a highly competitive market and thereby ensure their own long-term viability are therefore given powerful incentives to yield appropriate returns in a timely fashion.[9]

III. VC Investments

The dynamic between VC fund manager and VC fund investor affects the structure of the entire investment process. After raising capital from a variety of investors, VC fund managers select business projects based chiefly on their 'exit potential'.[10] VC fund managers then devote the first five years to nurturing their portfolio companies through a heavy 'hands-on' approach that stimulates growth within the short timeframe.[11] VC fund managers devote their remaining three to five years to cash in their investments through a variety of techniques such as: (1) initial public offerings (IPOs); (2) trade sales; (3) redemption of the venture capitalist's shares; or (4) liquidation – through bankruptcy, where appropriate – of the portfolio company (a so-called 'write-off').[12] Divestment typically generates highly skewed returns, with a relatively small number of 'winners' making up for the modest or non-existent returns of most of the portfolio.[13]

[7] For details and further references, see M Klausner and K Litvak, 'What Economists Have Taught Us about Venture Capital Contracting' (Stanford Law School John M. Olin Program in Law and Economics Working Paper 221/2001) (2001) 13–14, www.ssrn.com/abstract=280024. See also DJ Cumming and SA Johan, *Venture Capital and Private Equity Contracting*, 2nd edn (Oxford, Elsevier, 2014) 145–56 and 176–83.

[8] This duration range is stable despite the significant heterogeneity of the business projects to which VC extends its support. See Lerner and Nanda (n 4) 253.

[9] See RJ Gilson, 'Engineering a Venture Capital Market: Lessons from the American Experience' (2003) 55 *Stanford Law Review* 1089–1090 and 1091–92.

[10] See TT Tyebjee and AV Bruno, 'A Model of Venture Capitalist Investment Activity' (1984) 30 *Management Science* 1051–66, 1052–53.

[11] See eg Klausner and Litvak (n 7) 2–3 and 5–6.

[12] Cumming and Johan (n 7) 35.

[13] See eg Zider (n 5) 136.

In negotiating the terms of their cooperation with entrepreneurs, VC fund managers seek to address the market failures that generally prevent deals, as well as bargaining for terms that may accommodate the idiosyncratic timeline that governs the VC business model and allow for optimal portfolio diversification and portfolio value maximisation.

To this end, venture capitalists negotiate complex contracts with entrepreneurs, allocating cash flow- and control-rights that, being contingency-based, enable the venture capitalists to engage in adaptive decision-making and thereby adjust to the evolution of the business relationship.[14] They also enjoy largely disproportionate prerogatives with respect to their cash-flow rights. This allows for the acquisition of (principally) minority interests in portfolio companies and, hence, optimal portfolio diversification.[15] Moreover, they bargain for terms that expand their discretion in giving preferential treatment to one or more portfolio companies relative to others. Above all, 'contract' in this context seeks to intertwine the operational logic of the VC fund with that of VC-backed firms through so-called 'braiding'.[16] Braiding de facto embeds between the 'time to invest' with a focus on value-creation and a 'time to divest' dedicated to value-realisation, thereby trading-off contracting parties' shared ambition for value creation and the venture capitalist's unique need to generate liquidity in a timely manner.[17]

The aim of contracting parties to simultaneously pursue these goals, results in the adoption of a myriad of explicit and implicit arrangements,[18] whose overall richness and complexity, largely consistently with the predictions of financial contracting theory,[19] become apparent when observing the structure and contents of contracts governing VC-backed firms in the US and Delaware in particular.[20] Contracts assign venture capitalists conversion rights, liquidation preferences, board appointment and removal rights, share transfer rights, pre-emptive rights, buyout rights, redemption rights, registration rights, piggy-back rights, as well as

[14] See Gilson (n 9) 1078–84; and Klausner and Litvak (n 7) 7–11.

[15] See I Guler and MF Guillen, 'Institutions and the Internationalization of US Venture Capital Firms' (2010) 41 *Journal of International Business Studies* 105–205, 190.

[16] See Gilson (n 9) 1091.

[17] See above all, D Gordon Smith, 'The Exit Structure of Venture Capital' (2005) 53 *UCLA Law Review* 315–56, 317–18, but also passim; and, more recently, CA Nigro and JR Stahl, 'Venture Capital-backed Firms, Unavoidable Value-Destroying Trade Sales, and Flexible Fair Value Protections' (2021) 22 *European Business Organization Law Review* 39–86, 51–52.

[18] Such as the 'termination option', which grants the venture capitalist the right to divest once the VC-backed firm has entered its second phase and particularly as the VC fund's lifetime nears its end, regardless of the consequences that this decision may have on firm value. See also for references, Nigro and Stahl (n 17) 54–55.

[19] See the oft-cited work by SN Kaplan and P Strömberg, 'Financial Contracting Theory Meets the Real World: An Empirical Analysis of Venture Capital Contracts' (2003) 70 *Review of Economic Studies* 281–315.

[20] See B Broughman, JM Fried and D Ibrahim, 'Delaware Law as Lingua Franca: Theory and Evidence' (2014) 57 *Journal of Law and Economics* 865–95.

drag-along and tag-along rights. They also include bad leaver provisions, protective provisions, anti-dilution provisions, blank cheque shares provisions, ex ante waivers of fair value protections, fiduciary duty-based remedies and doctrines (such as the corporate opportunity doctrine), among others.[21]

IV. VC and Corporate Law

There is a broad-based though rather abstract consensus that building a VC market requires bringing together capital providers, entrepreneurs, and financial intermediaries.[22] It nonetheless remains unclear what the institutional framework required to attract them should look like.[23]

Despite this uncertainty, the literature does suggest that private ordering must play a central role. Among other things, private ordering enables venture capitalists and entrepreneurs to tailor the structure of their portfolio companies to address market failures, pave the way for optimal portfolio diversification and portfolio value maximisation, and follow the VC business model's idiosyncratic timeline.[24] This, however, presupposes a flexible corporate law.

The law and economics movement has given both theoretical and empirical credence to the importance of a flexible corporate law in allowing for contract formation in general.[25] Subsequent research has also underscored the importance of this flexibility for venture capitalists and entrepreneurs in particular,[26] as well as providing supporting empirical evidence.[27]

More recent and related scholarship has made theory-based attempts to investigate the correlation between the rigidity of a given corporate legal regime

[21] See chiefly, TH Maynard and DM Warren, *Business Planning: Financing the Start-up Business and Venture Capital Financing*, 2nd edn (New York, Wolters Kluwer, 2014) 479–615.

[22] This is the so-called 'simultaneity problem': see Gilson (n 9) 1070, 1090 and 1093.

[23] The literature has often stressed this point. For an overview of the relevant literature, see L Grilli, G Latifi and B Mrkajic, 'Institutional Determinants of Venture Capital Activity: An Empirically Driven Literature Review and a Research Agenda' (2019) 33 *Journal of Economic Surveys* 1094–1122.

[24] Gilson (n 9) 1069 (noting that 'the keystone of the U.S. venture capital market is private ordering').

[25] See R Romano, *The Genius of American Corporate Law* (Washington D.C., AEI Press, 1990); M Kahan, 'The Demand for Corporate Law: Statutory Flexibility, Judicial Quality, or Takeover Protection?' (2006) 22 *Journal of Law, Economics, and Organization* 340–65.

[26] See eg JA McCahery and EPM Vermeulen, 'High-tech Start-ups in Europe: The Effect of Regulatory Competition on the Emergence of New Business Forms' (2001) 7 *European Law Journal* 459–81, 464–67; as well as J Armour, 'Law, Innovation, and Finance' in JA McCahery and L Renneboog (eds), *Venture Capital Contracting and the Valuation of High-technology Firms* (Oxford, Oxford University Press, 2003) 133–61, 135–37; and, more recently, P Giudici and P Agstner, 'Startups and Company Law: The Competitive Pressure of Delaware on Italy (and Europe?)' (2019) 20 *European Business Organization Law Review* 149–205, 155–57.

[27] See chiefly Broughman, Fried and Ibrahim (n 20) 869 (explaining that one, albeit not the most important, reason why start-ups incorporate in Delaware is corporate law's flexibility).

and VC investment. The theory is the following:[28] corporate law lays down the default terms of the corporate contract, thereby allocating cash flow- and control-rights in a given way. Assuming no barriers to bargaining, venture capitalists and entrepreneurs, moved by the ambition to engage in prospectively value-creating cooperation, have incentives to depart from default arrangements and reshape the standard corporate contract as they see fit, with a view to eventually striking a presumably value-maximising deal.

Depending on its design, corporate law can facilitate or hinder this process. A flexible corporate law allows for venture capitalists and entrepreneurs to reach the equilibrium on which contract formation is contingent more easily. A rigid corporate law, by contrast, can create two sorts of frictions. First, it can prevent the adoption of one or more provisions. For instance, a given corporate law regime may prevent contracting parties from adopting solutions aimed at tailoring the duty of loyalty, particularly through the adoption of waivers of the corporate opportunity doctrine. Granted, contracting parties may then attempt to make up for an unfeasible term by allocating value through others, but this is not always possible. Secondly, a rigid corporate law may result in higher transaction costs (in the form of drafting costs, litigation costs, unenforceability costs, enforcement costs, renegotiation costs, and so on). For instance, a given corporate law regime may allow for the adoption of bad leaver provisions only if the triggering events are described in very analytical terms, increasing, inter alia, drafting costs. In some cases, a relative increase in transaction costs will not deter contracting parties from cooperating. In other cases, such an increase will prove an insurmountable hurdle. Either way, a rigid corporate regime can prevent, at the margin, venture capitalists and entrepreneurs from cooperating, leading to a corresponding decrease in the overall volume of VC investments.

Contemplating the role of corporate law in supporting VC investments gives rise to several pragmatic questions. The following will seek to deliver tentative answers to two: Have European policy makers adequately considered corporate law in framing their VC-related discourses? What factors influence their approach?

V. What Has the EU Done?

The VC market in Europe has always been small in relation to both the wider continental private equity sector as a whole and, above all, to its

[28] This part builds entirely on CA Nigro and L Enriques, 'Venture capital e diritto societario italiano: un rapporto difficile' (2021) 20 *Anal. Giur. Econ.* 155–57 and L Enriques, CA Nigro and TH Tröger, 'Venture Capital and European Corporate Laws: Bargaining in the Shadow of Regulatory Constraints' (2022) (on file with the Authors) 5–8. See also CA Nigro, 'Venture capital-backed firms, trade sales e tutela dell'imprenditore tra shareholder value maximization e equa valorizzazione (PhD Dissertation)' (2019), https://iris.luiss.it/handle/11385/201081 and Nigro and Stahl (n 17) 77–79.

US counterpart.[29] In fact, although VC funding in Europe grew an astonishing 6x over the period from 2011 to 2020, reaching $34.3 billion in 2019 and nearing $24 billion in 2020, this forward leap failed to narrow the gap: US VC investments topped $73.6 billion in 2020.[30]

Unravelling the intertwined reasons underlying the status quo is difficult, to say the least.[31] Industry representatives, some academics, and policy makers tend to assert that, while entrepreneurs abound, the construction of a VC market suffers from a shortage of VC capital supply due to a few systematic problems, such as the risk aversion of European investors and fragmentation in the continental VC industry due to high cross-border regulatory variance.[32]

European policy makers have made strenuous efforts to cope with these problems.[33] The EU's first such measures date back to the 1990s,[34] but the ambition to stimulate improvements has steadily gained traction ever since, particularly in the last decade or so. By exposing the functional limits of a predominantly bank-based financial system, the credit crunch that came with the 2007–08 Global Financial Crisis prompted the EU to announce policy actions aimed at strengthening the VC industry with an ultimate view towards offering innovative projects a wider range of funding options.[35] Later on, in 2015, the Capital Markets Union (CMU) project emerged with the ambition to create a single borderless

[29] For an overview of the European VC market, see eg F Bertoni, MG Colombo, and A Quas, 'The Patterns of Venture Capital Investment in Europe' (2015) 45 *Small Business Economics* 543–60. Reports of various types, academic research, and newspapers have long stressed the existence of a significant gap relative to the private equity sector and above all to the US VC market. See eg G De la Dehesa, 'Venture Capital in the United States and Europe' (The Group of Thirty – Occasional Paper n. 65, 2002) https//group30.org/images/uploads/publications/G30_VentureCapitalUSEurope.pdf, 11–12; A Oehler, K Pukthuanthong, M Rummer, and T Walker, 'Venture Capital in Europe: Closing the Gap to the U.S.' (2007) *Quantitative Finance* 3–17; and S Matveeva, 'Raising Venture Funding in Europe vs. the U.S.' (*Forbes online edition*, 31 May 2019) www.forbes.com/sites/sophiamatveeva/2019/05/31/raising-venture-funding-in-europe-vs-the-us/.

[30] I Pojuner and F Pratty, 'The Data: European vs US VCs' (*Sifted*, 3 May 2021) https://sifted.eu/articles/europe-us-vc/.

[31] For an attempt, See eg U Hege, F Palomino and A Schwienbacher, 'Venture Capital Performance: The Disparity Between Europe and the United States' (2008) https://papers.ssrn.com/sol3/papers.cfm?abstract_id=482322.

[32] Stakeholders often voice their concern over the persistence of the current situation. See AFME – Finance for Europe, 'The Shortage of Risk Capital for Europe's High Growth Businesses' (2017), www.afme.eu/portals/0/globalassets/downloads/publications/afme-highgrowth-2017.pdf. In the academic literature, see EPM Vermeulen, 'Capital Markets Union: Why Venture Capital Is Not the Answer to Europe's Innovation Challenge' in D Busch, G Ferrarini and E Avgouleas (eds), *Capital Markets Union in Europe* (Oxford, Oxford University Press, 2018) 201–02.

[33] See also for references, N Moloney, *EU Securities and Financial Markets Regulation* (Oxford, Oxford University Press, 2014) 312, nn 749 and 750; and, more extensively, Vermeulen (n 32) 193–94.

[34] See eg De La Dehesa (n 29) 25–27.

[35] See EU Commission, 'Communication from the Commission to the European Parliament, the Council, the European Economic and Social Committee and the Committee of the Regions 'Reigniting the Entrepreneurial Spirit in Europe' of 9 January 2013 [COM(2021) 795 final]' (2013) https://eur-lex.europa.eu/legal-content/EN/TXT/?uri=celex%3A52012DC0795, 8 and 13.

capital market in Europe. The goal remains the same and attempts to reach it are underway.[36]

Most broadly, European policy makers have moved in five directions.

The first and most general measure includes several policies aimed at redirecting investments towards the capital market with a focus on equity in particular.[37]

Secondly, and with a specific view towards the VC industry, the EU has adopted public interventions that aim to stimulate the private sector to increase the overall availability of VC in the market. The first part of this approach has consisted of the creation of the European Investment Fund (EIF) in 1996, which is now an operational arm of the European Investment Bank. It specialises in setting-up, managing, and advising a tailored fund of funds, mostly with resources entrusted to it by the European Investment Bank, the EU Commission, and several national and regional institutions.[38] The 2014 'Competitiveness of Enterprises and Small and Medium-sized Enterprises' programme complements that project by investing part of its budget into selected funds, which act as the EIF's financial intermediaries. They, in turn, provide firms with venture capital and mezzanine finance in the form of expansion and growth capital.[39] The most important and ambitious initiative thus far has been the 'SME Instrument', a programme that supports startups.[40] Within the frame of the CMU project, the EU has also created a pan-European VC mega fund, which provides cornerstone investments of €410 million in private VC

[36] See EU Commission, 'Communication from the Commission to the European Parliament, the Council, the European Economic and Social Committee and the Committee of the Regions Action Plan on Building a Capital Markets Union [Com/2015/0468 final]' (2015) https://eur-lex.europa.eu/legal-content/EN/TXT/?uri=CELEX%3A52015DC0468. The updated CMU action plan in 2020 does not contain any direct action concerning VC. See EU Commission, 'Communication from the Commission to the European Parliament, the Council, the European Economic and Social Committee and the Committee of the Regions "A Capital Markets Union for People and Businesses – New Action Plan" [com(2020)590 final]', https://eur-lex.europa.eu/legal-content/EN/TXT/?uri=COM%3A2020%3A590%3AFIN. It is nonetheless concerned with the financing of small and medium firms, whose improvement could have trickle-down effects for the VC financing. See eg P Schammo, 'Market Building and the Capital Markets Union: Addressing Information Barriers in the SME Funding Market' (2017) *European Company and Financial Law Review* 271–313; and K Langenbucher, 'Building a Capital Market – The Final Report of the High Level Forum on the EU Capital Market Union' (2020) 17 *European Company and Financial Law Review* 601–18.

[37] For a detailed account of how this policy goal has been shaped and achieved, See eg N Moloney, 'Building a Retail Investment Culture through Law: The 2004 Markets in Financial Instruments Directive' (2005) 6 *European Business Organization Law Review* 341–421.

[38] See EIF, 'Venture Capital' (Entry) www.eif.org/what_we_do/equity/venture/index.htm. The creation of funds of funds to support the expansion of the continental VC market had already been the subject of extensive discussion. See eg EU Commission, 'Assessing the Potential for EU Investment in Venture Capital and Other Risk Capital Fund of Funds' (2015) https://op.europa.eu/en/publication-detail/-/publication/8557bb3e-e10a-11e5-8a50-01aa75ed71a1.

[39] For more information, see EIF, 'COSME – Equity Facility for Growth (EFG)' (Entry) www.eif.org/what_we_do/equity/single_eu_equity_instrument/cosme_efg/index.htm.

[40] EPM Vermeulen (n 32) 200-01.

funds of funds. Their managers are then to raise at least three times as much from both public and private investors.[41]

Thirdly, recent measures have sought to encourage cross-border capital raising.[42] The European VC industry has had a difficult time expanding its investor base across borders due to a series of restrictions.[43] European VC funds have tended to be small, preventing them from engaging in costly cross-border capital raises due to the high associated costs. While their small size has allowed them to be exempt from the costly regulatory requirements set forth for the alternative investment fund industry in 2011,[44] this has come at the cost of exploiting the passport for alternative investment fund managers in order to market financial products to professional clients on a cross-border basis.[45] Concerned with the competitive disadvantage that this regime could create for the continental VC industry relative to other segments of the alternative fund realm,[46] in 2013 the EU passed a new regulatory measure providing eligible VC fund managers with an optional marketing passport for the pan-European institutional market. The measure is similar to the passport regime for alternative investment funds. The new regime also provided VC funds with the ad hoc label 'EuVECA', which is supposed to signal their peculiar nature within the alternative funds universe to the market.[47] The measure was initially exclusive to VC fund managers who fell outside of the purview of the general regime for the alternative investment fund

[41] For a short description of this initiative, see EU Commission, 'VentureEU – The European Union Venture Capital Mega-fund', https://ec.europa.eu/programmes/horizon2020/en/eu-pan-european-venture-capital-funds-funds-initiative. For an overview of the various initiatives that the EU has undertaken in this direction, see EU Commission, 'Venture Capital' (Entry) (2021) https://ec.europa.eu/growth/access-finance-smes/policy-areas/venture-capital_en.

[42] See eg EU Commission, 'Communication from the Commission of 21 December 2007 to the Council, the European Parliament, the European Economic and Social Committee and the Committee of the Regions – Removing obstacles to cross-border investments by venture capital funds [COM(2007) 853 final – Non published in the Official Journal], https://eur-lex.europa.eu/legal-content/EN/TXT/?uri=CELEX:52007DC0853.

[43] See Moloney (n 33) 312, n 755 and corresponding text.

[44] VC funds in Europe have on average a €60 million AUM. The US counterparts have on average a $130 million AUM. 98% of the EU VC fund managers have less than €500 million AUM overall. See EU Commission, 'Proposal for a Regulation of the European Parliament and of the Council on European Venture Capital Funds [Com(2011) 860 final]', https://eur-lex.europa.eu/legal-content/HR/TXT/?uri=CELEX:52012AE1036, 2, 10 and 26.

[45] See EU Commission, 'Directive 2011/61/EU of the European Parliament and of the Council of 8 June 2011 on Alternative Investment Fund Managers and amending Directives 2003/41/EC and 2009/65/EC and Regulations (EC) No 1060/2009 and (EU) No 1095/2010 [OJ L 174, 1.7.2011]', https://eur-lex.europa.eu/legal-content/EN/TXT/PDF/?uri=CELEX:32011L0061&from=EN. For a commentary, see Moloney (n 33) 269–311.

[46] The VC industry had voiced this concern. See eg KPMG, 'Navigating through AIFMD – A Guide for Private Equity and Venture Capital Funds in Ireland' (2014) https://assets.kpmg/content/dam/kpmg/pdf/2016/01/navigate-through-aifmd-july-2014.pdf.

[47] See EU Commission, 'Regulation (EU) No 345/2013 of the European Parliament and of the Council of 17 April 2013 on European Venture Capital Funds [OJ L 115, 25.4.2013], https://eur-lex.europa.eu/legal-content/EN/TXT/?uri=CELEX%3A32013R0345, Arts 1 and 2. In the literature, see Moloney (n 33) 313–15.

industry, but a 2017 amendment expanded its scope to the further benefit of the VC industry.[48]

Fourthly, the EU has repeatedly concerned itself with bankruptcy law. As oft-cited research suggests,[49] bankruptcy regulation can have adverse effects on the supply of entrepreneurs and the availability of good quality projects for venture capitalists[50] and therefore and ultimately on overall VC investment.

Finally, the EU has recently carried out a study of national tax incentives for VC with the aim of setting forth ideal practices for Member States' policy design and implementation.[51]

VI. What About Corporate Law?

This cursory overview of initiatives suggests that European policy makers have prioritised increasing the supply of capital to the VC market, while paying complementary, albeit limited, attention to other issues, such as taxation and bankruptcy law. But, given its newfound importance, what about corporate law?

European policy makers have been active in shaping corporate law since the late 1960s. Both the discourse and corresponding regulatory agenda, however, have mainly focused on public firms,[52] with harmonisation being the key driver.[53] Private firms have generally fallen within the regulatory remit of individual Member States. EU interventions regarding private firms did not then aim to harmonise Member States' respective corporate laws, but attempted to supplement them with a pan-European legal regime, the *Societas Privata Europea* (SPE).[54]

[48] See EU Commission, 'Regulation (EU) 2017/1991 of the European Parliament and of the Council of 25 October 2017 amending Regulation (EU) No 345/2013 on European venture capital funds and Regulation (EU) No 346/2013 on European Social Entrepreneurship Funds [OJ L 293, 10.11.2017]' https://eur-lex.europa.eu/legal-content/EN/TXT/?uri=uriserv:OJ.L_.2017.293.01.0001.01.ENG, Art 1.

[49] See J Armour and DJ Cumming, 'The Legislative Road to Silicon Valley' (2006) 58 *Oxford Economic Papers* 596–635; and J Armour and DJ Cumming, 'Bankruptcy Law and Entrepreneurship' (2008) 10 *American Law and Economics Review* 303–50.

[50] See in particular, EU Commission, 'Communication from the Commission to the Council, the European Parliament, the European Economic and Social Committee and the Committee of the Regions Overcoming the Stigma of Business Failure – For a Second Chance Policy' of 5 October 2007 [COM(2007) 584 final], https://eur-lex.europa.eu/LexUriServ/LexUriServ.do?uri=COM:2007:0584:FIN:en:PDF.

[51] See EU Commission, 'Effectiveness of Tax Incentives for Venture Capital and Business Angels to Foster the Investment of SMEs and Start-ups: Final Report' (2017), available at https://ec.europa.eu/taxation_customs/system/files/2017-09/taxation_paper_69_vc-ba.pdf.

[52] For a list of the initiatives that the EU has undertaken in this area over time, see EU Commission, 'Company Law and Corporate Governance' (Entry) (21 October 2020) https://ec.europa.eu/info/business-economy-euro/doing-business-eu/company-law-and-corporate-governance_en. Some of these measures affect also private companies.

[53] On harmonisation as a policy goal and a driver of regulation, as well as on its desirability and effects on national corporate laws, see L Enriques, 'A Harmonized European Company Law: Are We There Already?' (2017) 66 *International and Comparative Law Quarterly* 763–77.

[54] See EU Commission, 'Proposal for a Council Regulation on the Statute for a European Private Company of 25 June 2006 [COM(2008)396 Final]', https://eur-lex.europa.eu/LexUriServ/LexUriServ.

The SPE project was conceived as a regulatory tool with the ambition to meet 'the specific needs of [small and medium firms]', so as to allow 'entrepreneurs to set up [such firms] following the same, simple, flexible company law provisions across' the Single Market, thereby 'supporting the[ir] internationalisation' and 'hence, facilitate their growth'.[55] The SPE project failed, eventually. It is doubtful, however, whether the proposed statute could have fulfilled the promise of this full-fledged legal flexibility in practice.[56] To the extent that it would have made a more flexible corporate law available, it could have facilitated cooperation between venture capitalists and entrepreneurs. This potential outcome would not have been an intentional one. The SPE project was only intended to facilitate the internationalisation of small and medium firms. The proposal did not feature any references to 'start-up' or 'venture capital,' or more simply 'innovation' or 'innovative entrepreneurship'.

The EU has not undertaken any other comparable initiative since the SPE was left behind. A broader project 'Startup Europe' was nonetheless launched in 2019.[57] It grew to include the 2020 'EU Startup Nation Standards' initiative.[58] This initiative consists of several recommendations for Member States to adopt best practices so as to 'cause a sea change, effectively turning every Member State into a Startup Nation, and the EU as a whole into a [s]tartup [c]ontinent capable of rapidly adjusting to, exploiting and co-setting global trends'.[59] These recommendations include making incorporation procedures cheaper and faster, allowing for the issuance of stock options without voting rights and, more generically, simplifying domestic corporate laws.[60]

do?uri=COM:2008:0396:FIN:EN:PDF. In the literature, see the various contributions in H Hirte and C Teichmann (eds), *The European Private Company – Societas Privata Europaea (SPE)* (Berlin, De Gruyter, 2013) XII-508.

[55] EU Commission (n 54) 2.

[56] The proposed statute featured a significant level of flexibility. See eg M Siems, L Herzog and E Rosenhäger, 'The European Private Company (SPE): An Attractive New Legal Form of Doing Business?' (2009) 23 *Butterworths Journal of International Banking and Financial Law* 247–50. Yet, upon closer inspection, key regulatory components of the proposed statute seemed to be mandatory in nature (or at least interpreted as such). It also featured several significant gaps for Member States that did not necessarily favour flexible regulatory solutions. See eg EJ Navez, 'The Internal Organization of the European Private Company: Freedom of Contract under National Constraints' in Hirte and Teichmann (n 54) 147–181, 155.

[57] On this project, see EU Commission, 'Startup Europe – Shaping Europe's Digital Future' (2019) https://digital-strategy.ec.europa.eu/en/policies/startup-europe.

[58] See EU Commission, 'Start-up Nation Standards' (2021) https://startupnationsstandard.eu/.

[59] EU Commission, 'Declaration on the EU Start-up Nations Standard of Excellence' (2021) https://startupnationsstandard.eu/files/SNS-declaration.pdf.

[60] When announcing Startup Europe, the EU Commission explained that it would launch initiatives aimed at modernising corporate laws in the Member States. See EU Commission (n 57) main page. It reiterated this statement in the presentation of the Startup Nation Standards. See EU Commission (n 58) main page. References to this topic disappeared, however, in the following document detailing the initiative. See eg EU Commission (n 59) 5, where a vague reference is made to the desirability of measures aimed at 'promot[ing] a rigorous application of the "Think Small First" principle in view of avoiding unnecessary administrative burden/red tape'.

This soft law-based initiative does put a perceivable emphasis on start-ups. Yet, it has its main rationale in the EU Commission's ambition to provide small and medium firms with appropriate support throughout their lifecycle, so as to create the preconditions to scale up and reach maturity for an IPO or M&A transactions.[61] Granted, the suggestion for Member States, particularly as regards the simplification of their corporate laws, may, at least in its rhetoric and obviously depending on its actual implementation and ultimate outcomes, have a beneficial impact upon venture capitalist-entrepreneur cooperation. Yet, again, this would be a mere by-product. The locution 'venture capital' only appears in reference to increasing and diversifying access to finance for startups. No reference whatsoever is made to the importance of corporate law for VC investments, instead.

In conclusion, the EU has occasionally moved in the direction of facilitating cooperation between venture capitalists and entrepreneurs, but only as the indirect consequence of broader measures. Corporate law has not been a focus in its capacity as a regulatory apparatus for the venture capitalist-entrepreneur relationship at the portfolio company level. Accordingly, it has not been acknowledged by policy makers as a regulatory tool that may help to steer the fate of the continental VC market.[62]

Why? To begin with, one could speculate that European policy makers have considered the potential effects of corporate law on VC investments, but concluded that the costs of engaging in any attempt aimed at making it more flexible could exceed its benefits. One could alternatively point to policy makers' long-standing avoidance of measures that deal with private firms specifically, particularly after their experience with the SPE project.[63] One could also point to a broadly held assumption that a competitive continental market for corporate law already exists, which could provide for a sufficiently flexible corporate law.[64] These hypotheses, however, have limited explanatory power as the issue is never addressed. Policy documents make no mention of ruling out corporate law as a regulatory tool for supporting VC investments.

[61] See EU Commission (n 59) 2. For the uninitiated, 'M&A' stands for 'mergers and acquisitions'.

[62] This holds true even if, instead of considering corporate law measures for small and medium firms and startups, one pays attention to a larger number of policy documents that, while concerned with small and medium firms (eg, with their financing), do not really consider corporate law in its connection with firm financing. See eg EU Commission, 'Communication from the Commission to the Council, the European Parliament, the European Economic and Social Committee and the Committee of the Regions: Financing SME Growth – Adding European Value [COM(2006)349 Final]' (2006) https://ec.europa.eu/docsroom/documents/3315/attachments/1/translations/en/renditions/pdf.

[63] See above n 55 and corresponding text.

[64] Following the European Court of Justice's decisions as regards the Centros saga and other similar cases, the idea has gained traction that firms can incorporate in any EU Member State (that does not adhere to the real seat theory) and then operate in any other Member State without barriers. The existence of a continental market for corporate law is, however, largely disputable; the promise of freedom of establishment also comes with significant uncertainty as to the corporate law regime to which firms incorporating in one Member State but operating in another Member State would be subject to in practice. See also for references, Enriques, Nigro, and Tröger (n 28) 8.

A more credible hypothesis is that European policy makers have simply ignored the issue. European policy makers may share the perception that corporate law matters for small and medium firms, including startups, without understanding that the flexibility of corporate law matters for the cooperation between venture capitalists and entrepreneurs.[65]

This hypothesis is consistent with two observations regarding the EU's efforts. One observation concerns the EU's conception of corporate law as a tool to help firms grow without understanding its 'link' with VC: that is, without understanding that the complexity of the contract that venture capitalists and entrepreneurs negotiate is such that constraining their ability to modify its default terms can affect their inclination to cooperate. Another (and consequent) observation concerns the correspondingly generic nature of recommendations that the EU has brought in when it comes to modernising corporate law for the purposes of meeting the needs of startups. The generic nature of these recommendations suggests a lack of understanding of the specific terms of the corporate contract that should be made more flexible.

Whatever the ultimate cause, this lack of understanding is problematic. It may cause policy makers to miss factors which contribute to the disharmony between their various institutions, creating a major obstacle to holistic policy making.

Policy making with such a narrow focus can, in turn, lead to ill-designed policy recipes, which can frustrate ambitions to create a sounder institutional infrastructure for VC investments, so as to foster innovation and, ultimately, stimulate long-term, sustainable economic growth.

VII. Conclusion

VC, as a motor of innovation and economic growth, is a major objective for policy makers around the world.

VC-driven value creation depends, however, on a very peculiar capital management process, which requires venture capitalists to, among other things, negotiate a vast array of complex and interconnected contractual terms at the portfolio company level with entrepreneurs.

Recent scholarship has highlighted the importance of corporate law in order to facilitate VC investments by explaining that its rigid design may prevent, at the margin, parties from reaching the equilibrium on which contract formation depends, having a negative impact on VC investments.

[65] See EU Commission 'Venture Capital' (n 41), under the heading 'related Venture Capital Activities': none of the various documents listed there discusses corporate law in its connection to VC investments. See also EU Commission, 'Venture Capital Investments' (Entry), https://ec.europa.eu/taxation_customs/venture-capital-investments_en.

Although European policy makers have strived to foster the growth of VC over the last three decades and adopted several measures to this end, they have not paid adequate attention to corporate law. One plausible explanation is a narrow focus when it comes to VC-related policy making.

The absence of an adequate understanding as to the importance of corporate law for VC investments may have adverse consequences for elaborating effective policy recipes that facilitate VC investments and, ultimately, support innovation-based, sustainable long-term economic growth.

13

Policy Coherence for Corporate Sustainability in the EU: Can We Achieve Sustainable Corporate Governance Without Sustainable Finance?

ALEXANDRA ANDHOV AND LELA MÉLON

I. Introduction

Science speaks clearly. We live in a time of climate emergency,[1] however our collective actions do not indicate an accurate understanding of the situation, or a suitable response. Many believe that the warnings are unsubstantiated or exaggerated.[2] We are not acting as if our house is on fire and our existence threatened. Instead, we see smoke on the horizon and are unsure whether it actually is smoke, or just another cloud. This fundamental misconception has further been confirmed by the recently issued 'Glasgow Climate Pact',[3] which committed to double adaptation finance and asked countries to present more ambitious climate pledges next year while failing to provide the promised funds to developing countries for a sustainability transition.

As lawyers, we should listen carefully to the scientists. Naturally, we should ask hard questions, collect evidence, compare testimonies, apply analytical and

[1] Intergovernmental Panel on Climate Change, 'Climate Change 2021: The Physical Science Basis' (7 August 2021) (IPCC Report 2021) www.ipcc.ch/report/ar6/wg1/downloads/report/IPCC_AR6_WGI_Full_Report.pdf.

[2] D Hall, 'Climate explained: why some people still think climate change isn't real' (*The Conversation*, 8 October 2019) https://theconversation.com/climate-explained-why-some-people-still-think-climate-change-isnt-real-124763.

[3] UN Conference of the Parties serving as the meeting of the Parties to the Paris Agreement Third session Glasgow, 31 October to 12 November 2021, Glasgow Climate Pact. Available at unfccc.int.

critical thinking, and support meaningful change through legislative action. One excellent example is the *Urgenda* case, in which the court relied on scientific reports while carrying out a legal and policy analysis.[4] However, reflecting on the slow and gradual development in human rights or anti-corruption, we know that legislative actions aiming for sustainability across all industries require a multi-stakeholder approach. The various private and public organisations have to change their practices while condemning those who do not.[5] The legislative answers are not purely international agreements, protocols, or national laws that protect single segments of the environment (such as soil, water, or animals) or that prohibit deforestation, but rather those that compel the transformation of the entire society, both on an individual and corporate level. There shall be no doubt that all corporations must re-think and re-design their business practices, supply chains, and manufacturing methods. Nothing less will actually help us. As stipulated by the Intergovernmental Panel on Climate Change (IPCC), '[n]ow more than ever, unprecedented and urgent action is required of all nations'.[6]

As we have seen in our history, the only successful mechanism that can compel corporate behavioural change is through their financing and governance.[7] Ultimately, money talks. In terms of debt and equity financing, it is the financial institutions that dictate the tone. Even if we focus on publicly traded companies, due to the dispersed ownership across the major markets, various financial institutions represent the interest of shareholders, including the composition of the board of directors and other governance bodies. Simultaneously, corporate governance has become the mechanism to initiate corporate change. The European Union (EU) has recognised the interconnection between these two practices and introduced its initiative for a sustainable future through sustainable governance and finance. This chapter analyses the notion of sustainable governance and sustainable finance while exploring their policy coherence in the EU. Building on the renewed legislative impetus at the EU level in the two respective fields, this chapter highlights the areas for amelioration, and opens the door for further scholarly and legislative advancement that could achieve not only improved sustainability practices, but could also lead to a more efficient capital market union.

[4] *State of the Netherlands v Urgenda Foundation* ECLI:NL:HR:2019:2007; the Dutch courts found that the Dutch Government has obligations to urgently and significantly reduce emissions in line with its constitutional and human rights obligations. The decision in English is available at www.urgenda.nl/wp-content/uploads/ENG-Dutch-Supreme-Court-Urgenda-v-Netherlands-20-12-2019.pdf.

[5] See eg A Tamo, 'New Thinking on Transnational Corporations and Human Rights: Towards a Multi-Stakeholder Approach' (2016) 34 *Netherlands Quarterly of Human Rights* 147.

[6] Intergovernmental Panel on Climate Change, 'Climate Report' (2018).

[7] There have been various corporate scandals that have triggered new regulation, including Enron, Volkswagen, Siemens or Lehman Brothers.

II. The Urgency of the Climate Emergency

There is virtually no disagreement among the scientists who research climate change as to the current climate emergency. Presently, more than 97 per cent of climate scientists agree on the existence and cause of climate change.[8] The level of agreement among the scientists is astounding, as scientists tend to disagree on almost all subjects, including the reason why dinosaurs became extinct.[9] Thus, climate change should, in the eyes of lawyers, business people, and politicians, be considered a fact in the same way as humans needing to breathe to live.

The IPCC, a conservative body of researchers, concluded in 1995 that 'the balance of evidence suggests that there is a discernible human influence on global climate'.[10] The main driver of climate change is the greenhouse effect. Some gases in the Earth's atmosphere, similar to the gases in a greenhouse, capture the sun's heat and stop it from dissipating back into space, thus causing heating on the Earth. CO_2 produced by human activities is the most significant contributor to global warming. It is virtually certain that the global upper ocean has warmed since the 1970s.[11] In 2019, atmospheric CO_2 concentrations were higher than at any time in at least 2 million years.[12] There is naturally much more information and data available in the IPCC Report 2021. However, there are two main findings. First, the climate emergency is already present. There is no doubt. The planet is overheated, sea levels are rising, and we experience weather and climate extremes more regularly and on a grander scale. The scenarios and projects of the future that the IPCC offers show an existential threat to various nations and humanity. The second finding is that the source of the increased CO_2 is human activity. Hence, mathematics is elementary. In order to prevent further deterioration, human activity needs to change. We need to substantially reduce CO_2 emissions, and revise our behaviour and practices, on an individual, corporate and national level.

Once we recognise the emergency and realise that contemporary science does not offer any other alternative, our goal must be to reduce emissions and reform and innovate our industrial practices. From there on, we can address the issue on a strategic level. What strategy shall we (nations, corporations and individuals) undertake to reach the goal? As often is the case, strategy comprises various policy actions and activities. Focusing on corporate behaviour and industrial practices, as stipulated above, it can be seen that the only way to change these is through regulatory and multi-stakeholder change.

[8] See eg J Cook, N Oreskes, PT Doran at al, 'Consensus on Consensus: A Synthesis of Consensus Estimates on Human-Caused Global Warming' (2016) 11 *Environmental Research Letters* 1.

[9] See B Bosker, 'The Nastiest Feud in Science' (*The Atlantic*, September 2018) www.theatlantic.com/magazine/archive/2018/09/dinosaur-extinction-debate/565769/.

[10] See IPCC Second Assessment Climate Change 1995, 'A Report of the Intergovernmental Panel on Climate Change' (1995) 22.

[11] IPCC 'Climate Report' (n 1) 6.

[12] ibid 9.

III. State of the Art in the EU and the Renewed Impetus for Further Regulation

The latter EU green movement started in December 2019, when the European Commission launched the European Green Deal (the Green Deal), resetting the Commission's commitment to tackling climate and environmental-related issues.[13] The Green Deal represents an unprecedented effort to review and re-design EU laws and public policies. The Green Deal covers eight policy areas: biodiversity, sustainable food systems, sustainable agriculture, clean energy, sustainable industry, building and renovating, sustainable mobility, eliminating pollution, and climate action. In addition, the Green Deal stipulates numerous measures and goals, recognising that to achieve all these ambitions, there are significant investment and reformation needs for the financial systems in the EU and across the G7 and G20 countries.[14]

Since 2019, numerous activities in the Commission and other EU institutions have taken place, including the European Climate Law, the EU Renovation Wave Strategy, the EU Action Plan Towards Zero Pollution for Air, Water and Soil and several others.[15] Even though the COVID-19 pandemic has been an unforeseen hurdle, it became another reason for an economic transformation and recovery, emphasising the need to re-think the existing laws and structures. The two initiatives that represent the focus of this chapter are sustainable finance and sustainable corporate governance.

A. Sustainable Finance

The idea of changing finance policies to support industrial transformation has been discussed even before specific climate change targets were introduced in the Green Deal in December 2019. Sustainable finance has been one of the Commission's key priorities since March 2018, when the Action Plan on Sustainable Finance

[13] European Commission, 'Communication to the European Parliament, the European Council, the Council, the European Economic and Social Committee and the Committee of the Regions, The European Green Deal' COM(2019) 640 final.

[14] ibid 22. The European Commission has envisaged an investment of €1 trillion, half coming from the EU budget and the EU Emission Trading Scheme and half coming from Invest EU, combining funds from the EU budget, the European Investment Bank, and other public and private investments. Invest EU can be seen as a public-private investment partnership that will support innovative start-ups, SMEs, research, education, and more.

[15] See eg Regulation (EU) 2021/1119 of the European Parliament and of the Council of 30 June 2021 establishing the framework for achieving climate neutrality and amending Regulations (EC) No 401/2009 and (EU) 2018/1999 ('European Climate Law') [2021] OJ L243/1; Communication from the Commission to the European Parliament, the Council, the European Economic and Social Committee and the Committee of the Regions, Pathway to a Healthy Planet for All EU Action Plan: 'Towards Zero Pollution for Air, Water and Soil' COM(2021) 400 final.

(SF Action Plan) was adopted.[16] The SF Action Plan was built on the Paris Agreement and the UN 2030 Agenda for Sustainable Development and had overarching three objectives: (1) to reorient capital flows towards sustainable investment to achieve sustainable and inclusive growth, (2) to manage financial risks stemming from climate change, environmental degradation, and social issues, and (3) to foster transparency and 'long-termism' in financial and economic activity. The SF Action Plan supported a package of four legislative measures that were to be introduced in May 2018:

1. a unified EU classification system ('taxonomy');
2. investors' duties and disclosures;
3. low-carbon benchmarks; and
4. better advice to clients on sustainability.[17]

It is apparent from the above roadmap that the Commission has been aware that to achieve any of the three objectives, it must re-design some aspects of the decision-making processes, evaluation processes, and advisory processes within the financial system. The underlying theory behind this re-design is ultimately based on recognising that the existing monetary incentives and policies are neither achieving sustainable practices across the industries nor providing an enticement. However, the ongoing debate on sustainable finance tends to be polarised. Some scholars have adopted an optimistic perspective seeing the financial industry as the ultimate change maker.[18] Others dispute the ability of the finance industry to offer real solutions to the sustainability challenges that we are facing.[19] Even though there is an ambiguous relationship between traditional financial logic (that has been so far applied and promoted) and sustainability goals, the field of sustainable finance can become an established form of organising that combines different logics, orders of value preferences, organisational structures and identities.[20] Research suggests that even though these novel forms of organising can trigger conflicts and tension, they foster innovation, market transformation and societal impact.[21]

This chapter recognises that nothing is set in stone, and in the same way that legislation can be changed, so can policies and behaviours, if we are provided with a broader coherence and clarity of various legislative tools. However, the Commission continues to send mixed signals. On the one hand, it supports the Green Deal and introduces significant policy changes, but, on the other hand, it

[16] European Commission, 'Communication to the European Parliament, the European Council, the Council, the European Central Bank, the European Economic and Social Committee and the Committee of the Regions, Action Plan: Financing Sustainable Growth,' COM(2018) 97 final.
[17] ibid.
[18] See eg RG Eccles and S Klimenko, 'The Investor Revolution' (2019) 97 *Harvard Business Review* 106.
[19] See eg T Lagoarde-Segot, 'Sustainable Finance. A Critical Realist Perspective' (2019) 47 *Research in International Business and Finance* 1.
[20] See H Ahlström and D Monciardini, 'The Regulatory Dynamics of Sustainable Finance: Paradoxical Success and Limitations of EU Reforms' (2021) *Journal of Business Ethics*.
[21] See J Jay, 'Navigating Paradox as a Mechanism of Change and Innovation in Hybrid Organizations' (2013) 56 *Academy of Management Journal* 137.

continues to prolong its support for cross-border natural gas projects and fossil fuel gas subsidies for natural gas pipelines until 2027.[22]

Aside from achieving political consensus concerning transforming corporate practices and regulation, the second concern is translating ethical, social and environmental values into practice. There are still fundamental disagreements and radical differences among practitioners and researchers on what qualifies as sustainable finance or investment.[23] This uncertainty of such 'translation' opens doors to greenwashing and misrepresentation. Such an example is the German asset management company DWS, which is currently under investigation by BaFin, the German regulator, the Securities and Exchange Commission and the Department.[24]

The EU's classification system or the EU's Sustainable Finance Disclosure Regulation represent essential tools to translate the regulatory conundrum into understandable obligations and measurements for the institutions to work with. There might be parallels between the business and human rights and the contemporary sustainability literature, where both quantitative and qualitative translations should occur. The EU, together with diverse stakeholders, needs to find a solution to support the transition, despite the existing tension, while protecting the entire movement from sustainable finance greenwash. One of the most critical (almost preliminary) challenges in the transition towards sustainable corporate and financial practices is precisely one of translation of quantitative into qualitative indicators and measures, as some fields already acknowledged that some aspects and values cannot be shown in numbers.[25] Such transition will prove to become particularly challenging in the field of finance, as the field is quantitatively oriented and prone to dismissing or omitting non-quantifiable information. It is precisely at this point that not only The EU Taxonomy (the Taxonomy) but also sustainable corporate governance and the revised corporate sustainability reporting can provide some input as to the content of the non-quantifiable information. The following section focuses on sustainable corporate governance as an example of such content.

B. Sustainable Corporate Governance

To achieve corporate behavioural change, sustainable financing represents only one part of the story. The second part forms corporate governance.[26] The EU has

[22] See J Rankin, 'EU lawmakers vote to prolong fossil fuel gas subsidies until 2027' *The Guardian* (28 September 2021).

[23] See A Otani, 'ESG Funds Enjoy Record Inflows, Still Back Big Oil and Gas' (*The Wall Street Journal*, 11 November 2019).

[24] ibid.

[25] European Commission, 1 *Competition Policy Brief 1/2021 – Policy in Support of Europe's Green Ambition*.

[26] In the Action Plan for financing sustainable growth, Action 10 focused on corporate governance and undue capital market short-termism.

commenced the sustainable corporate governance initiative in 2020, focusing on directors' duties and sustainable corporate governance and supply chain due diligence.[27] This initiative and predominantly the EY Report on directors' duties and sustainable corporate governance (EY Report) have however been met with a substantial critique. The criticism was of the choice of EY as the principal of such research, similar to when the Commission planned to task BlackRock Investment Management to carry out a study on integrating ESG objectives into EU banking rules. However, the EY Report suffered from major material flaws of the conducted research, including the definitions or the lack of the terms, such as 'short-termism' and 'long-termism', a bizarre choice of economic indicators, biased use of literature and several others.[28] The criticism came from corporate law scholars, practitioners, and corporations from all over the world. Unfortunately, the entire initiative was a policy and political debacle, which shifted the focus from finding a solution to a significant problem to pinpointing the formal and material inadequacies of the EY Report. Thus instead of addressing the climate change issue, the majority decided to attack the messenger.

When reviewing the critical scholarly pieces, it is clear that even the corporate law scholars continue to ignore the responsibility and accountability of the corporations for their behaviour and effect on climate change. Many remain frozen in the 1970s with Friedman's claim that the taxes are the panacea for all the externalities.[29] The shareholder theory remains the holy grail that we grasp tightly even if an interdisciplinary scholarship has been playing its swan song for some time now.[30] Despite the years of research and studies showing repeatedly that corporate disregard towards human rights or the environment remains limitless unless there is enforcement, it truly amazes us. Corporate behaviour will not change until a clear regulatory framework is designed and an accountability system is introduced.[31] The corporate leadership's substantial salaries, bonuses, and other incentive payments must be mirrored with the responsibility to the corporation and its business. However, the success of the corporation is undeniably connected with various parties – the stakeholders. Moreover, the tone from the top is a

[27] European Commission, 'Study on directors' duties and sustainable corporate governance' (2020); European Commission, 'Study on due diligence requirements through the supply chain' (2020).

[28] See eg M Roe et al, 'The Sustainable Corporate Governance Initiative in Europe' (2021) 38 *Yale Journal on Regulation Bulletin* 133 or PK Andersen et al, 'Response to the Study on Directors' Duties and Sustainable Corporate Governance by Nordic Company Law Scholars' (2020) 100 *University of Copenhagen Faculty of Law Research Paper*, https://research.cbs.dk/en/publications/response-to-the-study-on-directors-duties-and-sustainable-corpora.

[29] See M Friedman, 'The Social Responsibility of Business Is to Increase Its Profits' *The New York Times* (13 September 1970).

[30] See eg LA Stout, 'New Thinking on "Shareholder Primacy"' (2012) *Accounting, Economics, and Law* 2; AM Lipton, 'What We Talk About When We Talk About Shareholder Primacy?' (2019) *Case Western Reserve Law Review* 69; B Sjåfjell et al, 'Shareholder Primacy: The Main Barrier to Sustainable Companies' in B Sjåfjell and BJ Richardson (eds), *Company Law and Sustainability: Legal Barriers and Opportunities* (Cambridge, Cambridge University Press, 2015).

[31] See eg O Hart and L Zingales, 'Companies Should Maximise Shareholder Welfare Not Market Value' (2017) *Journal of Law, Finance and Accounting* 247 f.

recognised phenomenon that changes the behaviour across the organisation.[32] There should be no question in our mind that we need to address the rights and duties of the corporate leadership to initiate the change.

The future of the sustainable governance initiative is unclear. The Commission closed the public consultation in February 2021. Originally, the 'Commission's adoption' was planned for the fourth quarter of 2021. However on 1 December 2021, the proposal in current form was withdrawn. It is presumed that the Commission will release a new proposal for a Directive on sustainable corporate governance, which should include new due diligence rules and new corporate directors' duties to integrate mandatory sustainable criteria into their decision-making. However, the specific wording is to be seen.

IV. Moving Forward with the EU Green Deal: Mapping of the Sustainability Regulation in Business Law

Despite the scholarly doubt being expressed as to the correctness of the analysis carried out by EY in its commissioned EY Report on 'directors' duties and sustainable corporate governance',[33] the need for change in the framework of corporate governance is practically indisputable. Requiring a reduction of net emissions by at least 55 per cent by the year 2030 while leaving corporate governance intact cannot be achieved no matter how many policy and legislative changes occur in the field of broader corporate law.

Some scholarly criticisms of the EY Report focusing on short-termism fail to note that while it is true that a certain amount of short-termism is a natural consequence of efficient business making, the threat of climate crisis does not allow for the notoriously unresolved scholarly topic on the existence of short-termism to continue as the academic 'business as usual'. It instead requires a reform of corporate governance in such a manner as to preempt attempts of short-termism that do not allow and/or support sustainable corporate behaviour under the given corporate governance systems. The analysis of the question of short-termism through such backwards induction yields a different result and calls for amelioration and modification of the current corporate governance systems,[34] if nothing else, to ensure its unambiguity in terms of legal certainty for corporate officers when pursuing environmentally and socially sustainable goals (particularly in

[32] See eg MS Schwartz et al, 'Tone at the Top: An Ethics Code for Directors?' (2005) *Journal of Business Ethics* 58.

[33] European Commission, 'Study on Directors' Duties' (n 27) 2020.

[34] L Dallas, 'Short-termism, the financial crisis, and corporate governance' (2012) 37 *Journal of Corporation Law* 265.

cases where there exists a doubt if such actions result in maximising the economic benefits for shareholders). While scholarly pushback against the EY Report has been potent, the market calls for change and creating a level playing field questions the claims made under that pushback.[35] Irresponsible business behaviour has been the cause of many environmental and social issues we are facing. While we most certainly cannot blame these developments entirely on the corporate governance framework, we cannot transform irresponsible behaviour into sustainable behaviour with the same certainty. This has also been highlighted by the Communication by the Commission:

> Through the EU Taxonomy Climate Delegated Act, the economic activities of roughly 40% of listed companies, in sectors which are responsible for almost 80% of direct greenhouse gas emissions in Europe, are already covered, with more activities to be added in the future. Through this scope, the EU Taxonomy can significantly increase the potential that green financing offers to support the transition, in particular for carbon-intensive sectors where change is urgently needed.[36]

As an expression of the recognition of the need for a changed corporate law framework, the EU Commission has been working on two crucial instruments: the proposal on sustainable corporate governance,[37] which is to implement due diligence concerns, as well as the revised Corporate Sustainability Reporting Directive.[38] These initiatives have been recognised as being closely related to sustainable finance, especially the Corporate Sustainability Reporting Directive, which is noted as a constitutive part of sustainable finance by the EU Commission. Indeed, and surprisingly enough, the sustainable finance taxonomy found its way almost directly into the proposal of the Directive on corporate sustainability reporting, closely tying the corporate reporting obligations on the definitions of environmentally and socially sustainable corporate activities in the sustainable finance taxonomy.[39]

These developments directly link corporate actions to the financial markets through regulation, placing a question mark on the scholarly arguments on the relative independence between the two fields in the recent scholarly criticisms of the EY Report and the EU Commission action in the field of corporate governance. Furthermore, envisaging directors' or corporate civil or criminal liability regarding

[35] ibid 30.

[36] Commission Delegated Regulation (EU) 2021/2178 of 6.7.2021 supplementing Regulation (EU) 2020/852 of the European Parliament and of the Council by specifying the content and presentation of information to be disclosed by undertakings subject to Articles 19a or 29a of Directive 2013/34/EU concerning environmentally sustainable economic activities, and specifying the methodology to comply with that disclosure obligation C(2021) 4987 final.

[37] European Commission, 'Inception Impact Assessment – Sustainable Corporate Governance', Ref. Ares(2020)4034032 – 30/07/2020, 2021.

[38] Proposal for a DIRECTIVE OF THE EUROPEAN PARLIAMENT AND OF THE COUNCIL amending Directive 2013/34/EU, Directive 2004/109/EC, Directive 2006/43/EC and Regulation (EU) No 537/2014, as regards corporate sustainability reporting COM(2021) 189 final.

[39] ibid.

sustainable corporate conduct and accompanying enforcement mechanisms does not represent an unsubstantiated intrusion in corporate governance, as has been repeatedly claimed by opposition to sustainable corporate governance. Rather, it is a logical continuance of the broader business law policy change in the EU that requires businesses to actively engage in sustainable corporate behaviour. Thus, while the whole business law policy in the EU is being reformed to achieve sectoral or product-focused sustainable outcomes, this creates a network of corporate obligations that requires their materialisation in the framework of EU corporate governance regulation.

A. Transversally Applicable Sustainability-related Policies – Aside from the Field of Finance

It is unimaginable that in the light of such substantive policy changes in EU business law, the content of corporate obligations in the sphere of general corporate law and corporate governance will remain intact. By way of example, to achieve climate neutrality, it is insufficient to only know the corporation's carbon footprint. Designing concrete strategies, plans and timelines that assure the mitigation of CO_2 emissions is a must, which by default requires the involvement of companies' strategic bodies and their responsibility for compliance with the set requirements. Climate action is an example of a transversally applicable policy that influences business in all sectors, creating obligations for businesses of all sizes, shapes and forms.

Another transversally applicable policy can be preserving Europe's natural capital under the EU Green Deal. It requires accounting for corporate impact on Europe's natural capital. Corporations need to understand Europe's natural capital in the context of the global natural capital through their environmental due diligence.[40] Such due diligence shall become part of the EU corporate governance, operationalised and directed to active corporate strategy and decision-making agents. This holds true when considering strategic corporate sectors with the most relative impact on the critical environmental sustainability challenges. By way of example, textiles have been defined by the EU Green Deal, the Circular Economy Action Plan,[41] and the Industrial Strategy[42] as a priority sector for achieving a carbon-neutral, circular economy, which resulted in the EU Strategy for Textiles.[43]

[40] Under the Proposal for a Corporate Sustainability Reporting Directive.

[41] European Commission, 'Communication from the Commission to the European Parliament, the Council, the European Economic and Social Committee and the Committee of the Regions, A new Circular Economy Action Plan For a cleaner and more competitive Europe' COM(2020) 98 final.

[42] European Commission, 'Communication from the Commission to the European Parliament, the Council, the European Economic and Social Committee and the Committee of the Regions, Updating the 2020 New Industrial Strategy: Building a stronger Single Market for Europe's recovery' COM(2021) 350 final.

[43] European Commission, 'EU Strategy for Textiles', Ref. Ares(2021)67453 – 05/01/2021 (2021).

Therefore, the companies in the textile sector encounter additional obligations regarding their corporate sustainability reporting and their core business obligations (eg, tackling the issue of release of microplastics, manufacturing and recycling processes).

Furthermore, the textile sector must set the targets for reuse, recycling and green public procurement through textile-specific and horizontal actions along the whole value chain (closely intertwined with the Sustainable Products Initiative). These additional requirements make it even harder to defend the view that the obligation of sustainable corporate conduct should not be regulated through the traditional channel of corporate law and corporate governance. The abovementioned requirements are beyond mere compliance. They require a bigger shift in business models and corporate modus operandi than merely adhering to an additional set of legal obligations outside of the core corporate purpose. The responsibility of such a core shift to a business model is without a doubt the task of the corporate management, which needs to have both rights and obligations to that effect accompanied by corresponding enforcement mechanisms. Moreover, one should not forget that creating innovative sustainable solutions and alternatives is dependent on the existence of sustainable investment.

B. Going Back to Basics: Finance as a Starting Point

In line with the arguments presented in this subsection, finance can be seen as one of the specific business sectors that is at the same time regulated by generally applicable rules and sector-specific rules. Suppose the finance industry is seen as one particular corporate sector. In that case, this changes the narrative on sustainable finance, and it becomes more than just instrumental in achieving a sustainable transition of corporate practices.

There are two functions that the finance sector carries out in the EU: it represents an indispensable tool for achieving EU sustainability-related goals[44] while still carrying out a general role of money management: acquiring and utilising funds necessary for the efficient operation of a business and private individuals. Within its second function, the field of finance closely resembles other industry 'sectors' having to re-design its principles, functioning and guiding principles to assure its environmental and social sustainability. Finance itself has to become sustainable no matter which particular subsection of finance we are discussing. Moreover, the financial system itself needs to account for changing the corporate environment and shifting from linear towards circular production, which at the moment seems to be an issue, as the current financial practices and regulations remain deeply rooted and embedded in linear production practices.[45]

[44] ibid 18.

[45] L Mélon, 'A Critical Assessment of the EU Circular Economy Action Plan in the Light of the Access to Finance for Circular Economy Projects' (2019) 20 *University of Oslo Faculty of Law Research Paper*, https://papers.ssrn.com/sol3/papers.cfm?abstract_id=3716255.

V. Need for Policy Coherence for Corporate Sustainability

It is well-recognised that the transition towards sustainable business presupposes a holistic transformation of the existing business law and policies,[46] as singular actions and minute changes have a minimal effect at best.[47] As described in this chapter, policy coherence for corporate sustainability represents such a holistic and organic change that does not impede but ideally supports and incentivises sustainable business practices in the broadest sense. Its operationalisation can be characterised by policy integration.[48] To illustrate, creating the sustainable finance taxonomy can be deemed void if not accompanied by requirements as to how much of the investment at particular levels of financing shall be 'sustainable'. Similarly, not tackling the challenge of excessive difficulty for circular businesses to access traditional finance leaves the EU circular action plan void of content. Furthermore, the Taxonomy could only have been built through a detailed understanding of the nature of underlying corporate practices that qualify as environmentally sustainable, creating a certain symbiosis between sustainable corporate practices, sustainable finance and corporate sustainability reporting. Without policy coherence in business law in the broader sense, and policy coherence in particular between corporate law and governance and finance law, the transition towards sustainable corporate practices will not be timely at best, and impossible at worst due to the clashing aims and goals of particular legal instruments in the two fields.

A. Regenerative Instead of Sustainable?

While the present chapter highlights the need for a swift and carefully tailored reform of EU corporate governance and EU finance law and policy, contributing to a long-standing debate on business sustainability, the climate emergency situation requires bold and ambitious action to ensure the material contribution of businesses to the fight against climate change.

The gap between where we should be in terms of CO_2 emissions level and where we are is becoming ever more significant. In terms of the challenges of protecting biodiversity, tackling resource depletion and preventing breaches of human

[46] OECD (2019) Recommendation of the Council on OECD Legal Instruments Policy Coherence for Sustainable Development, www.oecd.org/gov/pcsd/recommendation-on-policy-coherence-for-sustainable-development-eng.pdf.

[47] B Sjåfjell et al, 'Obstacles to Sustainable Global Business. Towards EU Policy Coherence for Sustainable Development' (2019) 2 *University of Oslo Faculty of Law Research Paper*, 10 *Nordic & European Company Law Working Paper*, https://papers.ssrn.com/sol3/papers.cfm?abstract_id=3354401.

[48] See eg D Azizi et al, 'Policy Integration for Sustainable Development through Multilateral Environmental Agreements' (2019) 25(3) *Global Governance: A Review of Multilateralism and International Organizations* 445.

rights, we are not doing any better. To be timely in terms of action on climate change, more ambitious action is required in terms of business transformation. Circular practices, their content, sustainable impact and financing should be at the forefront, so simplified legislation requiring corporations to 'know their impact' is insufficient. This fact should duly be accounted for when drafting and envisaging reformed EU policies and regulations as suggested in the previous subsections. While the existing EU legal instruments to a certain extent incentivise advanced sustainable practices,[49] the discourse is still primarily focused on establishing a framework of preferably mandatory requirements for understanding and consequently reporting on sustainable corporate conduct, informed by the business case for sustainability. Adding to the arguments exposed in this chapter on the indispensability of policy coherence for sustainability and the urgency of relevant action, the new legislation and the amendments envisaged shall strive for incentivising (or ideally requiring) regenerative business, as '… one that enhance[s], and thrive[s] through the health of social-ecological systems in a co-evolutionary process'.[50]

The regenerative business is one going beyond merely a business case for sustainability, organically and strategically embedding advanced sustainable practices in the core business strategy, and is as such more apt for achieving the ambitious change required for achieving global climate goals. Understanding this crucial difference between sustainable business, frequently characterised by mere enhancement of (productive and resource) efficiency, and regenerative business that requires a holistic reform of production processes and business practices allows for a more coherent and focused policy – and law-making for sustainable business conduct that materially aids the achievement of EU sustainability-related goals. Regenerative business is in more dire need of appropriate financing than the 'traditional' sustainable practices, as it requires an internal corporate transformation.

B. Translating Sustainable Policies vs Risk Assessment

One concern for the success of sustainable finance and governance that has been frequently put forward is its 'translatability' and its measurability. Some scholars and practitioners tend to question how quantifiable sustainability is. However, we see that several international commercial banks are able to translate and integrate various SDGs, CSR, ESG and/or sustainability standards into their

[49] The Corporate Sustainability Reporting Directive requires not only reporting on the current corporate environmental impact, but also presenting a clear strategy to lower the negative impact. See Proposal for a Directive of the European Parliament and of the Council amending Directive 2013/34/EU, Directive 2004/109/EC, Directive 2006/43/EC and Regulation (EU) No 537/2014, as regards corporate sustainability reporting COM(2021) 189 final.

[50] See T Hahn and M Tampe, 'Strategies for Regenerative Business' (2020) *Strategic Organization* 1, 2–11.

policies.[51] The EU Taxonomy with all the delegated acts represents a step towards a consistent terminology and technical standards that should be applied uniformly.[52] We can also expect to hear more from the European Central Bank, the Bank for International Settlement, and other international institutions to help navigate the process. However, it is envisioned by the authors that the standards will become only more relevant with time and with future scandals. One should not forget that little attention was paid to the accounting principles until the Enron or WorldCom scandals. The question remains, when will we start seeing cases.

Thus, the abovementioned concern regarding translatability and measurability of sustainable finance is not substantiated. Instead, the genuine concern is how to support sustainable finance, green transition and at the same time continue to earn a return and manage prudential and conduct risk. A taxonomy will not solve this concern. Instead, risk management tools, such as scenario analysis and stress tests, should be integrated into the standard financial risk measures commonly used by central and commercial banks.[53] These risks need to be made both for sustainable as well unsustainable investments.[54] Hand in hand with this goes managements' concern regarding their potential liability if the scope of their fiduciary duties is materially expanded. Looking back 15 years, certain business practices that today are seen as corrupt were considered good and legitimate. Will this happen in the case of oil investments? Presumably not, as long as the investment is not deemed illegal and the decision-makers can clearly show their due diligence and risk assessment. Verification needs to be a part of the process to mitigate the risk of greenwashing.

C. What are the Necessary Elements for Achieving Coherent Sustainable Policy?

Coherence, as regards sustainable policy in the framework of business and finance, presupposes the mutually recognised need for transition from the

[51] See eg BBVA, ASN Bank, Merkur Cooperative Bank or Triodos.

[52] See Regulation (EU) 2020/852 of the European Parliament and of the Council of 18 June 2020 on the establishment of a framework to facilitate sustainable investment, and amending Regulation (EU) 2019/2088; Commission Delegated Regulation (EU) 2021/1351 of 6 May 2021 supplementing Regulation (EU) 2016/1011 with regard to regulatory technical standards specifying the characteristics of the systems and controls for the identification and reporting of any conduct that may involve manipulation or attempted manipulation of a benchmark; Commission Delegated Regulation (EU) 2021/1349 of 6 May 2021 supplementing Regulation (EU) 2016/1011 with regard to regulatory technical standards specifying the criteria for the competent authorities' compliance assessment regarding the mandatory administration of a critical benchmark.

[53] T Ehlers et al, 'A Taxonomy of Sustainable Finance Taxonomies' (2021) 118 *BIS Paper*.

[54] An example of such a tool is the NGFS Climate Scenarios generated by Integrated Assessment Models, designed to monitor and mitigate climate risks before they materialise. See The Task Force on Climate-Related Risks (TFCR) of the Basel Committee on Bank Supervision which develops methodologies for measuring and assessing climate related risks.

quantitative-based system to a system that is quantified by underlying qualitative assessments. The longer we avoid acknowledging that a simultaneous shift away from policy informed by linear production systems of modern capitalism needs to happen to achieve truly sustainable outcomes, the more complex and inefficient our legislative efforts will prove. This partially answers the question as to how to ensure the credibility of taxonomy-related disclosure and prevent greenwashing. Even if we employ the traditional verification tools of external verification, either through assurance or credit rating agencies, this shift from purely quantitative to qualitatively informed quantification needs to occur. The detailed guidance and the general framework created by the Taxonomy was a very welcome initial development of firmly delineating and distinguishing between sustainable and unsustainable corporate practices, but requires a conceptual revision or reinterpretation of the description of those activities and the key performance indicators (KPIs) attached to those activities. This has been repeatedly recognised by the EU Commission throughout the work on EU Sustainable Taxonomy,[55] noting that the sustainability performance indicators cover the objectives of climate change mitigation and climate change adaptation and are not focusing on traditional KPIs for corporations and financial institutions.

Secondly, the current work on the interconnection between the substance of sustainable business and sustainable finance, as reflected by the renewed corporate sustainability reporting, needs to further the work on reducing duplication or overlaps, especially in sustainable finance. This is directly reflected in the upcoming European Financial Reporting Advisory Group (EFRAG) work on developing draft European sustainability reporting standards, harmonising the work on sustainability disclosure, bringing more legal certainty to the EU business framework and beyond. In the framework of the EFRAG's work, the need to address the corporate sustainability challenges in line with 'sustainability hotspots' is recognised, at the level of the entity in particular as well as more generally at the sectoral level.[56] While disclosure remains an essential guiding principle of corporate reporting related to finance and corporate governance, it needs to be informed in the given circumstances of climate emergency by the relevancy and (potential) impact of the corporate or financial practices on climate change and related sustainability challenges. As such, mere disclosure becomes insufficient, and it needs to become targeted in line with 'sustainability hotspots' of the entity and the industry.

[55] See eg COMMISSION DELEGATED REGULATION (EU) 2021/2178 of 6.7.2021 supplementing Regulation (EU) 2020/852 of the European Parliament and of the Council by specifying the content and presentation of information to be disclosed by undertakings subject to Articles 19a or 29a of Directive 2013/34/EU concerning environmentally sustainable economic activities, and specifying the methodology to comply with that disclosure obligation. COM(2021) 4987 final.

[56] European Reporting Lab EFRAG, 'Final Report Proposals for a Relevant and Dynamic EU Sustainability Reporting Standard-Setting' (2021) 9.

Thirdly, while top-bottom support for the transition towards sustainable corporate practices provided the initial impetus for corporate transformation, now the bottom-up pressures call for more ambitious policy and legislative efforts to assure a timely and efficient transition towards sustainable business practices. While there are similarities and common points between the corporate and financial sectors regarding the top-down and bottom-up transition, the two fields are sufficiently distinct to require a slightly different approach. The so-called 'social licence to operate' approach[57] requires, on the one hand, companies to disclose the relevant information in the given societal context, and in the case of financial institutions, it requires them to address in the current societal frameworks the types of financial products that are directly related to the society, eg pension funds, and assuring their alignment with the challenge of climate emergency. Such a nuanced 'impact-oriented' approach towards the sustainable transformation of financial systems requires further work based on the Taxonomy. At a minimum, financial institutions need to provide a comprehensive view of all investments, financial tools, and products that satisfy the necessary conditions for positive environmental sustainability. This comprehensive view should also provide relevant KPIs for corporations and financial institutions in the form of disclosure of taxonomy-aligned turnover and CapEx.

Last but not least, while focusing on the largest entities through initial sustainability-oriented policy and legislative changes at the EU level in the field of corporate law and finance, the inevitable next step is to address the policy coherence shortcomings that arose by leaving smaller corporate entities and financial institutions outside of the scope of legislative changes. In the finance framework, the focus on (institutional) shareholders and cross-shareholdings allowed traditional banking to escape the scrutiny of small and medium-sized enterprises (SMEs) in Europe. However, the SMEs represent the core of businesses across all EU Member States, and they also lie at the heart of bank financing. Therefore, to achieve sustainable business, SMEs need to change their corporate sustainability practices. One could argue that financial institutions should have initiated their policy transition, especially with regard to SMEs, as those are the entities in need of bank lending while carrying out the transition towards sustainable practices. Thus currently, in the EU, 99 per cent of business activity (that is the SMEs representation) continues to be financed and serviced by a banking system rooted in linear production practices, which are not suitable for financing and supporting advanced sustainable corporate practices (such as circular economy practices). The recognition of the need for such an enlargement of legislative focus is also shown by the inclusion of SMEs in the general obligation of corporate sustainability reporting by 2026.

[57] See eg K Wilburn and R Wilburn, 'Achieving social license to operate using stakeholder theory' (2011) 4 *Journal of International Business Ethics* 3–16.

VI. Conclusion: Corporate Finance and Sustainability in 2030 and the Capital Market Union

The policy coherence for sustainable finance and corporate governance has an additional benefit – achieving the Capital Market Union (CMU). We have witnessed decades-long challenges of bringing diverse financial industry segments closer together and building a functioning and integrated CMU.[58] In 2020, the Commission adopted yet another Capital Market Union Action Plan.[59] According to this plan, the CMU should provide the necessary funding for future sustainable growth. The CMU is envisioned as a channel for the Green Deal,[60] providing the necessary financing for sustainable businesses and supporting the transition to sustainable finance in all EU Member States. Furthermore, the CMU can help the EU attract truly sustainable investments worldwide and become more competitive in sustainable business models, as long as we can design coherent, sustainable policies across sectors.

Even though this chapter shows that policy coherence is challenging and easier said than done, it is indisputable that sustainability is the only way forward, and the EU, together with all its Member States need to re-design their sectoral policies to become sustainable. Even though there is no one-size-fits-all sequence, the finance industry and corporate governance obligations shall be the first that need to change. Clear financial sustainability standards and deliverables, combined with enforceable management rights and responsibilities, must be adopted in the shortest possible time.

We started this chapter by also indicating the climate change concerns. While we recognise that many of our corporate law colleagues will fail to fully understand our concern for the future and continue to beat around the bush with the shareholder vs stakeholder theory, the reality is dire. To showcase how misaligned the finance industry is with the sustainability goals, a recent analysis of over 16,5000 investment funds worth USD 27 trillion has revealed that under 0.5 per cent of their assets are aligned with the Paris Agreement.[61] Money talks loudly, and so far, they only whisper. This needs to change.

[58] See eg A Andhov, 'Fintech as a Facilitator for the Capital Market Union?' (2018) 15 *Nordic & European Company Law Working Paper*, 63 University of Copenhagen Faculty of Law Research Paper.

[59] European Commission, 'Communication from the Commission to the European Parliament, the Council, the European Economic and Social Committee and the Committee of the Regions, A Capital Markets Union for People and Businesses – New Action Plan' COM(2020) 590 final, 24 September 2020.

[60] ibid 4.

[61] CDP, 'Under 1% of $27 trillion global fund assets are Paris-aligned', www.cdp.net/en/articles/investor/under-1-of-27-trillion-global-fund-assets-are-paris-aligned.

14

FinTech in Luxembourg: A New Risk-management Approach

MARC PILKINGTON

I. Introduction

Historically, Luxembourg is a small country whose stability, high levels of per capita income, and geographical proximity with Belgium, France, and Germany, have ensured rapid growth, tamed inflation, and low unemployment rates. The industrial sector, under the initial impulse of the steel industry, progressively diversified toward other activities such as chemistry and rubber. We review the historical process that has seen Luxembourg come to the fore in Europe. The phenomenal rise of the FinTech industry,[1] Bitcoin and Blockchain technology[2] has refocused our concerns on e-money service providers and virtual currencies (VC), preferred to the cryptocurrency subset, their regulation, and their governance. We set out to examine these developments with the risk-management philosophy of the major players in mind. We propose a novel risk management framework taking into account the implementation of distributed ledger technology (DLT).

II. The Architecture of the Luxembourgish Financial Centre

A. The Growth of the Financial Centre

The *Banque internationale à Luxembourg*, the oldest private bank in the Grand Duchy, was founded in the middle of the nineteenth century, to help finance the

[1] M Wolf, 'Good news – fintech could disrupt finance' *Financial Times* (8 March 2016) www.ft.com/content/425cb3ca-e480-11e5-a09b-1f8b0d268c39.

[2] M Pilkington, 'Blockchain technology: principles and applications' in FX Olleros and M Zhegu (eds), *Research Handbook on Digital Transformations* (Cheltenham, Edward Elgar Publishing, 2016).

development of an economy mostly based on the steel industry. Luxembourg entered the small club of offshore financial centres in 1929 by adopting a new regime for holdings allowing them to establish subsidiaries in Luxembourg (whose *raison d'être* was ownership and asset management in foreign countries) exempted from capital gains and income tax. Another objective was to avoid double taxation (being taxed both in the home and host countries). However, this legitimate objective often morphed into double non-taxation that is fiscal evasion in both countries. Initially, and as the saying 'loans make deposits'[3] goes, these deposits were the outcome of short- and medium-term operations. Progressively, the market shifted to a long-term horizon. The turning point was the first issuance of offshore Eurobonds to finance the Autostrade investment project, the Italian motorway construction company in 1963. The growth of the Luxembourgish financial centre thus took place in the 1960s with the setting up of international loans and -Eurodollar markets. These were the dollar holdings owned by European residents and initially used in short and medium-run operations. These Eurodollars arose out of the US balance of payments deficit: European companies were earning dollars by exporting to the US and depositing them in European banks; or there were dollars accumulated by banks and financial institutions through American investments in Europe, not to forget the cash flow management of multinational corporations and central bank reserves. The market progressively shifted to the long-term issuance of eurobonds. The take-off occurred in the 1980s with the advent of financial liberalisation and the integration of capital markets. A Luxembourgish Big Bang has been singled out akin to the transformation of the British financial centre in the 1980s. Luxembourg began at the time to shelter an increasing number of asset management firms and subsidiaries of global banks.

B. The Current Configuration

The financial sector exceeds 35 per cent of GDP[4] against 28 per cent one decade earlier,[5] and more than offsets the decline of steel reflecting the large-scale sectoral changes throughout the twentieth century. The investment fund sector benefited from the launch and growth of cross-border funds (UCITS) in the 1990s. Luxembourg is the world's second-largest investment fund asset domicile, after the US. The majority of Luxembourg's banks are foreign owned, and involved in cross-border operations.[6] In the aftermath of the most severe financial crisis

[3] H Withers, *The Meaning of Money* (London, Smith Elder and Co, 1909).
[4] CIA, *The World Factbook 2014–2015*, 58th edn (Washington DC, Central Intelligence Agency, 2015).
[5] CIA, *The World Factbook 2012–2013*, 49th edn (Washington DC, Central Intelligence Agency, 2013).
[6] CIA (n 4).

since the 1930s,[7] the sovereign debt crisis exerted increased pressure, passed on by the UE and the OECD, on countries equated to tax havens. Luxembourg has lost some of its past comparative advantage in terms of jurisdictional competition,[8] exacerbated by the Luxleaks scandal.[9] The economy heavily relies on a highly qualified and cross-border labour force among which 52 per cent are French workers, a stable proportion between 2005 and 2019.[10] The unemployment rate was 5.36 per cent in 2019.[11]

The country experienced rapid growth between 2004 and 2007 before being hit hard by the global financial crisis with a 3.6 per cent GDP contraction in 2008. Government authorities were forced to recapitalise a number of banks, and put in place bailout plans. That year, the country recorded a 5 per cent public deficit. This short recession was followed by a sharp rebound in 2010–11 and a new slowdown in 2012 (−0.3 per cent). Growth has been exceptionally strong since (especially between 2013 and 2016, way above the EU average between 0 and 2 per cent during the same period).

Figure 1 Post-crisis GDP growth in Luxembourg (2012–2019)

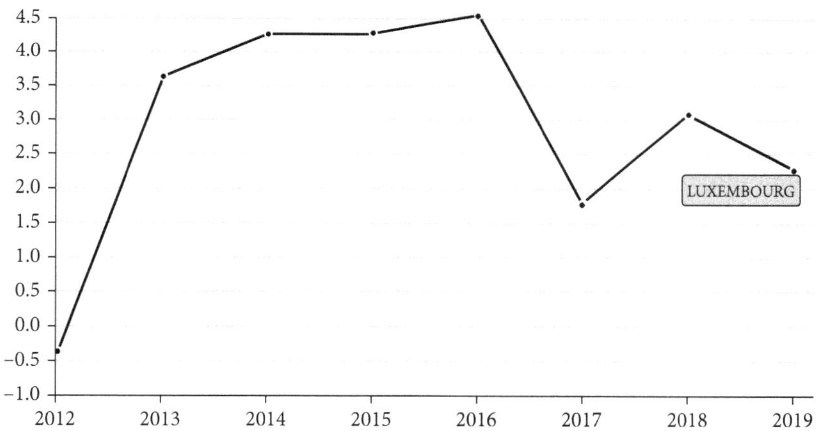

Source: https://data.worldbank.org/indicator/NY.GDP.MKTP.KD.ZG?end=2019&locations=LU&start=2012&view=chart (CC BY-4.0, https://creativecommons.org/licenses/by/4.0/).

The public budget generates a surplus, and debt GDP ratio is one of the lowest in the EU.[12]

[7] International Monetary Fund, 'World Economic Outlook: Crisis and Recovery' (2009).
[8] F Kieff and T Paredes, *Perspectives on Corporate Governance* (Cambridge, Cambridge University Press, 2010).
[9] CIA (n 4).
[10] Statec, 'L'impact des frontaliers dans la balance des paiements en 2019' (2020) 21 *Regards* 2.
[11] CIA (n 4).
[12] ibid.

C. A Multilevel Regulation Architecture

Finance is structured around a multilevel regulation architecture at the supranational level (UE, OECD, Financial Action Group, IMF, G20), at the state level (Central Bank of Luxembourg and the Commission de Surveillance du Secteur Financier), the intermediary dimension with representative bodies that take part in the self-regulation of banks, investment funds, mutual funds and insurance companies, and finally service providers forming a nexus of eclectic institutions (the Big Four, Clearstream, CETREL, business lawyers, notaries, fiduciaries etc) that complement the main actors.[13]

D. The Banking and Financial Industry

Universal banks, paramount in Luxembourg, are authorised to perform *all* banking activities both domestically and internationally. They enjoy international notoriety due to their expertise, their multilingual and highly qualified staff and their strict enforcement of laws and regulations. Universal banks are authorised on paper, but in practice, very few banks are effectively active in all segments of the banking industry.[14] The universal bank model, however, is a source of fragility, because the inefficiencies are overcompensated by implicit subsidies that they benefit from by virtue of their systemic nature.[15] Luxembourg is often described as an investment centre[16] geared at wealthy international institutional investors as shown by the weight of Private Banking and Wealth Management entities. Financial services are customised, of high quality, and often come hand in hand with related technical services. Luxembourg is replete with portfolio managers who deploy cutting edge techniques inspired by structured finance. Luxembourg is a global leader in Undertakings for Collective Investment in Transferable Securities (OPCVM in French). These financial services must comply with European Directives and obtain a passport enabling unrestricted commercialisation in the EU. Luxembourg can tap into a highly skilled labour force composed of product development experts, lawyers, accountants, service provider and so on. Venture capitalists enjoy a legislative framework defined by the Law of 15 June 2004, which enhances competitiveness and is favourable to investors from both legal and taxation standpoints. Specialised investment funds benefit

[13] P Pieretti, A Bourgain and P Courtin, *Place Financière de Luxembourg, Analyse des sources de ses avantages compétitifs et de sa dynamique* (Bruxelles, De Boeck, 2007) 26.

[14] ibid 27.

[15] JL Gaffard and JP Pollin, 'Pourquoi faut-il séparer les activités bancaires?' (2013) 36 *Les notes de l'OFCE*.

[16] ibid.

from an ad hoc legal structure (Law of 13 February 2007) for private investors, with lighter regulation and disclosure requirements. Because these specialised funds invest in financial, real estate, and money assets, they are well suited to the implementation of Blockchain technology for improving operational efficiency, security, client service, and capturing new revenue opportunities. Investment vehicles for microfinance are well supported by the Luxembourg Fund Labelling Agency (LuxFLAG) founded in 2006. Securitisation was facilitated by the Law of 22 March 2004. Other dynamic segments include vehicles for the pooling of pension funds, covered bonds issuing banks, the captive reinsurance industry, which has grown tremendously in the last three decades, consulting and auditing services, and financial engineering that requires multidisciplinary knowledge of complex transaction structuring, distribution expertise and cross-border management.

E. Luxembourg's Attractiveness

We formulate hereafter the hypothesis that the high adaptability of the regulatory environment is a source of competitive advantage endogenous to the development of the financial centre. Banking secrecy plays a pivotal role in the potential attractiveness of Private Banking. Luxembourg represents a substantial tax optimisation potential through financial engineering projects:

> The country draws on its political, economic and regulatory stability to foster a strong culture of investor protection. Financial services in Luxembourg benefit greatly from this stability.[17]

Luxembourg is a proactive country on a legislative level that offers an innovative framework for e-commerce, being a country, where Internet giants such as Skype, eBay and Amazon have opened their European headquarters. The latter multinationals specialise in intangible assets such as virtual files whose production is not anchored to any specific nation-state.[18] Luxembourg's small size is undoubtedly a source of competitive advantage.[19] It is a major international hub at the heart of Europe with 150 nationalities, 80 per cent of startup founders who are foreign, and is a pleasant place to live according to its residents.[20]

[17] Mondaini cited in R Pagnamenta, 'Alter Domus – Continuous Growth of New Private Debt and Real Estate Funds in Luxembourg' (2021) *Luxembourg Report*, www.alterdomus.com/media/615af4bef0276_pew-luxembourg-report-2021-continuous-growth.pdf.

[18] Red Herring, 'Luxembourg, Building on Old Habits, Births a Tech Ecosystem' (*Red Herring*, 3 March 2016) www.redherring.com/finance/luxembourg-building-old-habits-births-tech-ecosystem.

[19] ibid.

[20] ibid.

III. SWOT Analysis of E-Money Service Providers and Virtual Currency Issuers

A. The Global Level

The core of the global financial system is composed of banks and insurance companies.[21] The former manage payments systems, and act as financial intermediaries, market makers, and instruments designers, while the latter manage and assess a broad range of risks. The frontier between the two sectors is often porous. The FinTech sector can be considered disruptive for at least two reasons: (1) Blockchain technology that enables real-time settlement via distributed ledgers,[22] and (2) peer-to-peer lending that disintermediates the banking sector, and saves costs.[23] While cryptocurrencies open up the possibility of near-zero transactions costs outside the supervision of regulators,[24] FinTech pertains to innovative startup companies operating in the financial sector. The latter apply modern technology solutions in the financial services industry to offer digitally enhanced products, and allow widespread access to financial products at a lower cost than traditional players. The total value of investments into FinTech companies worldwide increased dramatically between 2010 and 2019, when it reached 215.4 billion US dollars. In 2020, however, FinTech companies saw investments drop by more than one third, reaching a value of 121.5 billion US dollars.[25]

B. The European Level

The 'E-Money Directive' (EMD)[26] enabled the conception of innovative e-money services, facilitated market access to European businesses, and promoted effective competition between the market actors, thereby benefiting consumers and businesses alike. EMD contains rules for electronic wallets used to store value

[21] Wolf (n 1).
[22] M Pilkington, 'Bitcoin through the lenses of complexity theory: Some non-orthodox implications for economic theorizing' in R Martin and J Pollard (eds), *Elgar Handbook of Geographies of Money and Finance* (Cheltenham, Edward Elgar, 2016) 610–36.
[23] Wolf (n 1).
[24] ibid.
[25] F Norrestad, 'Investments into fintech companies globally 2010–2021' (*Statista*, 11 January 2022) www.statista.com/statistics/719385/investments-into-fintech-companies-globally/.
[26] Directive 2009/110/EC of the European Parliament and the Council, of 16 September 2009, on the taking up, pursuit and prudential supervision of the business of the electronic money institutions amending Directive 2005/60/EC and 2006/48/EC and repealing Directive 2000/46/EC [2009] OJ L267/10.

via a computer, a mobile device or online. The Directive defines electronic money as follows:

- electronically, including magnetically, stored monetary value;
- as represented by a claim on the issuer which is issued on receipt of funds for the purpose of making payment transactions;
- a transaction is an act initiated by the payer or the payee, of placing, transferring or withdrawing funds, irrespective of any underlying obligations between the payer and the payee;
- as being accepted by a natural or legal person other than the e-money issuer.

The Directive on Payment Services (PSD2)[27] provides the legal foundation for the creation of an EU-wide single market for payments. PSD2 aims at establishing a ruleset applicable to all payment services in the EU. The target is to make cross-border payments as easy, efficient, and secure as national payments within a Member State. PSD2 seeks to improve competition by opening up payment markets to new entrants, thereby fostering greater efficiency and cost-reduction.

The European Banking Authority (EBA) distinguishes between e-money and virtual currencies or VC, the latter are not anchored to any fiat currency (FC), and are not redeemable at par value by an issuer:

> VCs are a digital representation of value that is neither issued by a central bank or a public authority, nor necessarily attached to a FC, but is accepted by natural or legal persons as a means of payment and can be transferred, stored or traded electronically.[28]

The e-money Directive initially referred to electronic value issued by electronic money institutions (EMI). In the absence of any central issuing body,[29] crypto-tokens do not represent any claim on a specific issuer, and lie outside the definitional scope of e-money. VCs are not legal tender, because the following features are not fulfilled: (a) mandatory acceptance, ie that the creditor of a payment obligation cannot refuse currency unless the parties have agreed on other means of payment; (b) acceptance at full face value, ie the monetary value is equal to the amount indicated; and (c) that the currency has the power to discharge debtors from their payment obligations.[30] El Salvador is the first country ever to

[27] Directive 2015/2366/EU of the European Parliament and the Council, of 25 November 2015, on payment services in the internal market, amending Directives 2002/65/EC, 2009/110/EC and 2013/36/EU and Regulation (EU) No 1093/2010, and repealing Directive 2007/64/EC [2015] OJ L337/35.

[28] European Banking Authority, 'EBA Opinion on "VC"', EBA/Op/2014/08, 7.

[29] Pilkington (n 22).

[30] European Banking Authority (n 28) 13.

make Bitcoin legal tender.[31] Slowly, the stance of central banks is evolving with the advent of central bank digital currencies (CBDC). ECB President Christine Lagarde[32] thinks that '[their] role is to secure trust in money. This means making sure the euro is fit for the digital age'. If a VC were to be backed by a governmental authority, it would become de facto a fiat currency.[33]

The Peoples Bank of China (2016) has planned to launch its own CBDC, owing to the untapped potential of emergent technologies for fighting off tax evasion, money laundering and criminal behaviour. In February 2021, PBC and the Central Bank of the United Arab Emirates (CBUAE) joined a CBDC project for cross-border foreign currency payments, the m-CBDC Bridge initiative, in partnership with the BIS Innovation Hub (BISIH), the Hong Kong Monetary Authority (HKMA) and the Bank of Thailand (BoT).[34]

C. The National Level

The Law of 10 November 2009 governs the transfer of funds and payment operations such as mobile and online payments as well as e-money activities. With the Law of 20 May 2011, a legal framework was set up for electronic money defined as monetary value representing a claim on the issuer. Value is electronically and/or magnetically stored, issued against funding for the purpose of electronic payments, accepted by a physical person other than the e-money issuer. EMI can provide payments services, grant loans linked to payments services, offer operational and auxiliary e-money services, or the provision of e-payments, to manage payments systems, and undertake commercial activities.

EMIs are subject to the agreement and the prudential supervision of the *Commission de Surveillance du Secteur Financier* (CSSF), the competent authority for the prudential surveillance of credit institutions, financial industry professionals, mutual funds, and securitisation firms, in Luxembourg. CSSF ensures that EMIs have a scheme for governance, detection, and management processes for potential risks, and a control and security mechanism for their computer systems. CSSF issued on 15 January 2020 a communiqué on virtual assets and virtual asset service providers, considering the Laws of 25 March 2020 amending the Anti-Money Laundering/Combating the Financing of Terrorism (AML/CFT) Law. Entities established or providing services in Luxembourg must register if they provide one or more of the following services on behalf of their clients

[31] BBC, 'Bitcoin: El Salvador makes cryptocurrency legal tender' (*BBC*, 9 June 2021) www.bbc.com/news/world-latin-america-57398274.

[32] European Central Bank, 'Report on a digital euro' (2020) 2.

[33] European Banking Authority (n 28) 11, fn.

[34] Bank for International Settlements, 'Central banks of China and United Arab Emirates join digital currency project for cross-border payments' Press Release (*BIS*, 23 February 2021) www.bis.org/press/p210223.htm.

or for their own accounts: exchange between virtual assets and fiat currencies, exchange between one or more forms of virtual assets, transfer of virtual assets, safekeeping and/or administration of virtual assets or instruments enabling control over virtual assets, including custodian wallet services, participation in and provision of financial services related to an issuer's offer and/or sale of virtual assets.[35]

VCs are scriptural (as opposed to fiduciary) money that dispenses with tangible writing. Furthermore, 'if VCs cannot be assimilated to legal tender currency, they may qualify for e-money and/or payment services. They would then fall on the regulatory scope of CSSF'.[36] VCs are regulated by the European Banking Authority (EBA) and the European Securities and Markets Authority (ESMA). CSSF issued its first statement on the legal treatment of VCs in February 2014.[37] VCs are considered as money, since they are accepted as a means of payment of goods and services by a sufficiently large group of people (CSSF 2014). Regarding risk management, CSSF points out that 'VC are obviously not legal tender, and they entail risks […] subject to a public warning issued by the EBA and ESMA'. All financial institutions must be authorised by the Minister of Finance, and subject to CSSF prudential supervision (Article 14 of the law of 5 April 1993). Consequently, all EMIs and VCs must define their business purpose with precision so that CSSF may recommend an adequate status ahead of ministerial authorisation. For instance, PayPal is a partnership limited by shares authorised to operate as a bank under Article 2 of the above law.[38] The next section offers a comprehensive strengths, weakness, opportunity, and threat (SWOT) analysis of e-money service providers and VC issuers in Luxembourg.

IV. SWOT Analysis

A. Strengths

Luxembourg is at the forefront in the promotion of the Virtual Agenda (EU Telecoms Council, Luxembourg 2013). This breakthrough mirrors the

[35] Blockchain and Virtual Currencies Working Group, 'Luxembourg's Commission de Surveillance du Secteur Financier issues a statement on Virtual Assets, VASPs and the related registration process, The Blockchain and Virtual Currencies Working Group (WG)' (2020).

[36] Wagner, cited in F Thibaut, 'Cet actif de première classe: la donnée' (*Paperjam*, 18 February 2016) https://paperjam.lu/article/news-cet-actif-de-premiere-classe-la-donnee.

[37] P Rizzo, 'Luxembourg Opens Dialogue with Bitcoin Businesses in New Statement' (*CoinDesk*, 11 March 2014) www.coindesk.com/policy/2014/03/11/luxembourg-opens-dialogue-with-bitcoin-businesses-in-new-statement.

[38] P Valcke, N Vandezande and N Van de Velde, 'The Evolution of Third Party Payment Providers and Cryptocurrencies Under the EU's Upcoming PSD2 and AMLD4' (2015) 1 *SWIFT Institute Working Paper* 58, fn 284.

consolidation of the new digital economy. The new Cybersecurity strategy 'An Open, Safe and Secure Cyberspace' represents the holistic vision elaborated by the EU, to tackle cybercriminal attacks (PricewaterhouseCoopers, 2016) and the disruption of the economy, while promoting values, such as freedom and democracy. The dynamism of the Single Market is contingent on trust building, enhanced accessibility for users of e-money, and data protection. The 'Draft regulation on electronic identification and trust services for electronic transactions' in the internal market was endorsed by Member States in February 2014. The Regulation enables students to enroll online at a foreign university, citizens to fill online tax returns in another EU country, and businesses to participate electronically in public calls for tenders. The electronic Authentication services in Europe (eIAS) come hand in hand with improved legal recognition and authentication processes.

B. Weaknesses

Notwithstanding its dynamism, the telecom industry has been hindered by regulatory shortcomings. The European Commission (EC) published a reasoned opinion intended for Luxembourgish State authorities within the 2009 EU Regulatory Framework for Electronic Communications; according to Article 16(6), the national regulator must analyse the market to ensure that the latter is competitive enough, and provides consumers with positive effects in terms of choice, prices, and innovation. The regulators must then notify the EC what steps they have undertaken within three years following the adoption of the last measure. Out of seven markets, Luxembourg failed to notify the EU in 2008 (2006 for certain markets), and request assistance from the Body of European Regulators for Electronic Communications (BEREC), as stipulated in Article 16(7).

The Digital Economy and Society Index (DESI) is a tool to measure the progress towards a digital economy and society, composed of five principal policy areas (connectivity, human capital/digital skills, use of Internet, Integration of Digital Technology, and Digital Public Services) representing overall more than 30 indicators.[39] In 2020, a dimension was added: fixed very high-capacity network (VHCN) coverage. The COVID-19 pandemic has demonstrated the relevance of these policy dimensions.[40] Luxembourg ranked tenth out of 28 EU Member States in 2020, one place lower than in 2019.[41]

[39] European Commission, Digital Economy and Society Index (DESI) 2020.
[40] ibid 2.
[41] ibid 3.

Figure 2 DESI index

Source: https://ec.europa.eu/commission/presscorner/detail/en/MEMO_16_385 (CC BY 4.0, https://creativecommons.org/licenses/by/4.0/).

C. Opportunities

The diffusion and adoption of Blockchain technology are compelling banks to undergo a process of diversification initiated in the late 1990s by the advent of e-banking,[42] conducive to increased market shares and reduced costs. A startup scene is gradually emerging for e-money service providers and VC issuers. Brexit has precipitated a relocation of London-based FinTechs to multilingual Luxembourg.[43] Numerous investment opportunities exist for which traditional business strategy tools such as Porter's five forces have lost their relevance,[44] and must be replaced by new approaches (see section III).

[42] Basel Committee on Banking Supervision, 'Risk Management for Electronic Banking and Electronic Money Activities', BS/97/122.

[43] T Thiel, 'If Luxembourg attracts UK-based Fintechs after Brexit, what's next?' (*PwC Blog*, 16 August 2018) https://blog.pwc.lu/luxembourgfintechhub/.

[44] T Pajak, 'DevOps at Seamless: The Why, How, and What' (*infoQ*, 29 November 2015) www.infoq.com/articles/devops-seamless-why-how-what. See also ME Porter, *Competitive Strategy* (New York, Free Press, 1980).

i. An Emerging Regulatory Environment

European legislation on crypto assets, previously defined as 'financial instruments' under the Markets in Financial Instruments Directive, have made a quantum leap forward with the integration of DLT under a new regulatory package[45] in the direct lineage with the FinTech Action plan in March 2018.[46] On 24 September 2020, the European Commission thus proposed a pilot regime for market infrastructures called the Markets in Crypto-Assets Regulation – MiCA. The regulatory package makes provision for trading and settlement using DLT;[47] it covers entities issuing crypto assets, firms providing crypto asset services (eg, digital wallets) and cryptocurrency exchanges.

ii. A New European Digital Money Identity

For Mertens, 'the "proclamation of identity" is one of the privileged means of mobilising and channeling the passions or political emotions that are set in motion in the name of a project'.[48] Identity is a complex and multifaceted concept. Vissol argues that the concept of identity belongs to the realm of belonging rather than that of being.[49] A new European monetary identity could thus be structured around the regulatory and technological sandbox called European Blockchain Partnership (EBP) and the EU Blockchain Observatory and Forum, two initiatives intended to develop a common EU strategy. Likewise, TOKEN (Transformative impact Of blocKchain tEchnologies iN public services) funded by the EU Horizon 2020 programme, aims to develop an experimental ecosystem for the adoption of DLT as a driver for the transformation of public services towards an open and collaborative government approach. TOKEN was developed by a consortium of 11 entities from eight EU Member States, including Luxembourg-based Infrachain (2021), a member of INATBA, a global forum for developers and users of DLT to interact with regulators and policy makers and bring DLT to the next stage. Infrachain[50] is convinced that Europe needs a vast community of operators and application providers to move toward a European DLT infrastructure.

[45] European Commission, 'Proposal for a Regulation of the European Parliament and of the Council on Markets in Crypto-assets, and amending Directive (EU) 2019/1937' COM(2020) 593 final.

[46] European Commission, 'Communication to the European Parliament, the Council, the European Central Bank, the European Economic and Social Committee and the Committee of the Regions – FinTech Action plan: For a more competitive and innovative European financial sector' COM(2018) 109 final.

[47] European Commission, 'Legal and regulatory framework for blockchain, Shaping Europe's digital future' (*European Commission*, 13 April 2021) https://digital-strategy.ec.europa.eu/en/policies/regulatory-framework-blockchain.

[48] J Mertens, 'The Euro and European Identity' (2005) N° Winter *European Political Economy Review* 171–72.

[49] T Vissol, 'The Euro: Outcome and Element of the European Identity' (2003) *YCIAS- European Studies Working Paper* 3.

[50] See https://infrachain.com/.

D. Threats

i. Operational Risk

Operational risk arises in the context of controls pertaining to the access to systems essential to risk management and accounting. This information can be potentially communicated to a third party, thereby causing severe risks of fraud or malfunctioning. Control of access to internal systems of financial institutions has become increasingly complex owing to constant computational power upgrading, the geographical distance from authorised access points to the system, and the use of various routes including public networks such as the Internet. E-monies coexist with the fraudulent use of banks liabilities following an internal breach in information systems security.[51] The growth of cryptocurrencies is hampered by doubts surrounding the security of transactions and data protection.[52] There is also the threat posed by terrorism and money laundering.

ii. The End of Banking Secrecy

Luxembourg was formerly known as the European 'death star' of financial secrecy but began to improve her image on 13 March 2009 after a dramatic turn during which she agreed to comply with OECD principles on the exchange of information and taxation cooperation.[53] European institutions are concerned with tax evasion in the aftermath of the Luxleaks scandal[54] wherein prominent multinationals were found guilty of engaging in secret pacts with Luxembourg's tax authorities, to lower their tax bills by channelling profits through the Grand Duchy. A law on the exchange of tax information took effect at the start of 2017; data on past deals began to be shared.[55]

iii. Conflicts of Interest in the Financial System

In a letter to former EU commissioner Michel Barnier,[56] the head of ProtInvest, an investor protection group criticised the decision to appoint Jean Claude Juncker's senior adviser as director of the Luxembourg Stock Exchange. Both institutions fall under the regulatory scope of CSSF. This example illustrates the conflicts of interest between the business community and the regulators.

[51] Basel Committee on Banking Supervision, 'Risk Management' (1997) 5.

[52] F Thibaut, 'Encadrer l'explosion des fintech' (*Paperjam*, 8 March 2016) https://paperjam.lu/article/news-encadrer-lexplosion-des-fintech.

[53] M Filipucci and O Wibratte, 'Echange automatique d'informations et coopération fiscale: l'épilogue est proche!' (PwC Luxembourg, 2013).

[54] A Christians, 'Lux Leaks: Revealing the Law, One Plain Brown Envelope at a Time Tax Notes International' (2014) 76 *Tax Notes International.*

[55] J Brunsden and P Spiegel, 'Sweetheart tax deals targeted as EU boosts information exchange' *Financial Times* (6 October 2015) www.ft.com/content/c3c1484c-6c33-11e5-aca9-d87542bf8673.

[56] E Kelleher, 'Luxembourg: "A flagrant violation of good governance"' *Financial Times* (6 October 2013) www.ft.com/content/958935c6-2643-11e3-aee8-00144feab7de.

iv. NGO and EU Criticism

For the World Forum on Taxation Transparency, Luxembourg is compliant on Phase 1, but has failed to validate Phase 2 (ie, lack of implementation of the regulatory framework). Luxembourg has indeed become a top destination for the profit-shifting activities of the top French banks with resulting distortions in banks' productivity statistics defying imagination; hence a Singapore-based banker is on average 42 times more 'productive' than his Paris-based counterpart.[57] Likewise, Luxembourg was ordered by the European Commission to recover millions in back taxes from a Fiat Chrysler Automobiles NV unit.[58] An investigation led by Bachero et al claims that despite reform efforts, Luxembourg is still an opaque jurisdiction, where mandatory disclosure rules for companies and individuals can be circumvented and sanctions are rarely enforced.[59] One year after the creation of a register of ultimate beneficial owners, barely half of all companies and one fifth of investment funds were compliant. Worse, dozens of foreign citizens linked to corruption, embezzlement of public funds, organised crime, and tax crime have opened companies in Luxembourg, without raising any red flags, suggesting regulatory failure in the corporate industry.

v. Rebranding Efforts

The Tax Justice Network evokes an internationally oriented centre with a strong offshore culture allowing multinationals and wealthy clients to take advantage of legal loopholes, by minimising tax liabilities. Of course, Luxembourg's reputation was seriously damaged by the Luxleaks scandal[60] and more recently by the Pandora papers.[61] There is little evidence that Luxembourg has substantially improved her image.[62] Yet Haag regrets that the country is reduced to this persistent fiscal-paradise-and-tax-evasion thriving country cliché.[63]

[57] B Cassel and M Pelloli, 'Les gros profits des banques françaises dans les paradis fiscaux' (*Le Parisien*, 16 March 2016) www.leparisien.fr/economie/votre-argent/les-gros-profits-des-banques-francaises-dans-les-paradis-fiscaux-16-03-2016-5631375.php.

[58] European Commission, 'EU study on the New rules for a new age? Legal analysis of a Single Market for the Information Society, European Commission's Information Society and Media Directorate-General' (2009).

[59] A Baquero, M Vaudano and C Anesi, 'Shedding Light on Big Secrets in Tiny Luxembourg' (*The Organized Crime and Corruption Reporting Project*, 8 February 2021) www.occrp.org/en/openlux/shedding-light-on-big-secrets-in-tiny-luxembourg.

[60] Christians (n 54).

[61] Y Hansen, 'Luxembourg named in new tax haven investigation' *Luxembourg Times* (4 October 2021) www.luxtimes.lu/en/business-finance/luxembourg-named-in-new-tax-haven-investigation-6159c52bde135b92369724e1#:~:text=In%202019%2C%20the%20EU%20parliament,and%20facilitate%20aggressive%20tax%20planning%22.

[62] ibid.

[63] E Haag, *The Rise of Luxembourg from Independence to Success, 1815–2015: Two Hundred Years of Modern Luxembourg History* (Luxembourg, Editions Saint-Paul, 2015).

Our brief overview of the multi-level regulatory architecture and our SWOT analysis of e-money services and virtual currencies in Luxembourg has helped us outline several salient features of the multidimensional environment of this small, yet fascinating country at the heart of the EU. As our chapter is geared at the emergent risk-management strategies of the FinTech industry in Luxembourg, our final section proposes a novel risk-management framework and toolkit in order to assist e-money service providers and VC issuers in the context of the increasing adoption of DLT (distributed ledger technology).

V. A New Risk Management Philosophy for Virtual Currencies and E-Money Services

Risks are 'the possibility that human actions or events lead to consequences that harm aspects of things that human beings value'.[64] Risk management is the collective 'process of reducing the risks to a level deemed acceptable [...] and to assure control, monitoring, and public communication'.[65] From a banking perspective, risk management is equated by Bauer and Ryser to a 'set of hedging strategies to alter the probability distribution of the future value of the banks' assets'.[66] A negative dimension of risk is attached to these definitions unlike the economic definition that refers to both gains and losses.[67] We agree with Klinke and Renn who state that the negative nature of a given event implies an underlying social judgement independent of the hazard itself.[68] However, we adopt a hybrid definition by equating risks in VC and e-money services to events threatening assets, future cash flows or any success factor of e-money and VC institutions.

Through recurrent scandals,[69] cryptocurrencies are under increased scrutiny, and justify the elaboration of a comprehensive risk-management framework. Our terminological choice in favour of VCs and e-money services, arguably more

[64] A Klinke and O Renn 'A new approach to risk evaluation and management: risk-based, precaution-based, and discourse-based strategies' (2002) 22 *Risk analysis: an official publication of the Society for Risk Analysis* 1071.
[65] R Zimmerman, 'The Management of Risk' in VT Covello, J Menkes and J Mumpower (eds), *Risk Evaluation and Management. Contemporary Issues in Risk Analysis, vol 1* (Boston, Springer, 1986) 436.
[66] W Bauer and M Ryser, 'Risk management strategies for banks' (2004) 28 *Journal of Banking & Finance* 331.
[67] Klinke and Renn (n 64) 1071.
[68] ibid.
[69] BBC, 'Hackers steal $600m in major cryptocurrency heist' (*BBC*, 11 August 2021) www.bbc.com/news/business-58163917.

outdated in view of the meteoric rise of cryptocurrencies in the public eye, may seem daring. Nonetheless, it is justified by an attempt at generality and abstraction for sheltering spectacular technological developments such as directed acyclic graph or DAG,[70] the pending and yet uncertain Ethereum 3.0[71] departing from first-generation cryptocurrencies.[72] However, we are convinced that DLT remains the most decisive game changer which inspired our framework (see Tables 1 and 2).

Our risk management philosophy is inspired by a few key questions. Why are we innovating? What is driving the innovation agenda? Is it demanded by customers or shareholders? Is it part of a broader strategic vision? Is it defensive (aimed at mitigating threats of virtual disruption and its negative consequences)? Is it offensive? Is it aimed at seizing market opportunities, and reaping the positive effects? What are we innovating in? Finally, how are we innovating?[73] The risk manager should choose between a constructive and a realist worldview,[74] and decide whether widespread public concerns (eg, criminal use of cryptocurrency for illegal activities or fears of Ponzi schemes) are legitimate and should be used as regulatory criteria.[75] Finally, the risk manager must consider different ontological categories of uncertainty.[76] The objectives of conventional KYC (know-your-customer) procedures include reasonable efforts to determine the identity and beneficial ownership of accounts, sources of funds, nature of customers' business, the assessment of reasonable account activity, identity of customers' customers etc. Given the idiosyncratic nature of e-money service providers and VC issuers, these objectives ought to be revised when defining a risk management philosophy, and once surfaced out, FinTech actors need a hands-on risk-management framework. The risk manager thus seeks to identify risks arising from their activities, prioritise them, describe their consequences, and take mitigating action if required.

As explained by Platen,[77] new methodological challenges arise from the need to integrate risk modelling in finance, insurance, and other areas of risk

[70] FM Benčić, and IP Žarko, 'Distributed ledger technology: Blockchain compared to directed acyclic graph?' (2018) *IEEE 38th International Conference on Distributed Computing Systems (ICDCS)* 1569–70.

[71] M Catmouse, 'Ethereum 3.0. What Would Happen After Ethereum 2.0?' (*Pensacola Voice*, 4 August 2021) www.pensacolavoice.com/ethereum-3-0-what-would-happen-after-ethereum-2-0/.

[72] G Claeys and M Demertzis, 'The next generation of digital currencies: in search of stability' (*Bruegel*, 2 December 2019) www.bruegel.org/2019/12/the-next-generation-of-digital-currencies-in-search-of-stability/.

[73] Ernst & Young (2015).

[74] Klinke and Renn (n 64) 1072–73.

[75] J Brito and A Castillo, *Bitcoin: A Primer for Policymakers* (Arlinghton, Mercatus Center at George Mason University, 2013).

[76] Klinke and Renn (n 64) 1073.

[77] E Platen, 'A benchmark framework for risk management' in J Akahori, S Ogawa and S Watanabe (eds), *Stochastic Processes and Applications to Mathematical Finance. Proceedings of the Ritsumeikan International Symposium World Scientific* (Singapore, World Scientific Publishing, 2004) 306.

management. The backbone of our risk-management framework is featured in Table 1. Horizontally, it consists of stylised facts that carry a risky dimension for EMIs. Vertically, it is divided into three columns: a short description of stylised facts equated to classes of risk, their potential negative outcomes, and finally the corrective measures to be implemented to remedy the abovementioned adverse effects. The latter cover a wide spectrum of events that might affect EMIs and VC issuers in every single dimension of their operations.

Although the following meta-categories (encompassing several stylised facts) are not highlighted directly in Table 1, some classes or risks are structured around: (1) clients' needs (eg, confidentiality), (2) hacking and cybercrime (eg, fraud, price manipulation, cybercriminal attacks), (3) IT deficiency phenomena (eg, systems obsolescence), (4) regulatory and legal matters (eg, exposure to foreign jurisdictions), (5) human resources (eg, outdated skills), and (6) the monetary and financial environment of the EMI (eg, macro-financial issues).

Table 2 steps back, and adopts a comprehensive and dynamic perspective on risk-management strategy that typically consists of three sets of risks defined according to the degree of persistence of negative outcomes following the implementation of DLT at the organisational level. These three sets of risks are complemented by a set of corrective actions outside the scope of DLT depending on the observed combination of outcomes and risks. Tables 1 and 2 provide EMIs and VC issuers with a risk management toolkit that includes DLT as a decisive technological environmental and strategic parameter.

Table 1 A technology typology for risk management (e-money or VC)

	Description	Potential outcomes	Corrective measures
Unauthorised access to information systems	- Hackers penetrate the information system of the VC protocol or e-money service provider, confidential client information is intercepted by unauthorised third party, e-wallet loss/hack, malfunctioning of the e-wallet, password/private key loss, faulty VC cash machines	- Data loss or theft, e-wallet or exchange theft or hack, identity theft, abusive use of client information - Shutdown of the information system or the whole protocol	- stress tests / vulnerability monitoring, anomaly detection - implementation of security / communication measures (firewall, password management, encoding, enhanced user authentication)

(continued)

Table 1 *(Continued)*

	Description	Potential outcomes	Corrective measures
Fraud, price manipulation, cybercriminal attacks	Data alteration (price manipulation) by employees of centralised VC schemes or e-money service providers, confidential information intercepted on money transfers, stolen chip, information system damaged by a cyber-attack (PwC 2016) causing a breakdown; fraudulent or Ponzi VC schemes[78] or exchange (eg MtGox scandal)	- refunding of the clients (costs), clients losses, - repurchase of e-money for which no pre-paid funds have received. - The reputation of the e-money service provider is tarnished – The latter is liable to legal sanctions, thereby reinforcing negative publicity	- implementation of screening policies (recruitment procedures and employee performance auditing) - intensified control of micro-chips - quantum encryption needed to secure payments (E&Y, 2015, p.5)
Counterfeiting	Hackers alter or duplicate the e-money or the VC to obtain funds or goods illegally	e-money service provider held accountable for counterfeited sums; costs for the repair of the system, image/reputation damage	- In centralised (not tamper resistant) protocols, monitoring and recording of all online interactions and all transactions - Immutable database of past transactions - tamper-evident devices incorporated in payment protocols and merchant hardware; "privacy by design" embedded in Fintech strategies; innovation-enhancing regulatory compliant privacy programs (EY, 2015, p.6)

(continued)

[78] See ECB, Virtual Currency Schemes at *27 (cited in note 4). Users go into the system by buying Bitcoins against real currencies, but can only leave and retrieve their funds if other users want to buy their Bitcoins, that is, if new participants want to join the system. Id. A Ponzi scheme is an investment fraud that involves the payment of purported returns to existing investors from funds contributed by new investors.

Table 1 *(Continued)*

	Description	Potential outcomes	Corrective measures
Internet service providers	- The Internet service providers do not provide the services announced to the e-money service provider - deficient systems, poor data integrity, lack of reliability	- e-money service providers held accountable by dissatisfied customers due to issues with Internet service providers, reputational damage	- due diligence before engaging with a service provider - contractual basis formation, performance benchmark, - take note of the recorded provisions - Establish backup procedures with the access provider - consider changing access providers
Macro-financial issues	unexpected fluctuations in the value of VC (exchange rate risk), unexpected tax requirements, losses incurred by VC-backed derivatives, high volatility of VC		
Mining / protocol issues	VC mining pool fails to remunerate the miner fairly for the mined VC units, deceptive publicity on VC features, abuse of the miner's computer capacity; opaque changes in the protocol		
System obsolescence	Delays or interruptions in transaction processing. Deficiency in the integrity of the data system or operational failure of the exchange,	- Hostile reaction from the public: legal action as a result of erroneous transactions - Costs related to possible chain repercussions / repair of damage to customer relation	- Make a regular technical and scientific review (hardware / software) - installation of a system for assigning responsibilities for system and equipment updates

(continued)

Table 1 *(Continued)*

	Description	Potential outcomes	Corrective measures
Outdated skills	Rapid technological change can surprise staff, management, service providers (i.e. upgrading) and higher education institutions (i.e. supply of skilled graduates)	- Poor installation of new technology. - Inability to provide continuous customer support - Poor data system integrity	- regular staff training plans - (HR policy)
Client security	Use by customers (card number, accounts) in unsecured transmissions. Risk of easy capture of confidential information by hackers.	Financial losses due to unauthorised transactions	- Information to clients ondue diligence - security measures incorporated into the products and services
Transaction repudiation	customer complaint to a merchant who wrongly debited his account, the latter asks for a refund	- the burden of proof is on the money-service provider - high loss risk in case of impossible proof	- implementation of security measures reinforcing customer authentication - Regularly audit transactions, monitor any anomalies
Acceptability of e-monies and VCs	poor acceptability of VCs by merchants	The use of the VC risk being limited to a narrow subset of economic agents	
General breakdown	Customers no longer have access to their account or their funds	Risk of leakage from impacted customers, aggravation if the issue is amplified and shared via social media	Stress tests conducted before implementation, backup procedures, crisis communications policy during the outage

(continued)

Table 1 ***(Continued)***

	Description	Potential outcomes	Corrective measures
Security alert	A virus is introduced into the system, damaging data integrity. Hackers gain access to the heart of the system.	Idem	Stress tests / penetration, other appropriate security measures, efficient anti-virus technologies Crisis communication
Competitor alert	Clients are suspicious with issues concerning one or more competitors that issue similar e-monies or VCs, information inequality regarding other VC ecosystem participants	Idem	Communication de crise visant à rassurer les clients
Legal uncertainty	e-money service provider or VC finds itself non-compliant by inadvertence (AML or electronic signatures); unexpected application of laws rendering contracts illegal or unenforceable, failure to meet VC-denominated contractual obligations	Legal sanctions, compliance costs	– Make a complete legal inventory before starting electronic money services activities – exercise a principle of prudence on the tolerated margins in a situation of legal uncertainty – Require precise interpretations from regulatory authorities – training policy (compliance)

(continued)

Table 1 ***(Continued)***

	Description	Potential outcomes	Corrective measures
Money laundering	The protocol of the internal system of the e-money service provider is captured for criminal or money laundering purposes	Legal sanctions related to breaches in KYC rules	– Set up identification procedures and screening techniques – Practice regular audit of transactions, monitor any anomalies – limit the amounts transferable at one time – regular inventory (compliance and training)
Client Information	Clients do not have an in-depth knowledge of their rights and obligations or litigation resolution mechanisms	prosecution for lack of information Legal fees (lawyers)	Check customer information systems before establishing an e-money service provider. Staff training (cost-benefit analysis of customer information beyond the legal threshold), Develop product information, regulatory audits etc
Client confidentiality	An e-money service provider inadvertently publishes a customer's transaction profile without his content	Legal sanctions, Legal fees (lawyers)	Confidentiality policies (regularly reviewed), additional security measures, compliance and training policies
Faulty hyperlink	A misleading hyperlink for customers is featured on the website of an e-money service provider	Legal remedies	Web design, analysis of the legal web browsing consequences, provide sufficient explanatory messages. Refrain from any comments about the products available on the sites offered as links.

(continued)

Table 1 *(Continued)*

	Description	Potential outcomes	Corrective measures
Certficate issues	Falsified certificates due to faulty verification procedures	Maintenance and repair costs. The (sustained) use of false certificates leads to prosecution. Reputational damage	Adequate security and control measures.
Exposure to foreign jurisdictions	e-money service provider based in Luxembourg can attract foreign clients, and be liable to foreign regulations. Overlap issues, e-monies or VC can be used outside the country it was issued.	- Money service provider may be in non-compliance with foreign jurisdictions. - Unanticipated legal expenses	- Evaluate potential for using e-money services outside Luxembourg legal space. - Principle of prudence vis-à-vis legal uncertainty - Legal and regulatory staff training (knowledge of neighbouring countries or economic partners)
Currency Valuation Issues	Opportunity costs of VC holdings (expected real return of holding the digital currency relative to other options), risk characteristics of the VC (probability of fraud, volatility, degree of anonymity etc); Time constraints of switching wealth from one VC to other assets; ideological preferences for specific currencies	If wrongly evaluated, these valuation risks incur a range of costs and other negative (non-monetary) consequences.	

Table 2 A risk management toolkit (before/after DLT introduction)

	Totally eradicated by the implementation of DLT	**Partly eradicated by DLT**	**Left unchanged by DLT**
Categories of risk	$risk_a$, $risk_b$, $risk_c$…	$risk_1$, $risk_2$, $risk_3$…	$risk_\alpha$, $risk_\beta$, $risk_\mu$…
Remaining corrective actions required (post-DLT implementation)		$action_1$, $action_2$, $action_3$…	See Table 1

VI. Conclusion

In this chapter, we have put forward a new risk management framework for virtual currency issuers and e-money service providers. The FinTech sector lies at the interface between political, historical, societal and economic evolutions. The rise of EMIs and VCs raise numerous issues related to data protection, confidentiality, consumer protection, online social interactions, business models, e-commerce law, private international law etc. The EMD paved the way for the growth of e-money and VC-backed services, facilitated market access for European firms, and promoted fair competition between the actors of the FinTech sector in Luxembourg.

The EU has opted for a single market approach for user-friendly and secured e-money services. Interestingly, the ECB is now contemplating the implementation of Blockchain technology, through the introduction of a digital euro.[79] An emerging scenario of a two-speed Europe is to be feared, however, with a polarisation between flexible proactive countries and more passive countries in the face of unwinding FinTech innovations.

[79] European Central Bank (n 32).

15

Some Thoughts on the Uneasy Fit between the ECB's Legal Mandate and its Crisis-Driven, 'Whatever it Takes', Policy Empowerment

MARTA BOŽINA BEROŠ AND MARIN BEROŠ

I. Introduction

In little more than two decades, the European Central Bank (ECB) has grown to become one of the world's most influential and powerful monetary authorities. In addition to the original price stability mandate anticipated by the drafters of the Maastricht Treaty in the 1990s, the ECB's policy capacity has grown over time to include broader policy objectives such as prudential soundness and financial stability. Although the process of ECB's gradual expansion of powers has been largely supported by the bank's exceptional political independence and monetary policy credibility,[1] there is no doubt that crisis events triggered the ECB's empowerment during this period in terms of extending and broadening policy capacities.[2] Arguably, the 'empowerment' of EU institutions – understood as the process by which national governments support the expansion of institutions' competencies in the face of 'external conditions of urgency and uncertainty' – has already been documented in EU policymaking.[3] This can clearly be discerned in the field of prudential policy where – to make an example – EU agencies, more specifically the European Supervisory Authorities, have gradually grown into powerful supervisory watchdogs with ample intervention powers. Nonetheless,

[1] D Howarth, 'The European Central Bank: The Bank That Rules Europe?' in K Dyson and M Marcussen (eds), *Central Banks in the Age of the Euro: Europeanization, Convergence, and Power* (Oxford, Oxford University Press, 2009) 73–88.

[2] CE Heldt and T Mueller, 'The (self-)empowerment of the European Central Bank during the sovereign debt crisis' (2020) 43 *Journal of European Integration* 83–98.

[3] ibid 86.

the empowerment of EU agencies drew harsh and widespread criticism in respect of their legitimacy, considering the boundaries set by EU jurisprudence and founding acts.[4] Similarly, the empowerment of the ECB, the key EU institution in monetary policy, raised and continues to raise important questions about the legal and political limits of its mandate.

Because of the political momentum galvanised by the crisis, the ECB was able to expand its mandate by implementing pioneering, non-conventional policy measures that brought the ECB closer to a redistributive role with fiscal effects, hence stretching the bank's mandate beyond the monetary domain. In 2012 all EU Member States of that time demonstrated wide support to the idea of 'more Europe' as a way out of the economic crisis, a stance that was then reflected in ECB's monetary strategy to 'do whatever it takes to preserve the euro'.[5] More specifically, the large-scale, expanded asset-purchase programme (EAPP) had a positive impact on the stabilisation of the EU financial system, yet the 'EAPP' drew widespread criticism not only for its distributional effects but also for undermining the ECB's democratic legitimacy.[6] The most important outcome from the heated debate about the evolution of ECB's mandate vs democratic legitimacy, has been the May 2020 ruling of the German Federal Constitutional Court (GFCC) that argued that the ECB acted beyond its powers or ultra vires during the crisis, violating the EU founding principle of proportionality and encroaching on Member States' sovereignty.[7]

Irrespective of these initial controversies, the COVID-19 pandemic emergency, which began in 2020, has allowed the ECB to further assert its monetary authority with the introduction of the Pandemic Emergency Purchase Programme (PEPP). Building on the contentious PSPP strategy of the EAPP, the PEPP is a massive asset purchase programme of public and private sector securities designed to be flexible in size and duration to allow the ECB to act proportionately to the risks confronting the EU economy. Essentially, the PEPP is a 'temporary and targeted measure'[8]

[4] For a detailed and insightful discussion on the topic of EU agencies' empowerment and their legitimacy see M Chamon, *EU Agencies: Legal and Political Limits to the Transformation of the EU Administration* (Oxford, Oxford University Press, 2016).

[5] M Draghi, 'Verbatim of the remarks made by Mario Draghi, President of the ECB at the Global Investment Conference in London 26 July 2012' (*European Central Bank*, 26 July 2012) www.ecb.europa.eu/press/key/date/2012/html/sp120726.en.html.

[6] See K McNamara, 'Banking on Legitimacy: The ECB and the Euro Zone Crisis' (2012) 13 *Georgetown Journal of International Affairs* 143–50; AL Högenauer and D Howarth, 'The democratic deficit and European Central Bank crisis monetary policies' (2019) 26 *Maastricht Journal of European and Comparative Law* 81–93; A Camous and G Claeys, 'The evolution of European economic institutions during the COVID-19 crisis' (2020) 6 *European Policy Analysis* 328–41.

[7] Bundesverfassungsgericht, 'ECB decisions on the Public Sector Purchase Programme exceed EU competences' Press Release No. 32/2020 (*Bundesverfassungsgericht*, 5 May 2020). The principle of proportionality is set out in Art 5(4) of the Treaty on EU and applies to the EU in the fields of monetary and prudential (supervisory) policy. See the Consolidated version of the Treaty on the European Union, 2012.

[8] Y Mersch, 'Legal aspects of the ECB's response to the coronavirus (COVID-19) pandemic – an exclusive but narrow competence' (*ECB Banking Supervision*, 2 November 2020) www.bankingsupervision.europa.eu/press/speeches/date/2020/html/ssm.sp201102~df871dcfe4.en.html.

to counteract exceptional economic circumstances caused by the COVID-19 crisis, and preserve the smooth functioning of the single currency area.[9] Politically, the PEPP has reaffirmed the ECB's unwavering commitment to the euro, but from a legitimacy standpoint the programme has reignited debates over encroachments on Member States' sovereignty as well as about the ECB's de facto departure from its original mandate. At the same time the PEPP demonstrates how ECB's institutional power and capacities can be extended to unprecedented degree in times of crisis.[10] Indeed, as the demarcation line between monetary and fiscal policy becomes blurred because of the bank's massive holdings of government debt thanks to the PEPP, the ECB is 'occupying terrain that would have been politically unimaginable and legally unfeasible before 2010'.[11]

From an institutional aspect, it appears as if crisis-events were the fuse, and the ECB the operative arm of policy recalibrations within the EMU.[12] Yet, even though the ECB has been engaging in transactions with important redistributive effects, the legality of its actions is – surprisingly – still upheld by the EU courts, as will be explained in the chapter. This leads us to the conclusion that, the legitimacy of the ECB's 'forceful actions'[13] in monetary policy is overshadowed by compelling political reasoning, first and foremost the need to preserve the common currency's singleness under circumstances that fuel disintegrative, centrifugal forces within the EU integration framework, such as crisis events. Therefore, regardless of the legitimacy issues of its controversial monetary strategy, we argue that the ECB will continue to support cohesion within the monetary union and the Single Market through an interventionist mandate that implicitly addresses economic policy concerns.

Against this backdrop, this chapter investigates, first, the political and legal arguments that helped sustain the evolution of the ECB's mandate, and secondly, it reflects on the concerns about the growing cleavage between the democratic legitimacy of the bank's actions and their integrationist aim. To substantiate its arguments, the chapter's analytical framework draws on two strands of scholarship: first, the literature on the ECB's political empowerment

[9] Although initially asset purchases were capped at 750 billion euros, the ECB has departed from the self-imposed purchase limits on the PEPP scheme and increased 'the envelope for the PEPP by EUR 600 billion' in June 2020, also announcing that net asset purchases under the PEPP will continue until June 2021 at least. See C Blot, J Creel, P Hubert, F Labondance and X Ragot, 'Setting New Priorities for the ECB'S mandate' (2020) *Monetary Dialogue Papers*, PE 648.812, 61.

[10] Heldt and Mueller (n 2); D Curtin, '"Accountable Independence" of the European Central Bank: Seeing the Logics of Transparency' (2017) 23 *European Law Journal* 28–44; F Schimmelfenning, 'European integration (theory) in times of crisis. A comparison of the euro and Schengen crises' 25 *Journal of European Public Policy* 969–89.

[11] M Dani, E Chiti, J Medes, AJ Menéndez, H Schepel and MA Wilkinson, 'Beneath the Spurious Legality of the ECB's Monetary Policy – Roundtable: Monetary Policy in the EU' (*Just Money*, 12 January 2021) https://justmoney.org/beneath-the-spurious-legality-of-the-ecbs-monetary-policy/.

[12] The authors would like to thank Dr Gabriella Gimigliano for bringing up this insightful and valid point.

[13] Mersch (n 8).

and leadership,[14] and secondly, on the buoyant legal scholarship on the (democratic) legitimacy of the ECB's emergency actions.[15] In addition, the chapter makes extensive use of secondary resources, such as ECB documents, policy papers, and briefs as well as statements from relevant monetary policy stakeholders.

The structure of the chapter is as follows: section II follows the introduction looking at how the legal description of the ECB's mandate in the founding treaties has been subject to 'contextualising exercises' in times of crisis, allowing the bank to engage in redistributive policies for a prolonged period irrespective of juridical contestations. Section III examines the emergence of political support for the ECB's interventionist mandate to tame centrifugal forces in the Single Market, which have been galvanised by unprecedented crisis events. The last section presents some concluding remarks on the ECB's monetary strategy in pursuit of monetary singleness, arguing how the ECB – in the absence of peers – will spare no resources to counter disintegration threats, even if this means engaging in monetary actions that teeter on the legal limits of its genuine policy responsibilities.

II. The ECB'S Mandate Expands: Reinterpreting the Mandate's Wording

The ECB's incremental empowerment into a monetary authority responsible for monetary, prudential, and economic policy would not have occurred if two conditions were not met: first, the interpretative versatility of the bank's legal mandate as outlined in the founding treaties, which allowed for contextual broadening, and secondly, the political momentum created by emergency events, which galvanised EU-wide consensus about the ECB's proactive role in times of crisis.

In terms of policy capacity, as defined by the bank's mandate, we can argue that the Eurozone and COVID-19 crises acted as catalysts for interpretative flexibility and 'mission creeps'[16] in the bank's policy responsibilities as spelled out by the bank's original mandate. The ECB's legal mandate emanates from the founding acts

[14] Heldt and Mueller (n 2); F Torres, 'The EMU's Legitimacy and the ECB as a Strategic Political Player in the Crisis Context' (2013) 35 *Journal of European Integration* 287–300; B Nielsen and S Smeets, 'The role of the EU institutions in establishing the banking union. Collaborative leadership in the EMU reform process' (2018) 25 *Journal of European Public Policy* 1233–56; A Verdun, 'Political leadership of the European Central Bank' (2017) 39 *Journal of European Integration* 207–21.

[15] J van t'Klooster, 'Democracy and the European Central Bank's Emergency Powers' (2018) 42 *Midwest Studies in Philosophy* 270–93; Högenauer and Howarth (n 6); Camous and Claeys (n 6); N de Boer and J Van t'Klooster, 'The ECB, the courts and the issue of democratic legitimacy after Weiss' (2020) 57 *Common Market Law Review* 1689–724; B Herzog, 'Hidden Blemish in European Law: Judgments on Unconventional Monetary Programmes' (2021) 10 *Laws*.

[16] J Einhorn, 'The World Bank's Mission Creep' (*Foreign Affairs*, 1 September 2001) www.foreignaffairs.com/articles/2001-09-01/world-banks-mission-creep.

of the EU, specifically Articles 127(1) and 282(2) of the Treaty on the Functioning of the European Union (TFEU), which clearly state price stability as the bank's primary policy objective. It is worth noting that the Articles also state that the ECB may pursue secondary goals, more specifically it can support the Union's general economic policies, but only as subordinate goals whose pursuit cannot jeopardise the price stability objective. Furthermore, Articles 101 TEU and 123 TFEU prohibit the ECB from engaging in monetary financing, while Articles 103 TEU and 125 TFEU establish the so-called 'no bail out rule',[17] which constitutes the cornerstone of EU's fiscal framework.[18] Although the monetarist paradigm ensures output legitimacy, it also limits the ECB to pursue broader economic policy objectives, even if they are for the sake of financial stability, because discretion is incompatible with the bank's legal mandate and therefore, the legitimacy of its actions. This paradigm also establishes a clear hierarchy in the achievement of policy goals (primary vs secondary), offsetting potential trade-offs in ECB's policy strategy.[19] As de Boer and Van t'Klooster rightly observe, this is a narrow, monetarist description of the bank's tasks and objectives,[20] but this view of the ECB's mandate has been enshrined in the monetary union's treaty foundations as well as in its legal stipulation. However, crises events have revealed that under pressure, ECB's mandate can be expanded through a flexible reinterpretation of the mandate's wording. De Boer and Van t'Klooster refer to this as the mandate's 'authorisation gap',[21] which emanates from the lack of a clear course of action or guidance in the bank's original legal mandate in the face of unprecedented economic emergencies, such as the Eurozone and COVID-19 crises.

Interpretative flexibility of its tasks and powers has allowed the ECB to declaratively uphold to the mandate's wording during crises by de facto compromising on its own rules, allowing for their much wider reinterpretation and therefore contributing to its own empowerment 'by stealth'.[22] One illustrative example is the ECB's pragmatic reasoning behind its intervention in the secondary government debt market during the Eurozone crisis, which fuelled Member States' concerns about the proportionality of this monetary measure, its adverse redistributive effects, and the possibility that the ECB was engaging in hidden monetary financing. In that case, the ECB argued that interventionist actions were prompted by 'potential second-round effects on wage and price setting threatened to adversely affect

[17] Högenauer and Howarth (n 6) 84.

[18] Herzog (n 15) 1.

[19] Blot et al (n 9) 7.

[20] de Boer and Van t'Klooster (n 15) 3.

[21] de Boer and Van t'Klooster (n 15) 10.

[22] V Schmidt, 'The Eurozone's Crisis of Democratic Legitimacy: Can the EU Rebuild Public Trust and Support for European Economic Integration?' (2015) *15 European Commission Discussion Paper, FELLOWSHIP INITIATIVE 2014–2015 "Growth, integration and structural convergence revisited"* 5; P Berés, G Claeys, N de Boer, PO Demetriades, S Diessner, S Jourdan, J van t'Klooster and V Schmidt, 'The ECB needs political guidance on secondary objectives' (*Bruegel*, 22 April 2021) www.bruegel.org/2021/04/the-ecb-needs-political-guidance-on-secondary-objectives/.

medium-term price developments', which necessitated 'a forceful monetary policy response'[23] to combat the deflationary pressures caused by the Eurozone crisis as well as to preserve the monetary transmission mechanism. Based on economic and monetary reasoning, the bank determined that its actions were necessary, proportionate, and effective.

Indeed, during the Eurozone crisis the ECB implemented pioneering, unconventional monetary policy measures that at times entailed discretionary decision-making and actual (re)distributive effects, thus blurring the distinction between the bank's monetary and fiscal activities. Within this package of non-standard policy responses, the Expanded Assets Purchase Programme (EAPP) was the key framework through which the ECB was able to purchase public sector securities, primarily government bonds issued by Eurozone countries and debt instruments issued by recognised agencies.[24] The EAPP consisted of the corporate sector purchase programme (CSPP), public sector purchase programme (PSPP), asset-backed securities purchase programme (ABSPP), and third covered bond purchase programme (CBPP3), whose goal was to support the smooth functioning of the monetary transmission mechanism and providing sufficient policy leeway to ensure price stability. Through this framework, the ECB amassed massive amounts of public securities, particularly under the PSPP, which totalled to EUR 2,088.100,00 million by the end of 2019.[25] Although this allowed governments and institutions selling the securities to maintain a 'level playing field' between EU Member States in terms of (inter)national debt market financing, as well as to reinvest the funds received to buy other assets or extend credit to the real economy, the EAPP deeply politicised reform efforts. In fact, politicisation was the by-product of the redistributive effects of large-scale central bank asset purchases, both on the micro- and macro-economic levels, which have already been documented in monetary economics. Not surprisingly, the ECB's monetary actions under the EAPP framework drew harsh criticism for their appropriateness in terms of moral hazard incentives and, more importantly, the legality and democratic legitimacy of monetary interventions.

In respect of moral hazard, it has already been pointed out that unconventional monetary measures may facilitate economic growth by providing ample liquidity and extended adjustment periods for Member States to use these funds to support structural reforms, but at the same time they also encourage risk-taking and can therefore lead to public debt expansions in the long run.[26] This means that instead of fiscal sustainability across Member States, the instruments deployed might undermine price stability and the ECB's anti-inflationary strategy. Admittedly, scholars and policy makers alike have yet to reach a clear and

[23] European Central Bank, 'ECB announces expanded asset purchase programme' (*European Central Bank*, 22 January 2015) www.ecb.europa.eu/press/pr/date/2015/html/pr150122_1.en.html.

[24] Decision (EU) 2015/774 of the European Central Bank of 4 March 2015 on secondary markets public sector asset purchase programme (ECB/2015/10) [2015] OJ L121.

[25] Bundesverfassungsgericht (n 7).

[26] Herzog (n 15) 2.

unanimous conclusion about the economic effects of the ECB's crisis measures. So far, empirical evidence suggests that the ECB's asset purchase programmes have effectively 'tamed' bond yield volatility on financial markets; however, the stabilising role has been more prominent for 'periphery' countries, and even in this group the effect was short term.[27] Because of the heterogeneity in inflation responses across member countries, the specific effect of the PSPP on inflation is much more difficult to disentangle, with better results more visible in member countries that experienced greater distress during the Eurozone crisis.[28] Yet, the question of whether ECB's asset purchase programmes pressure and challenge bank's anti-inflationary mandate cropped up with great prominence in the late Autumn of 2021 as the annual inflation rate within the Eurozone soared to unprecedented levels.

This leads us to the issue of legitimacy of ECB's actions in the monetary domain, where Högenauer and Howarth contend how these remain legitimate as long as the bank's decision-making process is specified, its decisions are justified, policy outcomes are sound, and the bank has the willingness and expertise to protect diverse interests.[29] The authors offer a broader account of legitimacy, primarily understood as output legitimacy or the ECB's problem-solving capacity in monetary matters. In other words, if the ECB achieves its numerically defined primary goal, it avoids politicisation and maintains legitimacy.[30] However, things become more complicated when the ECB pursues multiple objectives, particularly those involving discretion and redistributive effects, potentially overstepping the legal mandate, and encroaching on the political sphere.[31] Even if the link between monetary and supervisory policymaking is clear, and if interpretative flexibility allows for a wide range of other secondary objectives, too much ambiguity about how the ECB should pursue and rank these objectives in relation to its primary goal raises legitimacy concerns.[32] Consequently, after the ECB assumed a much more interventionist role in economic matters because of the PSPP and then the PEPP framework, while the bank's legal mandate remained unaltered, the bank found itself 'navigating unexplored waters'[33] in respect of the legality of its crisis-prompted actions.

[27] J Beckmann, S Fiedler, KJ Gern, S Kooths, J Quast and M Wolters, 'The ECB's Asset Purchase Programmes: Effectiveness, Risks, Alternatives' (2020) *Monetary Dialogue Compilation of papers: The ECB's Asset Purchase Programmes: Experience and Future Perspectives*, PE 652.749, 112.

[28] ibid 114.

[29] Högenauer and Howarth (n 6) 83.

[30] Again, the record-high annual inflation levels in the Eurozone prompt greater scepticism in this regard.

[31] M Božina Beroš, 'The ECB's accountability within the SSM: Mind the (transparency) gap' (2019) 26 *Maastricht Journal of European and Comparative Law* 5; D Fromage and R Ibrido, 'The "Banking Dialogue" as a model to improve parliamentary involvement in the Monetary Dialogue?' (2018) 40 *Journal of European Integration* 302.

[32] Berés et al (n 22).

[33] de Boer and Van t'Klooster (n 15) 1690.

Surprisingly, the ECB's policy and institutional empowerment is upheld by EU jurisprudence, although it sits uncomfortably with the ultra vires judgment of the GFCC on the ECB's PEPP assistance framework.[34] In what is known as the *Weiss* case, the GFCC challenged the legality of the ECB's government-debt purchasing framework, scrutinising both the bank's mandate and powers, arguing that the ECB acted well outside its delegated powers, engaging in monetary operations that clearly violated the monetary financing prohibition of Article 123 TFEU.[35] Violante notes how the German court did more than that,[36] it: 'delivered a serious warning as to the unsustainability of anchoring solidarity and redistribution processes on monetary means'. However, the opinion of the Court of Justice of the EU (CJEU) is in sharp contrast to the one of the German court.[37] In it, the CJEU set out essential clarifications in respect of proportionality, as well as the distinction between monetary and economic policy effects, therefore upholding the legitimacy of the ECB's interventionist actions. Essentially, the CJEU concluded that the means employed by the ECB to manage Eurozone's stability and attain its primary policy goal were effective and necessary.[38] While some authors note how the CJEU justified ECB's interventionist mandate in support of Eurozone's stability, with a 'clumsy' assertion that 'the authors of the Treaties did not intend to make an absolute separation between economic and monetary policies' and by accentuating the weight of the 'list of guarantees provided by the ECB that would limit the scope of its monetary policy measures',[39] other knowledgeable observers remind us that it is 'economically naive' to believe that a clear, non-ambiguous boundary between monetary and economic policy can be established, especially in multilayer governance frameworks like the EMU.[40]

Despite the convoluted legal reasoning, the ECB is more likely to reach again for the broader policy toolset, as the manoeuvring space for conventional monetary policy remains limited in circumstances of lower policy rates and prolonged disinflation.[41] Furthermore, as we explain in the following section, the ECB's

[34] See the BVerfG, Judgment of the Second Senate of 5 May 2020 – 2 BvR 859/15 – paras 1–237; ECLI:DE:BVerfG:2020:rs20200505.2bvr085915, hereafter the 'BVerfG PEPP case'. It should be noted that the GCC made no reference to any of the ECB's assistance measures in response to the pandemic emergency, even though the PEPP could have reignited the Court's interest in the matter and may well do so in the future.

[35] W Bateman, 'The Law of Monetary Finance under Unconventional Monetary Policy' (2021) *Oxford Journal of Legal Studies* 33.

[36] T Violante, 'Bring Back the Politics: The PSPP Ruling in Its Institutional Context' (2020) 21 *German Law Journal* 1056.

[37] Case C-493/17 *Weiss and Others* [2019] 2 CMLR 11 hereafter the '*Weiss* case'.

[38] K Pistor, 'Germany's Constitutional Court Goes Rogue' (*Project Syndicate*, 8 May 2020) www.project-syndicate.org/commentary/german-constitutional-court-ecb-ruling-may-threaten-euro-by-katharina-pistor-2020-05.

[39] N de Arriba-Sellier, 'Is monetary policy too important to be left to judges?' (*Leiden Law Blog*, 18 May 2020) www.leidenlawblog.nl/articles/is-monetary-policy-too-important-to-be-left-to-judges.

[40] Pistor (n 38).

[41] I Schnabel, 'A new strategy for a changing world. Speech at the virtual Financial Statements series hosted by the Peterson Institute for International Economics in Frankfurt am Main 14 July 2021' (*European Central Bank*, 14 July 2014) www.ecb.europa.eu/press/key/date/2021/html/ecb.sp210714~0d62f657bc.en.html.

mandate expansion and institutional empowerment will continue to benefit from wide support of main political actors which have recognised the eurozone and COVID-19 crisis as emergencies with unprecedented disintegration potential, necessitating proactive, supranational responses.

III. The ECB'S Mandate Expands: Political Momentum Propels Policy Capacities

The scholarship on the functional analysis of EU institutions[42] shows how Member States are willing to delegate greater agency to the supranational authorities because of their independent expertise in technically complex policy matters. This is especially true in times of adverse events – such as the Eurozone and COVID-19 crisis, where the complexity of specific economic policy issues, ie, monetary and prudential, effectively propelled the ECB's policy and institutional empowerment. With fiscal policy responses limited to individual Member State-jurisdictions, in both events the EU did not have access to substantive financial resources that could be used collectively to aid troubled banking sectors[43] or to tackle structural divergences between individual economies caused by the pandemic and thus, support an EU-wide recovery plan. Both the Eurozone and the COVID-19 crises demonstrated that the EMU's existing institutional and policy architecture was incapable of dealing with such extraordinary situations while also maintaining Eurozone stability without recurring to a far more proactive role of the ECB, one that stretches the understanding of its original mandate. As a result, when the economic crisis morphed into a sovereign debt crisis in late 2011, as well as when the protracted COVID-19 crisis began to threaten citizens' livelihoods and sovereigns alike, the EU did not hesitate to address problems in a political fashion, including the revamp of policy response of key institutional actors, most notably the ECB. According to one leading EU scholar 'as economies across the Eurozone boomed, interest rates on bonds remained low across Euro area countries (…) the ECB got high marks for its governance'.[44]

This is not to say that the ECB's more interventionist role has been easily accepted. Regardless of the crisis potential for disintegration, the concept of a more proactive ECB – a technocratic EU institution that is often accused of lacking democratic legitimacy due to inadequate accountability arrangements[45] – sparked

[42] M Blauberger and B Rittberger, 'Conceptualizing and Theorizing EU Regulatory Networks' (2014) 9 *Regulation & Governance* 367–76.

[43] Verdun (n 14) 211.

[44] Schmidt (n 22) 10.

[45] For further insight into ECB's (lack of) democratic legitimacy and accountability see F Amtenbrink, 'On the Legitimacy and Democratic Accountability of the European Central Bank: Legal Arrangements and Practical Experience' in A Arnull and D Wincott (eds), *Accountability and Legitimacy in the European Union* (Oxford, Oxford University Press, 2015) 147–63.

political outrage in individual Member States, particularly Germany. Wolfgang Schäuble, at the time the finance minister of the European Central Bank's largest capital subscriber, warned against the bank's 'activist role', emphasising how closely the ECB's intervention in secondary bond markets resembled outright monetary financing, at least in terms of discouraging Member States' governments from implementing important structural reforms. Nonetheless, from the start of the Eurozone crisis until recently, the ECB remained steadfast in implementing unconventional monetary actions, a stance pioneered by Jean-Claude Trichet, and which only intensified under Mario Draghi's leadership and then became de rigueur once the crisis subsided. This prompted Germany and its finance minister to repeatedly request that the ECB reassess its actions, with Schäuble even linking the continuation of the bank's loose monetary policy after the Eurozone crisis to the growth of right-wing and populist politics across the EU. Disagreements on the ECB's implicit mandate extension came not only from the political sphere, but also from the central banking community and the ECB itself. A proof of this is the ECB's Governing Council divide following the bank's decision to further cut interest rates into negative territory and restart the controversial asset purchase mechanism in mid-September 2019.[46] In that time a Memorandum on the ECB's Monetary Policy was issued and signed by former German, French, Dutch and Austrian central banker governors, who openly criticised ECB's 'accommodative policy' that had become the norm following the Eurozone crisis, stating that: '(f)rom an economic point of view, the ECB has already entered the territory of monetary financing'.[47] The criticism was then echoed by the heads of central banks on the ECB's Governing Council, as well as some members of the ECB's Executive Board, who opposed the bank's loose monetary policy for different economic reasons, but with a common concern that political pressures are undermining the ECB's monetary authority and consequently, ECB's legitimacy.[48] At the same time, the majority of Governing Council members supported the ECB's monetary actions, flanked by opinions of influential policy makers such as Jean-Claude Trichet, who stated that 'attacks on the ECB's monetary policy are misguided' given that the ECB delivered on its primary mandate in times of unprecedented crisis, preserving the monetary union's singleness and prompting public support for the euro.

In a similar fashion, the ongoing pandemic emergency prompted some policy makers to adopt starkly different stances toward the ECB's mandate and its crisis-management role in the current EU context of limited fiscal coordination. While

[46] European Central Bank, 'Monetary Policy Decisions' Press Release (*European Central Bank*, 12 September 2019) www.ecb.europa.eu/press/pr/date/2019/html/ecb.mp190912~08de50b4d2.en.html.

[47] H Hannoun, O Issing, K Liebscher, H Schlesinger, J Stark and N Wellink, 'Center for Financial Stability Memorandum on the ECB's Monetary Policy' (2019) https://centerforfinancialstability.org/research/Memorand.pdf.

[48] M Arnold, 'Splits at the ECB top table over Mario Draghi's last big stimulus' *Financial Times* (27 September 2019) www.ft.com/content/560b0edc-df98-11e9-9743-db5a370481bc.

the majority of Governing Council members reaffirmed their support for the PEPP and its acceleration, the governor of the Bundesbank argued for a gradual reduction in asset purchases in an attempt to reintroduce conventional monetary policy.[49] At the same time, the Finnish central bank governor suggested that the ECB should engage in 'inflation overshooting' for greater economic and social welfare, aligning its monetary strategy with that of other major central banks.[50] Surprisingly, given its clear inflation target, the ECB has not discarded the idea of temporary inflation overshooting, which sharply contrasts with the view of some leading Member State politicians, such as German Bundestag President Schäuble, that 'an independent central bank is only justifiable in democratic terms when it has only a limited mandate'.[51]

Nevertheless, from Draghi's 'whatever it takes' approach[52] to Lagarde's recent statement that 'extraordinary times require extraordinary actions',[53] EU policy makers have shown a readiness to empower this technocratic institution, primarily in terms of the scope of its competencies. This leads us to conclude that the uncertainty connected with the two exceptional crisis events has created enough political momentum needed for the ECB to 'self-empower'; in other words, 'to widen the scope of its action and material resources with the tacit consent of its masters' as Heldt and Mueller masterfully point out.[54] This is well illustrated by ECB's departure from its numerically set policy goals and traditional instruments that have brought the bank closer to the fiscal sphere, primarily through asset buying programmes. As for institutional power, Heldt and Mueller underscore how the notable expansion in ECB's policy responsibilities has also been met with an expansion of operational resources[55] – whereas before the Eurozone crisis and the pandemic emergency the average number of staff employed by the ECB amounted to 1,565, in 2015 this number has almost doubled to 2,722, and then swelled to over 3,500 in the pre-pandemic year.[56] As for current numbers, although the ECB hasn't disclosed the average number of staff employed in 2020, it is safe to presume that the number has grown, at least judging by the steady increase in total staff costs – from 566 million euros in 2019 and reaching 646 million euros in 2020.[57]

[49] M Arnold, 'ECB divisions open up over pledge to persist with negative rates' *Financial Times* (22 July 2021) www.ft.com/content/b329cbe7-1d93-41f5-8812-297f0e03de58.

[50] M Arnold, 'Rehn calls for change to ECB's inflation target in line with Fed approach' *Financial Times* (9 May 2021) www.ft.com/content/05a12645-ceb2-4cd5-938e-974b778e16e0.

[51] A Rinke, 'Germany's Schaeuble calls on Lagarde to respect ECB's "limited mandate"' (*Reuters*, 5 November 2019) www.reuters.com/article/us-germany-politics-schaeuble-idUSKBN1XF1J9.

[52] Draghi (n 5).

[53] S Belz, J Cheng, D Wessel, D Gros and A Capolongo, 'What's the ECB doing in response to the COVID-19 crisis?' (*The Brookings Institution*, 4 June 2020) www.brookings.edu/research/whats-the-ecb-doing-in-response-to-the-covid-19-crisis/.

[54] Heldt and Mueller (n 2) 4.

[55] ibid 2.

[56] European Central Bank, 'Annual Report 2010' (2011); 'Annual Report 2015' (2016) and 'Annual Report 2019' (2020).

[57] European Central Bank, 'Annual Report 2020' (2021).

Again, this confirms ECB's empowerment was made possible by supranational political support to the extension of ECB's policy toolkit into neighbouring policy areas,[58] something clearly not anticipated by the Maastricht treaty.[59]

IV. Concluding Remarks

Paraphrasing Verdun, we can say that there is no doubt that because of crises-driven events the ECB today is playing a much larger role in EU economic governance than one might have anticipated.[60] Although unchanged on paper, the ECB's mandate has been radically altered in its practice, partly because of the 'expansionary reading' of the bank's true responsibilities and partly because 'in the absence of strong political authority' crisis events pushed the ECB to embrace economic and political leadership.[61] Indeed, as shown in the preceding sections, the political leeway instigated by fast-ticking emergencies allowed the reinterpretation of the monetarist conception of the bank's legal mandate and broadened the ECB's policy toolbox by establishing quantitative easing programmes such as the EAPP and later the PEPP to address 'crisis-related problems, both in the financial sector (…) and in the public one'.[62] In response to the convoluted legal reasoning of German and EU courts on the legality and legitimacy of the ECB's policy conduct as a result of the bank's policy, political, and institutional empowerment, the ECB made public communication one of its more prominent policy tools,[63] emphasising that measures taken were 'necessary, suitable, and proportionate'[64] to preserve the monetary union's singleness, as the foundation of EU integration and an important component of our European identity. It is apposite to note how Verdun already argued that the ECB possesses a remarkable readiness for political leadership in times of crisis, a trait that is confirmed by its capacity to design and implement transformative, 'whatever it takes' monetary strategies which help withstand economic shocks caused by unprecedented and persistent emergencies.[65]

With this in mind, and in light of the historic ultra vires judgment, what will become of the ECB's interventionist monetary approach in the years to come? The ECB's monetary strategy review in July 2021 sheds some light on how the legacy

[58] Verdun (n 14) 216.
[59] Berés et al (n 22).
[60] Verdun (n 14) 208.
[61] Violante (n 36) 1054.
[62] PD Tortola, 'The Politicization of the European Central Bank: What Is It, and How to Study It?' (2019) 58 *Journal of Common Market Studies* 2.
[63] K Wheelan, 'The ECB's Mandate and Legal Constraints' (2020) *Monetary Dialogue Papers*, PE 648.808, 23; European Central Bank, 'An overview of the ECB's monetary policy strategy' (2021) 15 www.ecb.europa.eu/home/search/review/html/ecb.strategyreview_monpol_strategy_overview.en.html.
[64] Schnabel (n 41).
[65] Verdun (n 14) 217.

of the ECB's unconventional policy actions during the eurozone and COVID-19 crises will continue to shape how the bank interprets the 'spirit' of its legal mandate in the years ahead. Rather than revisiting the bank's primary policy objectives (or, in the words of the ECB 'what we do') the review emphasises all aspects of the ECB's monetary policy toolkit that allow it to remain 'fit for purpose' (or, in the words of the ECB, 'how we do it'). Indeed, in order to respond nimbly to future challenges, the ECB will continue to use: 'forward guidance, asset purchases and longer-term refinancing operations, as appropriate', even more so, it intends to 'consider (...) new policy instruments'.[66]

Regardless of how compelling the political and economic arguments in favour of the ECB's interventionist mandate are, it is important to remember that some of the limitations of the PSPP framework (eg, temporary nature, cap amounts) are not set by the PEPP, which may reignite legal challenges on monetary financing grounds before the CJEU.[67] Nonetheless, the prolonged period of economic and societal uncertainty that continues to fuel centrifugal forces and fragmentation forces within the EU integrative framework, combined with the remarkable expansion of the ECB's powers over the last decade and the pioneering extension of the effects of its operative toolkit, suggest that the ECB is unlikely to 'return to its old knitting' even if monetary policy responses become politicised as a result of (perceived) distributive effects.[68] All things considered, it appears that the ECB possesses sufficient policy capacity and political clout to withstand the uneasy fit between its legal mandate and unconventional monetary actions.

[66] European Central Bank, 'An overview' (2021) 10.
[67] Wheelan (n 63) 16, 25.
[68] Högenauer and Howarth (n 6) 88.

INDEX

www.ingramcontent.com/pod-product-compliance
Ingram Content Group UK Ltd.
Pitfield, Milton Keynes, MK11 3LW, UK
UKHW020802290926
15470UKWH00003B/902

9 781509 956791